AGAINST LIBERALISM
SOCIETY IS NOT A MARKET

by

ALAIN DE BENOIST

TRANSLATED BY
F. ROGER DEVLIN

Middle Europe Books
Budapest
2024

Cover image:
Rembrandt, *Syndics of the Draper's Guild*, 1662
Rijksmuseum, Amsterdam

Cover design: Kevin I. Slaughter
Layout: Greg Johnson
Editing: Greg Johnson, John Morgan, Michael Walker,
& David Zsutty
Index & Proofing: James J. O'Meara

Published in Hungary by Middle Europe Books, Kft.
www.MiddleEuropeBooks.com

Hardcover ISBN: 978-1-64264-041-0
Paperback ISBN: 978-1-64264-042-7

To David L'Epée

CONTENTS

INTRODUCTION

When liberalism is said to be the dominant ideology of our time, there are always those who protest by citing, for example, the amount of public expenditures or the level of taxation in our country. But this is looking at the problem through the wrong end of the telescope. A liberal society is not exactly the same thing as a liberal economy. On the other hand, it *is* a society dominated by the primacy of the individual, the ideology of progress, the rights-of-man ideology, an obsession with growth, a disproportionate emphasis on mercantile values, the subjection of the symbolic imagination to the axioms of self-interest, and so on.

As the principal heir of the Enlightenment philosophy that affirms the supremacy of reason and establishes it as a universal principle to which all men naturally have access, liberalism has acquired a universal scope since "Globalization instituted capital as the real historical subject of capitalist modernity, and market value as a universal norm for regulating social practices."[1] It is at the origin of globalization, which is merely the transformation of the planet into an enormous market. It inspires what is nowadays called "political correctness." And of course, like any dominant ideology, it is also the ideology of the dominant class.

When we speak of liberalism, we are ensnared by words from the start. If by "liberal" we mean open-minded, tolerant, a partisan of free examination and freedom of judgment—or even being hostile to bureaucracy, welfare, and a centralizing and invasive statism—the present author would obviously have no problem in claiming the label for himself. But the historian of ideas knows that such senses of the word are trivial. Liberalism is a philosophical, economic, and political doctrine, and it clearly

---

[1] Maxime Ouellet, "Les 'anneaux du serpent' du libéralisme culturel: pour en finir avec la bonne conscience" ["The Ouroboros of Cultural Liberalism: Putting an End to Good Conscience"], *Collectif Société*, online.

must be studied and judged as such.

The old Left-Right division is not very useful in this respect. As Jean-Claude Michéa has reminded us, liberals "constituted the business wing of the original Left through the early twentieth century."[2] It was only afterwards that liberalism found itself displaced toward the Right—along with the ideology of progress—at least in Europe, since in the United States liberals are even today regarded as Leftists. Whereas in Europe "liberals"— whether "men of the Right" or "national liberals"—define themselves above all as partisans of the market economy and free trade, in the United States "liberalism" has an exclusively political sense and only refers to the doctrine of individual liberty, limited government, and contract. "Liberals" can thus be considered Left-wing opponents of conservatives, which is usually not the case in European countries.

Moreover, it is obvious that within liberalism there exist a great number of different authors and tendencies: "classical" and "modern" liberalism, continental and Anglo-Saxon liberalism, "evolutionary" and "rationalist" liberalism, etc. Just as political liberalism has been distinguished from and even opposed to economic liberalism, some have identified two great principal currents, one running from Burke to Hayek, the other from Locke to the American libertarians.[3] Others prefer to distinguish between those who see in liberalism the application of universal

---

[2] Jean-Claude Michéa, *Le complexe d'Orphée: La gauche, les gens ordinaires et la religion du progress* [*The Orpheus Complex: The Left, Ordinary People, and the Religion of Progress*] (Paris: Climats, 2011), 169.

[3] Libertarians divide themselves into two tendencies: proponents of the "minimal state" or "minarchists," who at least admit that a state can exist without necessarily violating rights, such as Robert Nozick (*Anarchy, State, and Utopia* [New York: Basic Books, 1975]) or James M. Buchanan, founder of the "Public Choice" school (*The Limits of Liberty: Between Anarchy and Leviathan* [Chicago: University of Chicago Press, 1975], and the "anarcho-capitalists" according to whom every state is by definition illegitimate and immoral, such as David Friedman (*The Machinery of Freedom* [Chicago: Open Court Publishing, 1989]), Karl Hess, and Murray Rothbard (*The Ethics of Liberty* [Atlantic Highlands, N. J.: Humanities Press International, 1982]).

principles and those who see in it a means of peaceful coexistence, those hostile to state regulation in the name of economic efficiency and those hostile to it in the name of liberty. Still others, sensitive to certain recent developments, oppose "neoliberalism" to classical liberalism.[4] We shall not enter into this teeming debate, which is certainly interesting but is not the subject of this book.[5]

Nor is it the goal of the texts collected here to discuss the well-foundedness of this or that point of the stock arguments of

---

[4] One of the leading characteristics of "neoliberalism" is a changed perspective on the state, which is no longer seen as an intrinsic obstacle to the free development of exchange but, because of its decreasingly political character and its rallying to the principles of "governance," becomes an auxiliary of the market, tasked especially with introducing rules of competition and deregulation where they have not previously existed. In other words, neoliberalism requires the state to intervene in favor of non-intervention by applying rules without which the market economy cannot function. The recourse to the authority of the "rule of law," in addition to the blackmail preventing capital export, thus permits the overcoming of the old Manchesterian "laissez-faire." This development, which was already emerging at the celebrated Walter Lippman Colloquium organized in Paris in 1938 at the initiative of Louis Rougier, has become stronger since the Reagan-Thatcher era, which relaunched the fashion of the "new economists" in the 1980s. The conclusion to be drawn from this is that the state no longer constitutes a rampart against the encroachments of the market today as one might still have believed in the time of Keynes. As Christian Laval writes, "If there is a lesson to be learned from the events of 2008–2011, it is that the state is not simply opposed to the market, that it is not merely external to the market, but that it is more than ever an internal element of the market whose intervention is indispensable to the functioning of the capitalist system" ("Les gauches françaises et la nature du néoliberalisme" ["The French Left and the Nature of Neoliberalism"] in Juliette Grange and Pierre Musso, eds., Les socialismes [Socialisms] [Lormont: Le Bord de l'eau, 2012], 339).

[5] On the diversity and ambiguities within the liberal family, cf. especially Françoise Orazi, L'Individu libre: Le libéralisme anglo-saxon de John Stuart Mill à nos jours [The Free Individual: Anglo-Saxon Liberalism from John Stuart Mill to the Present] (Paris: Classiques Garnier, 2018), a work recently added to an already considerable literature.

economic liberalism, to assess the comparative merits of free trade and protectionism, the advantages of the flat tax, or the need to reduce public expenditures. Still less is it meant as a challenge to the reputation of first-rate authors such as Raymond Aron or Alexis de Tocqueville—who are not satisfactorily defined by the label "liberal" in any case. It is rather a work of political philosophy that strives to go straight to the central point, the heart of liberal ideology, beginning from a critical analysis of its foundations, viz., an anthropology essentially based on individualism and economism. Along with the theologian John Milbank, we believe liberalism is above all an "anthropological error." This is why we use "liberalism" to refer to this ideology and its natural correlate, capitalism, rather than "ultraliberalism," an equivocal formulation that suggests liberalism would be acceptable as long as it did not fall into certain excesses.

The culture of narcissism, economic deregulation, the religion of the rights of man, the collapse of the collective, gender theory, the defense of hybrids of all sorts, the emergence of "contemporary art," virtual reality, utilitarianism, the logic of the market, the primacy of the just over the good (and of right over duty), subjective "freedom of choice" set up as a general rule, the taste for shoddy merchandise, the reign of disposable goods and planned obsolescence: all this is part of a contemporary system in which, under the influence of liberalism, the individual has become the center of everything and is set up as the universal criterion of value. To understand liberal logic is to understand what connects all these elements and their derivation from a common matrix.

Liberalism does not contain all of modernity within itself, but is its most illustrious representative ("the most coherent form of the modern project," as Michéa says, "but not its exclusive form"). Modernity has often been described as the age when the heteronymous way of life gave way to the autonomous, i.e., the moment when we passed from a society where behavior was subjected to the norms of the superego consisting of beliefs or traditions to a society where man conceives himself as a power free to create himself from himself alone. This conception obviously contains some truth but also quickly reaches its limits, for modernity has only put an end to certain forms of dependence and constraint in order to replace them with new forms of alienation: the exploitation of living labor, subjection to the law of value, transformation of the subject into an object, mass loneliness, the absurdity of forced labor, the collapse of the interior life, inauthentic existence, conditioning through advertising, the tyranny of fashion, the disappearance of intimacy, the judicializing of everything, the lies of the media, social control, the reign of political correctness, and so on.

Modernity is better understood by seeing in it the moment when society is no longer posited as primary, but when the individual is considered as prior to the social whole, which then becomes a mere aggregate of individual wills. Considered as a being fundamentally independent of his fellows, man is at the same time redefined as an agent permanently seeking to maximize his self-interest, thus adopting the behavior of a businessman with regard to the market (*Homo oeconomicus*). This unprecedented transition is precisely the work of liberalism. "The fundamental axis of modern European history can be summarized in this formula: the abstract individual becoming concrete," observes Marcel Gauchet.[6] In this sense it is not an exaggeration to speak of an individualist revolution, a revolution that must obviously be appreciated over the long term, for it has not only affected society but also transformed personalities, customs, and ways of thinking.

Individualism legitimizes egoistical behavior,[7] but it would be a serious mistake to make it a mere synonym for egoism, or to reduce it to egocentrism or the narcissistic bombast of egos.

---

[6] Marcel Gauchet, "Les métamorphoses de la personnalité contemporaine" ["Metamorphoses of the Contemporary Personality"], lecture delivered at La Salpêtrière, January 18, 2018, 7.

[7] This affirmation that man is above all else an egotistical being has led many authors to attribute to liberalism a pessimistic conception of human nature. But one could see in it the liberal form of optimism, since it is by acting in his own interest that the individual is supposed to serve everyone's interest the best: egoism then becomes a virtue.

There is an anarchistic individualism and even an aristocratic individualism, but the individualism spoken of here, individualism in the full sense of the term, is first of all tied to the rise of the bourgeois class and its values. Moreover, the individual is not the person, nor does individualism correspond to improved recognition of the person.

Marcel Gauchet has well described the difference between biopsychic and social individualism. Ancient societies in which legitimacy rested on beliefs, shared customs, or ancestral traditions were societies without social individuation, something that in no way hindered individual personalities from standing out prominently. Gauchet writes, "Societies without individualism involve very strong individuation, whereas individualism as we know it makes individuation very problematic."[8]

As a structural component of modernity, social individualization is inseparable from the rise of rights discourse—insofar as for liberalism man is defined above all as a bearer of rights, with law itself supposedly cognizant of nothing but equally free individuals. Liberalism is based on the conviction that there exist fundamental individual and inalienable rights both prior to and superior to any human institution, and that the first of these is the right to pursue one's own best interest freely. Such rights are obviously purely formal (the right to work has never provided anyone with a job), but this is not the important point: the fundamental right is the right to have rights. The society of individuals is both a society of which individuals are in the last instance the only and ultimate component (the *indivisible* social atom) and a society in which legitimacy is based exclusively on law: "The society produced by individuals is the society charged with producing the individuals that compose it by giving them the means of conducting themselves as individuals."[9] To say that man possesses rights *qua* man amounts in fact to saying that to be a man is to have rights: a society of individuals is one where the individual bearer of rights is the only source of legitimacy, for the separate individual human holder of rights is alone truly

---

[8] Gauchet, "Les métamorphoses," 3.
[9] Gauchet, "Les métamorphoses," 8.

human. This is why, in such a society, forms of communal assertion are easily seen as pathological even when they are not violent. This is also why whatever may remain of non-contractual
collective structures, beginning with the family, has been permanently delegitimized.[10]

For liberals, the sovereignty of individuals is based firstly on
their property in themselves: it is insofar as they own themselves
that they have the right not to be "owned" by anyone else, i.e.,
not to be dependent, as a matter of principle, on anyone else.
This is the very principle of the theory of possessive individualism that defines human beings as the proprietors of themselves.
In a book that has become a classic, Crawford Brough MacPherson[11] shows that the right of property in liberal doctrine is only a
secondary expression of this property in oneself, which establishes that man only possesses the character of man if he is independent of the will of another and is in no way beholden to society for his person, abilities, or choices. This theory supports the
idea that man is above all what he has freely chosen to be, that
he is entirely the master of his choices, and that he constructs
himself not from anything already there, but from nothing.

The consequences are considerable. Since the only legitimate
social actions are those based on the will of individuals, every
contract is based on an implicit or explicit calculation of the contracting parties' self-interest. Individual rights may thus be opposed to any social obligation or any political imperative. Marcel

---

[10] "No one appealed to the rights of man in court 50 years ago,"
Marcel Gauchet reminds us.

The idea would have appeared bizarre. Today, in all democratic
countries, the rights of man have become positive rights, inscribed in the legal code and to which courts refer with increasing frequency. . . . We are living in a social universe of individuals psychically constituted by their identification with their legal
status as individuals and according to the rights belonging to
them. ("Les métamorphoses," 9–11)

[11] Crawford Brough MacPherson, *The Political Theory of Possessive
Individualism: Hobbes to Locke* (Oxford: Clarendon Press, 1962).

Gauchet observes:

> An individual who defines himself purely by the rights he
> originally holds from the mere fact of his existence is an
> individual who owes nothing to society. He has a freedom
> with respect to it. He is, of course, able to influence its de-
> cisions and, if he wants, can participate in collective life
> and play a role in it. But nothing obliges him to do so.[12]

In the name of individual prerogatives, rights can turn into a
rejection of any power and any limit. As Pierre Manent writes,
"This is how, in the name of human rights, some people want to
forbid nations from making laws they may consider necessary or
useful for preserving or encouraging the common life and common education that give each nation its physiognomy and *raison
d'être*."[13]

Since the individual is the owner of himself, each should be
left entirely free in his preferences and choices as long as he does
not infringe other people's ability to do the same. The liberal
conception of individual rights can be summarized in this formula: as long as I do not prevent others from doing the same, I
have the right to do with myself anything I want (take drugs,
sell my bodily organs, rent out my uterus, work on Sunday, dis-
inherit my children, etc.). As a matter of principle, there is no
collective rule I must respect, and no public power can order me
to sacrifice my life for any cause at all. The right of property in
oneself thus takes no account of the praiseworthy or degrading
character of the way we intend to make use of ourselves. Similarly, according to strict liberalism nothing allows limits upon
the financing of electoral campaigns by private companies or
industrial lobbies, opposition to drug trafficking, or, as Michael
J. Sandel remarks, objections to cannibalism between consenting
adults . . .[14] The concept of political society thus disappears in

---

[12] Gauchet, "Les métamorphoses,"12.

[13] Pierre Manent, *La loi naturelle et les droits de l'homme* [*Natural Law
and the Rights of Man*] (Paris: PUF, 2018).

[14] Michael J. Sandel, "Do We Own Ourselves?" in *Justice: What's the*

favor of "civil society." This is perfectly logical, since civil society is never anything but an aggregation of private interests, and not a political community to which citizens must bear allegiance in order to participate in the common life. The result is what Pierre Manent observes: the undivided reign of individual rights automatically kills off the idea of the common good.

By the same token, the liberal conception of liberty is clarified. Liberalism, of course, is no more synonymous with liberty than egalitarianism is with equality, Communism with the common good, or humanism with humanity. Liberalism is not the ideology of liberty, but the ideology that puts liberty in the service of the individual alone. The only liberty proclaimed by liberalism is individual liberty conceived as emancipation from everything that goes beyond the individual.

In October 1841, in a letter addressed to John Sterling, the young John Stuart Mill already defined liberalism as the doctrine "that is in favor of allowing each man to be his own guide and sovereign" and of "acting exactly in the way he considers best for himself."[15] Later, in one of the best-known passages of his book *On Liberty* (1859), he writes:

> [A man] cannot rightfully be compelled to do or forbear because it will be better for him to do so, because it will make him happier, because, in the opinions of others, to do so would be wise, or even right. . . . Over himself, over his own body and mind, the individual is sovereign.

This way of looking at things is common to all currents of liberalism. L. Susan Brown writes, "A group cannot be liberated — it cannot, as a group, exercise freedom — only individuals can be free."[16] Jeremy Waldron adds, "The liberal rejects the view that the social order is constitutive of individual freedom."[17] From

Right Thing to Do? (New York: Farrar, Straus & Giroux, 2009).

[15] *The Earlier Letters of John Stuart Mill, 1812–1848*, ed. Francis E. Mineka (Toronto: University of Toronto Press, 1963).

[16] L. Susan Brown, *The Politics of Individualism: Liberalism, Liberal Feminism, and Anarchism* (Portland: Black Rose Books, 2003), 22.

[17] "Theoretical Foundations of Liberalism," in Jeremy Waldron, ed.,

the liberal point of view, "neither the common good, nor the country, nor any other value can justify restricting liberty."[18]

Liberals can insist all they like that the counterpart of liberty is responsibility; it is in fact obvious that as concerns ethics, they cannot develop the least conception of the good without contradicting their own principles. Léon Walras in his *Elements of Pure Economics* (1874) already said that from the liberal economy's point of view "There is no taking into account of the morality or immorality of the need that the useful thing corresponds to, and whose satisfaction it allows." Praise of egoism reaches almost caricatural proportions in the writings of Ayn Rand, the idol of libertarians, who goes so far as to claim "Altruism is incompatible with freedom."[19]

The principle of equal liberty is also based on the primacy of the individual insofar as he is no longer considered as a political and social being but as an atom not naturally bound to any other.

> Only beings posited as independent can be conceived as "similars," since that is the soul of equality. . . . The individual independence acknowledged in individuals means there is no legitimacy except what flows from the rights they hold from the fact of [their] equal original liberty.[20]

The social bond henceforth depends entirely on the contractual system. Liberalism affirms that anything can be negotiated — except individual liberty, which by nature is non-negotiable (the paradox then arising that it can only guarantee individual liberty on the condition that everyone agrees to consider it an essential value, which is rarely the case).

But the principle of undifferentiation holds not only in the

Liberal Rights: Collected Papers 1981–1991 (Cambridge: Cambridge University Press, 1993), 42.

[18] Françoise Orazi, *L'Individu libre,* 16.

[19] *The Objectivist Newsletter,* April 1963.

[20] Marcel Gauchet, "Pourquoi 'L'avènement de la démocratie'?" ["Why 'The Advent of Democracy?'"], *Le Débat,* January–February 2017, 184.

moral domain. The primacy of the abstract individual also operates in the sense of a generalized neutralization, of the expansion of the *neutral* effected by the ideology of Sameness at the expense of differences. It erases collective singularities between peoples and cultures just as it relativizes sex differences, for legal individuals have no sexed characteristics: "The order of priorities is reversed. It is tacitly established that we are first of all abstractly identical individuals and then, incidentally, of the male or female sex."[21] Laurent Fourquet puts it well: "To go ever farther in the neutralization of man: this means to tear from all concrete men their non-rational particularities so that men increasingly resemble that unique, ideal man who in humanist teachings is alone rationally able to govern a rational world."[22]

Just as protectionism is not autarky, autonomy must not be confused with independence. The former holds accountable; the latter separates. Liberals flatter themselves with emancipating man and thus making him more "autonomous." They do not see that autonomy does not consist in cutting oneself off from one's peers but in the capacity to think and act on one's own without eliminating all relation to others. (It is in this sense, for example, that by opposing the "slavery of salaried employment" the first socialists were fighting for the autonomy of the proletariat.) Liberalism claims to aim at autonomy, but in fact what it idealizes is the independence of individuals with respect to one another. Since individual initiative is only fruitful when framed by collective rules, the interaction of egoisms stimulates mimetic rivalry and the desire to eliminate competitors while it increases inequalities—much more than it favors the autonomy of agents. Just as free competition unavoidably ends in the formation of oligopolies and monopolies, abstract liberty involves a rise in inequalities and strengthens the hold of class. "The market can only emancipate human beings *according to its own laws*," to cite the excellent formulation of Jean-Claude Michéa. This may be

---

[21] Marcel Gauchet, "La fin de la domination masculine" ["The End of Masculine Domination"], *Le Débat*, May–August 2018, 81.

[22] Laurent Fourquet, *Le christianisme n'est pas un humanisme* [*Christianity is Not a Humanism*] (Paris: Pierre-Guillaume de Roux, 2018), 81.

paired with Guy Debord's observation that "The economy transforms the world, but only into an economic world." In liberal
society man is neither emancipated nor rendered more autonomous; he is transformed into a monad, atomized.

Pierre Manent explains: "For the Greeks, nature is what binds
us, what brings us together. . . . For us moderns it is the other
way around: nature is what separates us, for we are 'naturally'
separate individuals." Whence the paradox that "living together"[23] must today be preached on the "exclusive basis of a principle that strictly separates and dissociates. . . . We want to 're-
make the social bond' and reject the only idea that could give
meaning and content to this bond: that associative human nature
in which we find our goods and our ends."[24]

The liberal way is obviously not the only way of conceiving
liberty. Since Benjamin Constant, we have known of all the ways
that the liberty of the Ancients, understood as the ability to participate in public life, is opposed to the liberty of the Moderns,
defined as the right to free oneself from public life. Another way
of understanding liberty is in the republican and neo-republican
manner, those terms here designating the political tradition that
runs from Titus Livius and Machiavelli (*Discourses on the First
Decade of Titus Livius*) through James Harrington (*Oceana*, 1656),
all the way to authors such as Quentin Skinner and John Pocock.[25] If for liberals liberty is defined as that which escapes all
interference capable of limiting individual choice, for republi-
cans liberty is defined as non-domination and is never, as a matter of principle, restricted to the individual sphere: I cannot be
free if the political community to which I belong is not. This conception of society as a field of forces whose course is never determined in advance obviously implies the primacy of politics,
which alone can impose and guarantee the freedom of a people

---

[23] "*Vivre ensemble*," an expression recently popular with French politicians. —Trans.

[24] Interview in *Le Figaro Magazine*, June 8, 2018.

[25] Cf. Philip Pettit, *Républicanisme: une théorie de la liberté et du gouvernement* [*Republicanism: A Theory of Liberty and Government*] (Paris:
Gallimard, 2004).

or a country. Republican liberty is concerned with society as such, while liberal liberty proudly ignores it.

The work of the Quebecois sociologist Michel Freitag is part of this "neo-republican" current. We owe to him a fundamental critique of liberal liberty whose principal merit is directly tying the concept of liberty to that of the symbolic imagination.[26] As Daniel Dagenais explains:

> Freitag illuminates from the start, and contrary to a narrowly modern philosophical tradition, all that liberty owes to primordial conditions, rooted as it is in the autonomy of living things. Moreover, if liberty is made possible by the opening that allows access to the symbolic, if therefore it constitutes a human attribute par excellence, Freitag never ceases to insist on the substantial historical rootedness of symbolism in the concrete forms of society.[27]

Indeed, liberty does not fall from the empyrean of pure ideas. It is not an abstraction; on the contrary, it is always concretely situated. To ask ourselves about liberty is firstly to ask ourselves both about its limits (unconditional liberty is totally void of meaning) and about the conditions of its possibility — and to recognize that it is created and maintained above all by historical and political action, and that in this sense it is not so much a matter of justice in the legal sense as a matter of political choice or will. Freitag writes, "The subject cannot emancipate himself simultaneously from all his particular anchorage points without shedding his inmost humanity and everything accessible and concretely appropriable in it and through it."[28] This means that,

---

[26] Michel Freitag, *L'abîme de la liberté: Critique du libéralisme* [*The Abyss of Liberty: Critique of Liberalism*] (Montreal: Liber, 2011); Michel Freitag and Yves Bonny, *L'oubli de la société: Pour une théorie critique de la postmodernité* [*Forgetting About Society: Toward a Critical Theory of Postmodernity*] (Rennes: Presses Universitaires de Rennes, 2002).

[27] Daniel Dagenais, ed., *La liberté à l'épreuve de l'histoire: La critique du libéralisme chez Michael Freitag* [*Freedom in the Test of History: Michael Freitag's Critique of Liberalism*] (Montreal: Liber, 2017), 9.

[28] Freitag, *L'abîme de la liberté*, 382.

as for Hannah Arendt, liberty must not be founded on the individual, but on the social relation by which a world is constructed: all liberty is the manifestation of a concrete form of being much larger than itself.

For liberalism, man—far from being constituted as such by his bonds with others—must be thought of as an individual unbound by any constitutive form of belonging, i.e., outside any cultural or socio-historical context. Liberalism does not so much oppose liberty to constraint or domination as to the determination that would make the individual less than entirely free in his choices. Liberal freedom rejects all determination from the first, especially those forms that involve historical anchoring or cultural belonging that are not voluntarily chosen. In this sense it rests on what Jacques Dewitte has called "the denial of what is already there."[29] John Rawls, for example, explains that the choice of the form of justice to implement should be made behind a "veil of ignorance," abstracting from all the contingent factors of individual identity (ethnocultural belonging, social situation, sex, etc.). Thus what presents itself as a program of emancipation from all that might force us to be something, culminates in reality in an explosion of subjectivities and a clash of egos. Alasdair MacIntyre reminds us that "From the standpoint of individualism, I am what I myself choose to be."[30] This is why it is so difficult to give any account in the language of moral individualism of the sense of obligation we may feel toward our family, our community, our country, our people, and so on. From a liberal point of view, these feelings, tied as they are to a form of belonging upstream from ourselves, are illusory; there is no occasion for them to exist, for they have no meaning.

Jean-Claude Michéa writes:

---

[29] Jacques Dewitte, "Le déni du déjà-là. Sur la posture constructiviste come manifestation de l'esprit du temps" ["The Denial of What Is Already There: On the Constructivist Posture as a Manifestation of the Spirit of the Times"], *Revue du MAUSS*, no. 17, 2001, 393–409.

[30] Alasdair MacIntyre, *After Virtue: A Study in Moral Theory* (South Bend, Ind.: University of Notre Dame Press, 1981), 220.

One of the philosophical problems with which a liberal state is necessarily confronted comes from its excluding by definition any concept of devotion to one's community and, *a fortiori*, any idea of sacrifice (e.g., as by a resistance fighter). When "the country is in danger," the liberal state cannot count on any of its citizens to assure its defense at the risk of his own life.[31]

Michéa also notes that "the liberal watchword 'no countries, no borders,'" the natural complement of *'laissez faire, laissez passer,'* seems to have first appeared in 1777 in a book by the physiocrat Guillaume-François Le Trosne."[32] Thus, liberalism has no fundamental objection to globalism, all the less so in that globalism is in harmony with liberalism's intrinsic universalism (individuo-universalism) and contributes by definition to the limiting of national political sovereignty.

Ernest Renan used to say that "A nation is a soul, a spiritual principle." For the very liberal Bertrand Lemennicier, a member of the Mont-Pèlerin Society and Vice President of ALEPS (Association pour la liberté économique et le progrès social), the nation is nothing but an "elusive political fetish," a "concept with no counterpart in the real world," and a "representation of something that does not exist." He writes:

France is simply an *aggregate* of human beings. . . . What can the behavior of a group be if not the behavior of the members that compose it? How can a society have values or preferences independent of its members? It does not have any. . . . Nor should we be fooled by the sentiment of belonging. *We do not belong* to a nation, nor to a territory, not to state, none of which exist, unless we alienate our

---

[31] Michéa, *Le complexe d'Orphée*, 285.

[32] Jean-Claude Michéa, *Notre ennemie, le capital: Notes sur la fin des jours tranquilles* [*Our Enemy, Capital: Notes on the End of Quiet Days*] (Paris: Climats, 2017), 37. The expression *"laissez faire, laissez passer"* (or *"laisser faire, laisser passer"*) was coined in 1752 by the economist and international businessman Vincent de Gournay.

free will and our condition of human *qua* human [*sic*].

From that point, there can no longer be any question of the necessity in certain circumstances of dying for one's country: "Our lives cannot be sacrificed to an abstraction that has no intrinsic existence."[33] We note that the author does not ask himself for one second whether the inalienable rights he attributes to individuals are not also abstractions with no intrinsic existence. But at least he states matters clearly.

Also significant is the position of most liberals on the issue of immigration. Liberalism approaches this question from a purely economic point of view: immigration amounts to an increase in the supply of labor and in the potential mass of consumers thanks to individuals who come from abroad, in which respect it is positive. It is also justified by the imperative of the free circulation of men, capital, and commodities, while allowing a downward pressure on native wages. A million non-Europeans coming to settle in Europe is simply a million individuals coming to add themselves to other millions of individuals. The receiving nation, itself a mere aggregate of individuals, gets a certain supplementary number of economic agents. The liberal reasons as if people were interchangeable — which they are, in fact, as long as we only take the economic and quantitative side of things into account — forgetting along the way, as the historian Gilles Richard reminds us, that "The enormous abyss of inequality on a planetary scale due to triumphant neo-liberalism is itself what is provoking migratory waves."[34]

For a liberal such as Joseph Carens, immigration above all

---

[33] "La nation, fétiche politique introuvable" ["The Nation, an Undiscoverable Political Fetish"] on the website www.contre-points.org, February 21, 2018. Lemennicier uses the same argument to respond to the Nobel Prize-winning economist Jospeh Stiglitz, who stated that "Market economies are incapable of regulating themselves," viz., that "A market economy has no individual conscience and thus cannot lose its mind"! This clearly does not prevent him from speaking of "liberalism" as if it were a person.

[34] Gilles Richard, *Histoire des droites en France de 1815 à nos jours* [*History of Rights in France from 1815 to the Present*] (Paris: Perrin, 2017).

must not be regulated, for that would amount to violating the liberal principle according to which one cannot allow the consideration of contingent aspects of individuals' identities, starting with their origin or sociocultural belonging, to legitimize "inequality of treatment." Since citizenship status itself is usually determined by contingent factors, it must be considered arbitrary.[35] John Rawls also considers that each person must be left free to settle wherever he wants. This is also the position of the libertarians, of course (Murray Rothbard, David Friedman, Tibor R. Machan), for whom any regulation of immigration infringes on individuals' sovereignty.[36]

Milton Friedman thinks the best way to put an end to immigration is to dismantle the welfare state completely, which would have the effect of drying up welfare payments. He only forgets that in such cases, the first victims will be the poorest classes of the native population! Moreover, he does not see that for most immigrants the most attractive element is not so much welfare payments as the difference in average salary between their country of origin and their destination.[37] As for the liberal economist Gary Becker, he has found a solution in perfect conformity with his utilitarianism by proposing to have immigrants pay an entrance fee of an amount to be determined, which would have the advantage of admitting only the wealthiest, a measure of control by price that unavoidably reminds us of the "right to pollute" that certain economists propose granting to the most successful multinational companies.[38]

---

[35] Joseph Carens, *The Ethics of Immigration* (Oxford: Oxford University Press, 2013).

[36] Tibor R. Machan, "Immigration into a Free Society," *Journal of Libertarian Studies*, Summer 1998, 199–204.

[37] Cf. George J. Borjas, *Immigration Economics* (Cambridge, Mass.: Harvard University Press, 2014).

[38] Among the few liberals in favor of restricting immigration, we may cite Jean-Philippe Vincent, champion of an improbable alliance between conservatives and liberals (*Qu'est-ce que le conservatism? Histoire intellectuelle d'une idée politique* [*What Is Conservatism? An Intellectual History of a Political Idea*] [Paris: Belles Lettres, 2016]). His main argument is that "classical" liberalism proclaims the moral equality of indi-

Communitarians, on the other hand, recognize that the state has the right (and sometimes the duty) to regulate, limit, or forbid immigration, because once it reaches a certain level it infringes on cultural habits, the ways of life — in short, the mores — of the receiving population. It risks threatening their identity or destabilizing their social cohesion, the latter largely based on the confidence members of the society have in each other, which is itself largely dependent on the ease with which they recognize themselves in their neighbors and identify with them.[39]

Liberalism, as we have seen, rejects the idea that there are things or values that can be called intrinsically good even if some individuals do not accept them. The liberal state thus abstains as a matter of principle from any judgment concerning the way people choose to live. It has no business deciding between

---

viduals, but not their political equality: "Moral equality does not stop at national boundaries; but boundaries create a previously non-existent situation that legitimizes a political treatment that differentiates between nationals and foreigners, including candidates for immigration" (*Éthiques de l'immigration* [*Ethics of Immigration*] [Paris: Fondation pour l'innovation politique, 2018], 11). The whole question is whether (and to what extent) moral equality can be dissociated from political equality. We can also ask whether such a dissociation, which many liberals would not accept, can be considered a liberal principle. It should be noted that the President of the Foundation for Political Innovation's Scientific Evaluation Council is Laurence Parisot, who loudly came out in favor of immigration while serving as President of the Movement of the Enterprises of France.

[39] Cf. Russell Hardin, *Trust* (London: Polity Press, 2006); and Niklas Luhmann, *La confiance: Un mécanisme de réduction de la complexité sociale* [*Trust: A Mechanism for the Reduction of Social Complexity*] [1968] (Paris: Economica, 2006). Other authors come to the same conclusion by arguing from state sovereignty or, like Christopher Heath Wellman, from its autonomy of decision (cf. Christopher Heath Wellman and Phillip Cole, *Debating the Ethics of Immigration: Is There a Right to Exclude?* [Oxford University Press, 2014]). Wellman, who takes great care never to make use of the concept of sovereignty, also argues from freedom of association: if a country is free to choose with what other countries it wishes to associate or not, it is hard to see why it would not be free to do the same with this or that category of foreigners.

competing conceptions of morality; it must not contribute to giving a meaning to existence; it is not to encourage certain attitudes or discourage others — unless some of these contradict the rights of others. The government, as Robert Nozick emphasizes, must be "scrupulously neutral between its citizens."[40] Originally, liberalism hoped to pacify society and put an end to the wars of religion by attributing to the state a position of axiological neutrality based on the impersonal mechanisms of law and the market. The underlying idea was that passions and values could only divide society by fomenting conflict, whereas "peaceful commerce," fueled by rational egoism and the mere pursuit of private interests, was intrinsically pacifying. But we may imagine that at that time liberalism was still concerned not to damage the social fabric irremediably. It was not able to realize that public authority's disengagement in matters of norms and morality would result in a much more alarming dissolution of bonds, for no society could maintain itself on the basis of legal contract and commercial exchange alone.

This neutrality, of course, was largely artificial and cannot be assimilated to a pure relativism: even if he considers them equally legitimate as opinions, no liberal can think that a liberal and an anti-liberal proposition have the same value. Moreover, liberalism would have plenty of difficulty in considering all values to be equal since it makes individual liberty a supreme value. When he is attacked, he does not hesitate to defend himself — and, on the pretext of exporting his opinions across the world, he does not even shrink from preventive wars. In this we see the limits of his "pluralism." Contrary to appearances, neutrality does not favor pluralism, but the destruction of landmarks and the vanishing of the meaning we can give to collective life.

For Aristotle, justice consists in giving each person what he deserves (which involves determining who deserves what); for liberalism, it consists in making sure everyone enjoys equal rights. These are two different conceptions of justice, the former oriented toward the good, the latter indifferent regarding ends. The whole question, then, is whether the rights of which liberalism

---

[40] Robert Nozick, *Anarchy, State, and Utopia*, 33.

speaks can be justified by "justice" alone, i.e., without presupposing any conception of the good. On this point, as too often goes unnoticed, the liberal state, because of the very axiological neutrality it demands, cannot limit itself in any way:

> It can only really be fulfilled as a right to have rights, extensible to infinity. . . . The question of how to accord rival freedoms in a world of individuals conceived as egoistical [then] becomes philosophically insoluble. This is why, under the liberal management of societies, the war of all against all, is destined to continue forever.[41]

Political neutrality *vis-à-vis* different conceptions of the good is also at the heart of the logic of the market, which obviously passes no judgment on the preferences it satisfies, just as political neutrality is the legal basis of liberal doctrine. Now, the "neutrality" of the market is also merely apparent, for there are many circumstances where commercial exchange modifies the very nature of the good being exchanged (think, for example, of the sale of "rights to pollute" or the transformation of a particular good into an object of consumption). Moreover, it has the most serious consequences from the political, sociological, and anthropological point of view since it claims to abstract from all the ethical, philosophical, and religious convictions of the members of society, and by making the equality of individual freedoms the only legitimate basis of justice, it breaks with the traditional idea that public safety and the common good come about mainly by way of taking conceptions of the good into account in political debate. How can one be surprised, then, at the inability of liberal societies to legislate coherently on "social questions" (bioethics, assisted procreation, homosexual marriage, immigration, etc.) which inevitably involve a judgment in terms of substantive morality?

It is in light of the foregoing that one can understand the

---

[41] Jean-Claude Michéa, *La double pensée: Retour sur la question libérale* [*Doublethink: Return to the Liberal Question*] (Paris: Flammarion-Champs, 2008), 151, 154.

precise nature of capitalism, which, far from being an economic system tied to private property in rents and capital, is a "total social fact" (in the words of Marcel Mauss) from which issues the fetishized form that social relations assume in liberal societies. The society of individuals is quite naturally a market society, for the limitlessness of desire and the inflation of rights are counterparts to the limitlessness that is the very principle of capital reproduction. "Economic" man aims to maximize his self-interest, just as Form-Capital aims to maximize profit: both seek to increase themselves in the single category of *having*. They do not favor happiness but make it more problematic, since they imply permanent dissatisfaction and the unleashing of mimetic rivalry. As Jean-Claude Michéa remarks:

> A system based on mimetic rivalry and whose only obligation, as Marx said, is "to produce for the sake of producing and to accumulate for the sake of accumulation," can only favor the war of all against all and thus lead to the dissolution of all collective foundations of individual happiness and the common good.[42]

For his part, Alfredo Gómez-Muller writes: "Capitalism is not simply a mode of production, but also and above all a regime of enclosing the human within a purely instrumental and calculating rationality oriented toward the absolute finality of cumulative possession."[43] Capital is first of all a social relation that forms its own specific kind of imagination and involves ways of living in, and also conceiving of, the world. Those who think capitalism is a philosophically neutral system stubbornly fail to see this. Thus they mistakenly think that capitalism can be reformed, corrected, or reconciled with radically opposed values.

Thus, the fundamental trait of capitalism is not merely the

---

[42] Jean-Claude Michéa, "Solidaire et solitaire" ["Solidarity and Solitude"], debate with François Jullien, *Philosophy Magazine*, December 2014–January 2015, 70.

[43] Alfredo Gómez-Muller, *Nihilisme et capitalism* [*Nihilism and Capitalism*] (Paris: Kimé, 2017), 8–9.

abusive exploitation of living labor. Its fundamental characteristic, as soon as one conceives it as founding a social order that is really only an established disorder, is its orientation toward endless accumulation in both senses of the term "endless": a process that never stops and which has no goal other than increasing the value of capital, a system in which every surplus is employed to reproduce and increase itself — what Marx called "capital as value that adds value to itself in the cycle of its existence." The activity of the privative and accumulative appropriation of human and non-human reality, thus posited as the root of human behavior, presupposes a general representation of the world as an object susceptible of being appropriable, calculable, and rationalizable from one end to the other. The expansionist logic of capitalism hardly differs in its fundamentals from the process of the rationalization of the world that Heidegger calls the *Gestell*, or machination (*Machenschaft*). Perceived as an object without intrinsic meaning, the world is treated as fundamentally exploitable; it is called upon to become lucrative, a source of profit, in other words "value" in the economic sense of the term. It is this limitlessness in its aims as in its practice that makes capitalism a system resting on excess (*hybris*), the negation of any limit, and solely preoccupied with producing ever more value in order to increase capital ever further.

That the liberal philosophy implies the primacy of the economy, however, does not merely lead to the obsession with growth and the endless expansion of the market. It also feeds a directional and vectoral conception of history of a type fully comparable with that of the great historicist systems of the nineteenth century that were engendered by the philosophy of progress. As David Djaïz observes: "Political economy rests on the postulate of an indefinite process of production that brings with it growth, technical progress, and the perfecting of humanity. It favors linear and teleological representations of history."[44]

It also contributes to Western ethnocentrism, which tends to undermine the basis of traditional societies everywhere, since

---

[44] David Djaïz, "Un 'moment républicain'?" ["A 'Republican Moment'?"], *Le Débat*, March–April 2018, 173.

what today most characterizes the West "is capitalism *qua* impossibility of remaining within a border, *qua* passing beyond any border; it is capitalism as a system of production for which nothing is impossible except not being an end in itself." [45]

Using the image of a Moebius strip, Jean-Claude Michéa has shown the profound unity of economic, political, cultural, and "social" liberalism. He sees in it a double entry chart, specifically "two parallel and (more importantly) complementary versions of a single historic and intellectual logic."[46] Economic liberalism based on the market economy and universal competition is in fact structurally identical to political liberalism based on the rule of law and the reign of the individual, as well as to social liberalism ("libertarian liberalism") based on value relativism and the liberation of mores. This, by the way, allows us to understand how the postmodern "counter-culture" of the years after 1970 was able to feed into a new discourse legitimating capitalism, beginning with its theme of the "struggle against all forms of discrimination" that aimed to emancipate all identities not recognized at the time of the Fordist compromise; and secondarily why the Left, by rallying to the market, definitively cut itself off from the people.

From this it follows that economic liberalism and "liberal-libertarian" liberalism are bound to meet. As Michéa adds, "A Right-wing economy can only function in a lasting manner with a 'culture of the Left.'"[47] Already in his book *Impasse Adam Smith*, he had written:

> To simplify greatly, we can say that the modern man said to be "on the Right" has a tendency to defend the premise (the absolutely competitive economy) but is still having difficulty admitting the conclusion (civil unions, crime, the *fête de la musique*, and *Paris-Plages*), while the modern man officially "on the Left" tends to make the converse choices.[48]

---

[45] Pierre Clastres, "Ethnocide," *Encyclopedia Universalis*, online.

[46] Michéa, *La Double pensée*, 13–14.

[47] Michéa, *La Double pensée*, 65.

[48] Jean-Claude Michéa, *Impasse Adam Smith* (Paris: Flammarion, 2002). The *fête de la musique*, in which people are encouraged to play music in

Michéa has proven himself a good prophet, since it was when the financial crisis was constantly imposing austerity policies on societies headed toward pauperization, when industrial jobs had left the Western world, when sovereign debt had doubled since 2008, when income inequality was becoming enormous, when the share of salaries in the gross national product of Western nations fell to 57% as the income on capital continued to grow, when the disciplinary tutelage of the financial markets was daily furthering the dispossession of democratic sovereignty, when the national debt of France was on its way to passing 100% of the annual gross domestic product, when there were over three million unemployed and ten million poor, when 85% of employment contracts were for a limited term, when layoffs and "social plans" succeeded one another in a cascade, when the popular classes were hit directly by recession while the middle classes were for the first time threatened with downward mobility — that the French government chose, under François Hollande, to abandon all welfare policy in favor of "social issues" — of which the tussles over "marriage for all" were the most striking example.

The Left's rallying to the logic of the market and the mystique of growth has led it to believe that the arrival of a more just society would require tearing its members from their traditional forms of belonging (obstacles to the expansion of the market), uprooting them, abolishing borders, and forgetting the past. This conviction was already at the heart of the ideology of progress that the Left has never given up, but which has also received a new impulse from the demands for "efficiency" inherent in capitalist limitlessness. A high priority was then assigned to denouncing "ontological" inequalities linked to sexism, racism, religious fanaticism, etc., at the expense of all the concrete inequalities produced by social policies of liberal inspiration. Equality is henceforward assimilated to the critique of "stereotypes" and the "overcoming of taboos," while economic exploitation is passed over in silence. Social deprivation is no longer interpreted in

---

public spaces, takes place every June 21. The *Paris-Plages* are temporary artificial beaches created in the summer along the Seine. — Trans.

terms of class, but of the sociology of victimhood, individual setbacks, or identitarian categories associated with the critique of exclusion. The person whose identity has been "excluded" — the cultural or sexually marginal person—has replaced the worker, while celebrities [*les* people] replace the people [*le peuple*]. Justice is reduced to the struggle against all forms of discrimination and the extension in all directions of "for everybodyism."

"Progressivism" has rallied to the market all the more easily in that capitalism has at the same time taken up a culturally libertarian program. The liberal Right, for its part, has proceeded to the commercial recovery of critical thought by capitalizing on the decomposition of traditional social forms. In this way the great ideological osmosis of a financial Right that has betrayed the nation and a "permissive" Left that has betrayed the people has been realized. The two aspects of liberalism very naturally go together and, in the final analysis, liberalism has triumphed all along the line.

On the Right, the defense of liberalism has been carried out most especially by those milieus known as "national-liberal" or "conservative liberal," which believed (and still believe) they can reclaim economic liberalism and even political liberalism without conceding anything more than they want to the extreme individualism that philosophical liberalism inspires. Unfortunately, this position is untenable. How can one claim to regulate immigration while adhering to a liberal economic order that rests on an ideal of mobility, flexibility, the opening of borders, and generalized nomadism (*laissez faire, laissez passer*: "Let us build within a moving world!"[49])? How can one rely upon the "efficiency of the market" without acknowledging that such efficiency requires treating as non-existent the boundaries that separate and thus distinguish the different cultures of humanity? How does one defend the identity of peoples or nations while considering these collectivities as nothing more than aggregates of separate individuals? How does one deplore the serial bankruptcies of small businesses while celebrating competition and

---

[49] This is the slogan of the Crédit industriel et commercial (CIC), the fourth largest banking group in France. — Trans.

the logic of free trade that causes them? How can one appeal to "morality" while simultaneously reasoning from a doctrine that legitimates forms of individual behavior (the maximization of particular interests) that all authentic morality has always condemned? How can one restore "traditional values" without questioning a capitalism that works everywhere to suppress them?

"Conservative liberals" refuse to see that "it is precisely the continual development of the market economy that erodes the anthropological basis of these traditional values a little more every day, even as it destroys the ecological conditions of human life."[50] They do not want to understand that the perpetual movement of capitalist *hybris* can only involve ruptures that make it incompatible with any genuine form of conservatism. They often defend the idea that conservatives should defend the market because it is based on a spontaneous order, "the same as tradition." But the market is anything but spontaneous. We could even say in Hayekian terms that it results from a pure constructivism to which the state has not been alien.[51] As Laurent Fourquet has quite rightly said:

> Whoever takes up the struggle against the universal deregulation of the family is only acting meaningfully if his struggle against the universal deregulation of the family is coupled with a struggle against the universal regulation of the world by commercial contract. The activist who fights "for the family" but enthusiastically preaches so-called ultra-liberalism as soon as the talk turns to economics is not merely inconsistent: he is useless.[52]

Liberalism has in fact no choice but to oppose conservatism, which it perceives as the heir to the old order that the rise of capitalism ended. Conservatism defends the existence of a certain number of anthropological constants that liberal individualism

---

[50] Michéa, *Le complexe d'Orphée,* 138.

[51] Cf. Wendy Brown, *Les habits neufs de la politique mondiale* [*The New Clothes of World Politics*] (Paris: Les Prairies ordinaires, 2007), who does not hesitate to describe liberalism as a "constructivist project."

[52] Fourquet, *Le christianisme n'est pas un humanisme,* 279.

automatically deconstructs the moment it ceases to consider man a social and political being by nature. Roger Scruton, who wants to consider himself both conservative and liberal, implicitly recognizes this when he states, "It is important that in each society certain goods escape a commercial logic because they are considered sacred" — but he knows very well that it is impossible to adopt such a position starting from a liberal premise:

> We see a certain paradox emerge here. Individual liberty requires that the individual be free to circulate and exchange, but the individual does not exist independently from a social body, and when economic liberties are exalted like a new form of religion, they increasingly threaten the social bonds and thereby the individual's own existence.[53]

This problem also occurs for believers. Christianity certainly shares responsibility for the historical emergence of liberal ideology, since it was Christianity that "invented" the individual and began the process of disenchanting the world. But at the same time, the church has had the merit of always remaining faithful to the Aristotelian definition of man, as accepted by Thomas Aquinas, as a naturally political and social being. It also has the merit of having always condemned egoism, the search for profit at any cost (even if it has not always provided a good example of that itself).

Thomas Aquinas does not limit himself to condemning those forms of economic activity necessary to the development of modern capitalism (beginning with the credit system), but also takes a clearly holist position inherited from antiquity. For two centuries the church's teaching has not ceased to condemn the evils of cutthroat competition (*Quadragesimo anno*, 1931) and the

---

[53] Roger Scruton, Interview in *Le Figaro Magazine*, May 18, 2018, 36. *Cf.* also his interview with the journal *Limite* (January 2017): "There is a problem which has never been resolved: how to reconcile the free market with a controlled capitalism not based on the creation of new appetites and the replacement of spiritual values by material values" (22).

shortcomings of free trade doctrine (*Populorum progressio*, 1967), to criticize the principal of state non-intervention, to reject the idea of absolute private property, and to reaffirm the primacy of the common good ("Freedom of trade is only equitable if in accord with the demands of social justice"). The church has also condemned the belief according to which what comes from spontaneous order (in Hayek's sense) is better than what is socially organized and decided. John Paul II said that

> There is a risk in the spread of a radical ideology of the capitalist type that rejects any consideration of human needs as such, affirming *a priori* that any attempt to face them directly is destined for failure, and that, on principle, awaits the solution from the free development of market forces. (*Centesimus annus*, 42)

This, he adds, is why "We cannot accept the statement that the defeat of so-called 'real socialism' leaves only the capitalist model of economic organization." And it is well-known that Pope Francis has gone farther in this same direction, especially in his encyclical *Laudato si'* (2015).[54]

Attempts to reconcile Christianity and liberalism have not been lacking, but they have never succeeded for the simple reason that any consistent liberalism goes back to an explicit or implicit philosophy incompatible with the imperatives inherent in any genuine ethics (effective egoistic behavior must be judged insofar as it is egoistic, not insofar as it is "effective," i.e., not in a consequentialist fashion). This argument regularly recurs in the writings of Christian philosophers or theologians such as Alasdair MacIntyre, John Milbank, and William T. Cavanaugh, or essayists close to Radical Orthodoxy such as Rod Dreher, who forcefully criticize the liberal order and denounce the modern loss of the sense of community on the grounds that communities

---

[54] Cf. also the document published by the Roman Curia on May 17, 2018, under the title *Economicae et pecuniae quaestiones* ("Economic and Financial Questions").

are also the locus of real forms of solidarity.[55]

But let us return to French politics. As Régis Debray has observed, the presidential election of 2017 caused an old class division to reappear that some had thought gone forever. On the one hand, those with high to very high incomes, those elites belonging to the Caste, the middle and upper levels of management, and the *grande bourgeoisie*, the "self-employed," and the bobos; on the other hand, those with low to modest incomes, the unemployed, workers, and farmers, the lower middle class: everyone who no longer lives where jobs are created and wealth is accumulated. On the one hand, the inhabitants of the great metropolises; on the other, the "peripheral France" (in Christophe Guilluy's phrase) of the mid-sized towns, the deindustrialized zones on the edges of cities, and the rural communes. On the one hand, the believers in a France "open to the world" and adapted to the demands of the global market, their hands on their wallets as they sing the "Marseillaise"; on the other, a people that wants to perpetuate its immaterial patrimony, conserve its specific forms of sociability, and retain sovereignty over the conditions of its own social reproduction: in short, the winners and losers of globalization, the "party of tomorrow" and the party of always.

But above all, the election of Emmanuel Macron has brought with it a complete reconfiguration of the political landscape and the forces in play. In working to gather liberals of all stripes into a "central bloc" over the ruins of the great institutional parties attached to the old Left-Right divide, Macron—whom Marcel Gauchet has called "the first true liberal in the proper philosophical

---

[55] Cf. Alasdair MacIntyre, *Ethics and Politics* (Cambridge: Cambridge University Press, 2007); John Milbank, *Theology and Social Theory: Beyond Secular Reason* (Malden, Mass.: Blackwell, 1990); John Milbank, Catherine Pickstock, and Graham Ward, eds., *Radical Orthodoxy: A New Theology* (London: Routledge, 1999); William T. Cavanaugh, *Being Consumed: Economics and Christian Desire* (Grand Rapids, Mich.: Eerdmans Publishing, 2008); and Rod Dreher, *The Benedict Option: A Strategy for Christians in a Post-Christian Nation* (New York: Sentinel, 2017). According to Dreher, "Liberalism and consumerism are the two words that weaken the West and render it vulnerable to Islam" (interview in *La Nef*, January 2018, 14).

sense of the term to arise on the political stage in France for a very long time" — has confirmed the emergence of another divide that will impose itself lastingly in the coming years, for it ultimately involves an ideological redefinition confronting all the parties today. This great divide of the near future, both in France and in Europe, is that between liberals and anti-liberals, which is also a divide between political universalism and the specific socio-cultural features of each people.

This represents a double challenge. It remains to be seen if the Left can go back on its commitment to the market society and return to its original socialist inspiration. The future of the Left lies in its ability to turn back from this commitment and reappropriate the original principles of the socialist critique of capitalism, which saw in the traditional forms of belonging not an archaic residue, but a powerful tool of solidarity and protections (the "bonds that protect"), and which also knew that one never arrives at the universal except by way of particular rootedness (what Hegel called the "concrete universal," as opposed to abstract universalism). On the Right it remains to be seen if conservatives will be capable of regrouping to form a confederation between the popular classes and at least a part of the middle classes in a new "hegemonic bloc" by unambiguously repudiating the liberal doctrine championed by the dominant class and understanding once and for all that "national liberalism" and "conservative liberalism" are mere oxymorons.[56]

Let us sum up. Man is a "social animal" whose existence is consubstantial with that of society. Justice in the first instance is not a matter of rights but of measure, i.e., it is only defined as a relation of equity between persons living in society, so there are no holders of rights outside social life, and within it there are only those to whom rights are attributed. Economic life represents not a "sphere," but a dimension of social life that every traditional society has always placed at the lowest rung of its

---

[56] On this subject, cf. Guillaume Bernard, *La guerre à droite aura bien lieu: Le mouvement dextrogyre* [*The War on the Right Will Take Place: The Dextrorotatory Movement*] (Paris: Desclée de Brouwer, 2016).

hierarchy of values. Politics is the locus of sovereignty and legitimacy. Society is not the sum of the individual atoms that compose it, but a collective body whose good takes precedence over (without suppressing) mere party interests. Ethics involves never seeking one's own personal interest first but contributing to the organic forms of solidarity that strengthen the social bond. Civic belonging obliges people to work first of all for the common good. Liberty is not defined as the chance to escape political authority or exempt oneself from public life but as the chance to participate in it.

It is certainly not the state's job to substitute itself for business leaders nor for economic agents in general. The economic agent should be free in his activity . . . as long as it remains purely economic. The problem is that many social facts have both an economic and a political or cultural dimension. The state should intervene in economic matters each time an economic activity has a political dimension, for in regard to this dimension it is political authority that ought to be affirmed. Thus, the state need not accept the "law of the market" when the latter not only fails to contribute to the common good of the community of citizens over which it has authority but endangers its system of values, its social coherence, its cultural *habitus*, the integrity of its patrimony, or even its independence and thus capacity for action. Such a state has nothing in common with today's welfare state, the essentially "therapeutic" state that mothers its citizens and deprives them of responsibility, any more than with a "minimal state" charged only with managing the externalities that exceed the capacity of private agents.

It is also important not to make the "state" synonymous with politics or public life as liberals (but also statists) too often do by opposing "public" and "private" without nuance. When the welfare state is beginning to tire under the effect of its own excesses and is no longer able to offer citizens the guarantees of solidarity and the capacity for decision that formerly constituted the essence of its prerogatives, and this would be a false alternative. The idea of conferring on "civil society" the tasks of which we want to relieve the state is very ambiguous from this point of view. Applying the principle of subsidiarity rightly understood

certainly does not consist in conferring on the private sphere
what is withdrawn from the state, which would lead to passing
from one excess (universal welfare) to another (all sorts of exclusion), but rather in organizing public and private roles differently by recreating spaces open to participative democracy and citizen initiatives. Withdrawing into the private sphere can only
favor individualism, whose inevitable consequence is indifference to others, if not disguised civil war. We must therefore encourage a renewed citizenship based on participation and collective grassroots action. From this perspective, as Chantal Delsol
has rightly remarked:

> Tasks in which everyone has a stake cease to be the exclu-
> sive affair of the state — that, however, remains the guaran-
> tor of their effective and complete realization. Thus they
> do not become private business; they become, more pre-
> cisely, political affairs in the sense of everybody's affair.
> There is no doubt that citizenship itself would be deeply
> transformed by such a change.[57]

Incantatory recourse to the virtues of the "market" is similarly nourished by ambiguities. Speaking historically, the capitalist
system has indisputably shown itself to be more efficient than
the economic systems of the "countries of real socialism." But
what is meant by "efficient"? Efficiency is never an end in itself.
It only ever refers to the means chosen to bring about a certain
end, without telling us anything of the value of that end. Here it
seems the end is the production of an ever-increasing number of
commodities, a condition indispensable for the expansion of
capital. But what price must be paid in other areas for a further
gain in growth or productivity? It has often been observed that
the more societies are materially enriched, the poorer they become spiritually. Is there a relation of cause and effect here? Is it
possible that the endless development of the market encourages
man to reason exclusively in cost-benefit terms that can only be

---

[57] Chantal Delsol, *Le principe de subsidiarité* [*The Principle of Subsidiarity*] (Paris: PUF, 1993).

expressed within a purely material order? The reign of liberalism induces an economistic obsession that prevents the great majority of our contemporaries from asking themselves about the ultimate purpose of their activities and the very meaning of their presence in the world. As Marcel Gauchet writes: "A market society is a way of life in which mercantile values insinuate themselves into even the smallest aspects of human affairs. It is a place where social relations are refurbished on the model of the market."[58] The farther mercantile values spread, the more they tend to eliminate non-mercantile values, the ideal being attainment of a society where absolutely everything can be bought or sold.

Beyond a certain level of well-being, the amounts of happiness and unhappiness within a society barely depend on its wealth *at all*. We are not happier today than when we lived in less opulent societies. Perhaps we are even less so, for that opulence has come at the price of undoing the social bond and deconstructing a realm of symbolic imagery that helped us live. The good society is not fundamentally that which provides the means of existence, but that which gives reasons to live—i.e., *meaning*. Economic activity, efficient or not, provides only means.

Liberal capitalism was largely accepted by the population for decades for three main reasons: it favored growth, raised the average standard of living, and allowed an increase in consumption well beyond material need. Today, these three forms of legitimacy have disappeared. Growth is stagnating or barely progressing in the most developed countries, and no one knows how to make it "come back." The middle classes are falling back into the working class, if not into oblivion. Purchasing power is sinking, and economic inequalities (inheritance and income) are becoming more serious, even as states are no longer able to stand up to the financial markets and correct their effects. This loss of legitimacy is expressed in a dissociation between capitalism and democracy, which used to work. Unable to keep its

[58] Michael Sandel, *What Money Can't Buy* (New York: Farrar, Straus & Giroux, 2012).

promises any longer, capitalism finds itself in a critical situation utterly unlike the circumstantial crises that beset it in the past.

From a liberal point of view, in which markets are automatically in equilibrium as long as nothing interferes with their spontaneous functioning, crises can only be incidental events that do nothing worse than slow down the market's planetary expansion. The very concept of systemic crisis is foreign to liberal analysis. Yet, the capitalist system has been in crisis for a long time. To hide this, it first had recourse to credit in order to maintain the dynamic of overproduction and overconsumption that allowed the contradictions of industrial capitalism in the Fordist Era to be regulated, but this was merely a way of postponing the reckoning. Since the real economy was no longer able to bear the system, the latter became increasingly speculative and financial—not because it had "gone astray" as many believe, but quite simply to survive: financialization is merely a reckless way to avoid facing the facts of decreasing profits and the devaluation of value. But this resort is itself reaching its limits. To private debt is now added sovereign debt—i.e., state debt, which has multiplied exponentially over the past 20 years, and which everyone knows will never be paid off, in spite of austerity policies.

Lacking any better options, the system is trying to buy a little time by printing money as fast as it can, as for example by fabricating ever more fictitious capital. Previously meant merely to watch over the monetary system, the central banks to which states have abandoned their economic policies have chosen to create unlimited money. These injections of massive liquidity that favor speculation over production may artificially (and temporarily) secure the banks themselves, but they do not get the economy moving again. And just as capitalist progress has now destroyed everything that might regulate or limit it, a new global financial crash, much worse than that of 2008, is starting to appear on the horizon.

For his part, Marcel Gauchet thinks that if capitalism was so well received in the Western countries, this was not so much due to its efficiency, and even less because it has been perceived as "natural," but because it was profoundly consistent with a way of thinking long since won over to the primacy of the individual.[59] Capitalism is, as it were, the logical correlate of a society of individuals. But the paradox is that liberalism cannot function except through what survives of a non-liberal spirit within society. In this regard, Jean-Philippe Vincent is not wrong to write that "Adam Smith's invisible hand can do nothing without the second, conservative invisible hand of trust."[60] But how can supposedly self-sufficient individuals put in competition with everyone around them trust one another? The efficiency of the markets is not enough to produce the preconditions for its own existence, beginning with social cohesion and trust—all the more so in that its capacity for self-correction is largely illusory.

Jean-Claude Michéa observes:

> The liberal state is philosophically forced to launch a permanent cultural revolution whose aim is to eradicate all historical and philosophical obstacles to the accumulation of Capital, beginning with what in our days constitutes the absolute precondition of this possibility: total individual mobility—a mobility whose ultimate form is obviously the invitation, broadcast to all the most dangerous characters, to circulate without restrictions across all the sites of the global market.[61]

Herein lies the destructive power of liberalism. It must remove all obstacles to the expansion of the market but also methodically destroy any philosophical or religious system that condemns egoism and cupidity. The very idea that letting individuals follow their self-interest is enough to achieve economic efficiency and social harmony, which amounts to a complete reversal of the norms that have presided over the human presence in the world, suggests a kind of deconstruction that can only result in the total destruction of everything that has no commercial

---

[59] Marcel Gauchet, *Le nouveau monde. L'avènement de la démocratie, IV* [*The New World: The Advent of Democracy, IV*] (Paris: Gallimard, 2017).

[60] Vincent, *Éthiques de l'immigration*, 2.

[61] Michéa, *La double pensée*, 115.

value or that can be sacrificed to commercial value. This is also emphasized by the philosopher Jean Vioulac, who writes:

> The arrival of the consumer society imposes the dissolution . . . of everything capable of restraining the purchase of commodities, and thus the abolition of any morality that rejects the immediate satisfaction of desire. Liberalism, insofar as it is defined by the demand for deregulation and the de-institutionalizing of all forms of human activity, is the political project that seeks the complete dismantling of the legal order, and in this respect it is one of the most powerful motors of nihilism.[62]

Finally, the reign of capitalism expresses itself in a closure of meaning nearly without historical precedent.[63] This closure of meaning, which is also a closure of the possible, leads unavoidably to nihilism:

> Nihilism is the historical product of a social and economic regime in which the human capacity to create and recreate existential meaning and values tends to melt away, and where social activity tends to be reduced to the perpetual reproduction of means and ends subordinate to the absolute finality of having, and of power over the human and non-human. Since the nineteenth century, this model of society has been characterized as capitalist. . . . Capitalism is intrinsically a regime that devastates the human as well as non-human nature, a regime incompatible with culture.

---

[62] "The icy waters of egoistical calculation," *Esprit*, March–April 2014, 136. Eric Deschavanne observes, "Liberalism liberates the forces of historical transformation that permanently destabilize societies. Liberty especially liberates the forces that tend to destroy it," www.atlantico.fr, February 25, 2018. Cf. also Dany-Robert Dufour, "Du vrai, du beau, du juste et du bien: Hypothèses sur le déclin des idéaux de la culture occidentale," *Revue de MAUSS*, first semester of 2018, 174.

[63] Cornelieus Castoriadis spoke of a "total vacuum of meaning" (*La montrée de l'insignifiance: Les carrefours du labyrinth IV* [*The Show of Insignificance: The Crossroads of the Labyrinth IV*] [Paris: Seuil, 1996], 61).

. . . Nihilism is the overall representation of the world underlying capitalism.[64]

Liberalism has been able to play a useful role at certain historical moments by opposing dogmas that had become overly
cumbersome, but that does not make its principles any less false.
By basing itself on individualism, liberalism adopted an anti-
political stance from the start, for the simple reason that there is
no politics of mere individuals. There is only politics with reference to peoples and communities. The rise of individualism accompanied the collapse of the "grand narratives" which were
the vehicles of collective projects. But it also led to a corruption
of democracy. If democracy is fundamentally a political regime,
it is because it presupposes that the individual, rising above the
private sphere and perceiving himself as a citizen, identifies with
a collective cause and a general interest irreducible to any mere
addition of particular interests (whence the distinction Rousseau
draws between the general will and the "will of all," which is
never more than the sum of individual wills). The language of
rights has today become a discursive strategy that allows individuals and groups, on the basis of their subjective feelings or
desires, to launch a permanently escalating series of demands
without having to ask about their compatibility within a common world. From this point, the social bond can only result from
the harmony between individuals and from the confrontation
between their interests and rights. Insofar as liberalism claims to
place institutions in the service of the individual, it inevitably
opposes the common good. The liberal world is the *non-common*
world.

Just as one can oppose despotism without adhering to the
ideology of the rights of man, the alternative to liberalism is obviously not a return to the institutions and corporations of the
now-vanished *Ancien Régime*, nor in recourse to totalitarianism,
which consists, as Louis Dumont has shown, in trying to recreate a society of the holistic type artificially, working from individualist premises. It is better to seek to recreate the common by

---

[64] Gómez-Muller, *Nihilisme et capitalisme*, 8.

starting from the base—i.e., the social bond. Non-liberal society maximizes what individuals must do together and place in common. Giving priority to the common once again, to being-in-relation, is at the same time working toward the rebirth of the figure of the citizen, based on active participation, and remedying the desymbolization of social life.

It is not an accident that in the past "demands on behalf of the common were called forth by social and cultural struggles against the capitalist order" (Pierre Dardot and Christian Laval). Throughout European history, great popular revolts have taken the form of "communes" seeking local self-government, starting with the great Commune of 1871 that was of socialist, mutualist, federalist, patriotic, and Proudhonian inspiration (the "federation of the communes of France"). Conversely, in the nineteenth century it was with the suppression of the *commons*—those lands and pastures used collectively in conformity with customary law, and the establishment of areas for the privatization of fields and meadows—that the logic of the market triumphed in England. Men who enjoyed the use of what was held in common without ever possessing anything were stripped and robbed, while a vast movement to replace use-value with exchange-value, inaugurated at the end of the Middle Ages, became universal. From this point of view, we might say that present-day globalism represents the enclosure of the totality of the world.

That which is held in common is a matter of the social bond (and not of "connection"). It is the very principle of all life in society, but it is not a thing, a substance or quality, nor even an end aimed at or sought. Nor is it a synonym for the universal or public (as opposed to private). The common good is not beholden to any moral definition but to a political definition. At the beginning, the "com-mun" is the collective enjoyment of a *munus*. The *munus* belongs to the vocabulary of reciprocity and gifting (munificence, municipality, mutuality, communion), this Latin term being associated with the Aristotelian "put in common" (*koinônein*) which, by announcing the distinction between property and use, presupposes a relation of reciprocity between those who adhere to the same values and lead the same kind of life. The common (*koinôn*) refers to what belongs to the community (*koinônia*), but not to any of its members in particular. The common cannot be divided or shared: it need not be appropriated to fulfill its social function. It is even inappropriable by nature, for the excellent reason that it can only be enjoyed in common. It is defined as that which each can enjoy without dividing it. Moreover, it is inseparable from the practical activity necessary to institute it, which means that it is to be thought of mainly as the result of a coactivity rooted in *praxis* (the common use of what is held in common), and it is in this respect that it can also become a social force as well as a political principle for transforming society.

From this point of view, the common good means nothing other than a good which has been instituted in common. In the expression "common good," the second term counts for as much as the first, because the common by itself is already a good. Restoring the common and the common good is the program that offers itself today to all anti-liberals.

WHAT IS LIBERALISM?

Not being the work of a single man, liberalism has never presented itself as a unified doctrine. The authors who have laid claim to the name liberal have sometimes given divergent and even contradictory interpretations of it. Yet there must have been enough points in common between them to consider them liberal authors. It is precisely these points in common that allow us to define liberalism as a school.

We shall pick out the two most important.

Liberalism is firstly an economic doctrine that tends to make the self-regulating market the paradigm for all social facts. What is called political liberalism is merely a way of applying principles deduced from this economic doctrine to political life, principles that tend precisely to limit the role of politics as much as possible.

Secondly, liberalism is a doctrine based on an anthropology of the individualist type, i.e., a conception of man as not a fundamentally social being. Both characteristic traits have a descriptive and a normative side: the individual and the market are described as factual data as well as presented as models.

Thus, we cannot understand anything about liberalism as long as we oppose its principal forms (economic, political, cultural, philosophic) to one another, just as we cannot understand anything about capitalism if we see in it merely an economic system and not a "total social fact" (in Marcel Mauss' words). The deep unity of liberalism resides in its anthropology — an anthropology whose basis is individualism and economism, each inseparable from the other.

Louis Dumont has demonstrated the role played by Christianity in Europe's transition from a traditional society of the holist type to a modern society of the individualist type. From the beginning, Christianity posits man as an individual who, before any other bond, is in an inner relationship with God, and who can thence hope to achieve his salvation thanks to his personal transcendence. In this relationship with God, the value of man as an individual is affirmed, a value in relation to which the world is inevitably lowered or devalued. Moreover, the individual is, by the same title as other men, the holder of an individual soul distinct from his body (since destined to survive it), a prerogative that distinguishes him from other animals. Egalitarianism and universalism are thus introduced at the ultramundane level. The absolute value that the individual soul receives from its filial relationship to God is shared by all of humanity. This is the very logic of monotheism: if all men are equally sons of the same unique God, these men must be considered as belonging to the same family, which relativizes the specific cultures to which they belong. Hence the Apostle's well-known statement: "There is neither Jew nor Greek, there is neither slave nor free, there is neither man nor woman, for all of you are one in Christ Jesus" (Gal. 3:28). God's people have no borders.

Marcel Gauchet concurs with this observation of a causal connection between the emergence of a personal God and the birth of an *inner man* whose fate in the beyond depends only on his individual actions and whose independence is foreshadowed by this possibility of an intimate relationship with God, i.e., one involving only himself. He writes:

> The farther God recedes into his infinitude, the more the relationship with him tends to become purely personal, to the point of excluding any institutional mediation. Raised to the absolute, the divine subject can have no legitimate terrestrial counterpart except in intimate presence. Thus the interiority with which we began becomes a thoroughgoing religious individualism.[1]

The Pauline teaching reveals a dualistic tension that makes the Christian, at the level of his relationship with God, an "individual outside the world": becoming a Christian originally involved renouncing the world in some sense. Over the course of

---

[1] Marcel Gauchet, *Le désenchantement du monde* [*The Disenchantment of the World*] (Paris: Gallimard, 1985), 77.

history, however, the individual outside the world gradually came to contaminate worldly life. In 380 AD, under the Emperor Theodosius, Christianity became a state religion. As it acquired the power to make the world conform to its own values, the individual originally posited as outside the world gradually returned to immerse himself in it and deeply transform it. This process occurred in three main steps. At first, life in the world was no longer rejected but relativized: this is the Augustinian synthesis of the two cities, which shows both what opposes them and what connects them. In a second phase, the papacy assumed political power and itself became a temporal power. Finally, with the Reformation, man completely invested himself in the world, where he worked for the glory of God by seeking a material success that he interprets as the very proof of his election. The principle of equality and individuality, which at first only functioned at the level of the relationship with God and could thus coexist with an organic and hierarchical principle structuring the social whole (this was the case during the entire Medieval period), thus finds itself gradually brought back to Earth to end up as modern individualism, which represents its secular continuation. As Alain Renaut writes, expounding the theses of Louis Dumont: "For modern individualism to be born, the individualist and universalist component of Christianity had to 'contaminate' modern life, so to speak," to the point that the two representations gradually united, the initial dualism was erased, and "Life in the world was conceived as capable of being wholly compatible with the supreme value." At the end of this process, "The individual-outside-the-world became the modern individual-within-the-world."[2]

By this point, the organic society of the holistic type had disappeared. To cite a celebrated distinction, we had passed from community to society, i.e., to a common life conceived as a mere contractual association. It would no longer be the social whole that came first but the individual holders of rights bound to one

---

[2] Alain Renaut, *L'ère de l'individu. Contribution à une histoire de la subjectivité* [*The Era of the Individual: Contribution to a History of Subjectivity*] (Paris: Gallimard, 1989).

another by rational and hardly disinterested contracts.

One important stage in this evolution corresponds to nominalism, which affirmed with William of Ockham in the fourteenth century that no being exists apart from particular being (it was also from Spanish scholasticism that the subjective theory of value derives[3]). Another key moment corresponds to Cartesianism, which already posited the individual in the philosophical field, as would later be presupposed by the legal perspective of the rights of man and the intellectual perspective of Enlightenment reason. From the eighteenth century, this emancipation of the individual with respect to his natural bonds would regularly be interpreted as marking humanity's accession to "adulthood" within a narrative of universal progress. Underpinned by the individualist impulse, modernity would be characterized primarily by a process through which kin and local groups, as well as larger communities, gradually disaggregate in order to "liberate the individual," i.e., in fact to dissolve all organic relations of solidarity.

Being human has always meant asserting oneself both as a person and as a social being, with the individual and collective dimensions being irreducible to one another, yet inseparable. In the holist view, man constructs himself on the basis of what he has inherited and with reference to his socio-historical context. It is this model, historically the most common, that individualism (which must be regarded as a peculiarity of Western history) directly opposes.

Individualism in the modern sense of the term is the philosophy that considers the individual as the sole reality and takes him as the principle of all evaluation. Liberalism posits the individual and his supposedly "natural" liberty as the only normative courts of appeal for life in society, which amounts to saying

---

[3] Cf. Wim Decock, *Theologians and Contract Law: The Moral Transformation of the Ius Commune (ca. 1500–1650)* (Leyden: Martinus Nijhoff, 2013). On the "theological thoughtlessness at the heart of economic rationality," cf. also Sylvain Piron, *L'occupation du monde* [*The Occupation of the World*] (Brussels: Zones sensibles, 2018).

that it makes the individual the one and only source of values and of the ends he chooses for himself. This individual is considered *per se*, abstracting from all social or cultural context. While holism expresses or justifies existing society with reference to inherited, transmitted, and shared values—i.e., in the final analysis, with reference to society itself—individualism posits its values independently of society as it is met with. This is why it recognizes no autonomous state of existence belonging to communities, peoples, cultures, or nations. In these entities, which it apprehends by way of methodological individualism, it sees mere aggregates of individual atoms and posits that they alone have value.

At the same time, man is posited as a producing and consuming being, egoistic and calculating, who always and only seeks to maximize his own utility rationally, i.e., his best material interest and private profit. This thesis makes of man a being of calculation and interest. The model is that of the tradesman in the market: the *Homo oeconomicus*. From that point, society consists only of a series of market relations.

This primacy of the individual over the collective is at once descriptive, normative, methodological, and axiological. The individual is supposed to come first, whether considered prior to the social in a mythical representation of "prehistory" (the priority of the state of nature), or whether a mere normative primacy is attributed to him (the individual is what is most valuable). Georges Bataille stated that "At the base of every being there exists a principle of insufficiency"; liberalism by contrast affirms the full sufficiency of the singular individual. In liberalism, man can apprehend himself as an individual without having to think of his relationship to other men within a primary or secondary society. As an autonomous subject who is the owner of himself and moved by his own particular interest, he defines himself (by opposition to the person) as a "moral being, independent, autonomous, and thus essentially non-social."[4]

---

[4] Louis Dumont, *Homo aequalis. Genèse et épanouissement de l'idéologie économique* [*Homo aequalis: Genesis and Flourishing of Economic Ideology*] (Paris: Gallimard, 1977), 17.

In liberal ideology, this individual is the holder of rights inherent in his "nature," whose existence in no way depends on political or social organization. Here we are within the horizon of the theory of subjective rights that Michel Villey has shown to oppose on every point natural right as posited by the Ancients, which limited itself to determining the just share to be attributed to everyone ("*suum cuique tribuere*"[5]). Governments must guarantee these "natural" rights but cannot provide the basis for them. Existing prior to any social life, they are not immediately paired with duties, for duties imply precisely that there has been a beginning of social life: there is no duty to others where there are not already others. The individual is thus himself the source of his own rights, starting with the right to act freely according to the calculus of his own particular interests. Thus he finds himself at war with all other individuals, since they are all supposed to act the same way within a society conceived as a competitive market.

Although individuals can indeed choose to associate with one another, the associations they form have a merely conditional character, contingent and transitory, since they remain dependent on mutual consent and have no goal other than satisfying the particular interests of each party as fully as possible. Social life, in other words, is no longer a matter of anything but individual decisions and discriminatory choices. Man behaves as a social being not because it is part of his nature, but because he is supposed to find it advantageous, i.e., it has no ethical relation to him. If he finds no more advantage in it, he can break the agreement (at least in theory). It is even by thus breaking the agreement that he would best display his own freedom. As opposed to the liberty of the Ancients, which consisted primarily in the opportunity to participate in public life (in Rome there was an indissoluble connection between *civitas* and *libertas* that we also find in Greece), the liberty of the Moderns consists above all in the right to withdraw from public life. The fundamental right for liberals is the right of secession: the "right to leave," as Baudelaire said. This is why liberals always tend to define liberty as

---

[5] "To give each his own" — Trans.

synonymous with independence.[6] Thus Benjamin Constant celebrates "the peaceful enjoyment of private individual independence," adding that "To be happy, men only need to be left in perfect independence regarding everything related to their occupa-
tions, undertakings, sphere of activity, and fancies."[7] This
"peaceful enjoyment" is to be understood as a right not subject
to any duty of belonging, nor to any of those allegiances that, in
certain circumstances, can in fact reveal themselves as incompatible with "private independence." Society only exists to satisfy
individual desires that are immediately transformed into
"needs" and "rights," something that robs the concept of the
common good of all meaning.

Liberals particularly insist on the idea that individual interests should never be sacrificed to the collective interest, the
common good, or public safety, concepts they consider inconsistent with individual interests. This conclusion follows from
the idea that only individuals have rights, while collectivities,
being mere sums of individuals, cannot have any rights properly
belonging to them. Thus, Ayn Rand writes, "The expression 'individual rights' is redundant; there is no other source of rights."[8]
Benjamin Constant says, "Individual independence is the first of

---

[6] Some liberal authors, however, have distinguished between independence and autonomy, while others (or the same ones) have striven
to distinguish between the subject and the individual, or between individualism and narcissism. Unlike independence, autonomy remains
compatible with submission to supra-individual rules, even when the
latter arise from a self-based normativity. This, in other words, is the
view defended by Alain Renaut (*L'ère de l'individu*, 81–86). This way of
proceeding is not very convincing. Autonomy is in fact very different
from independence — in certain respects it is even its contrary — but this
is not the essential question. The essential question is what can, from a
liberal point of view, force an individual to respect any limitation on
his freedom if such a limitation contradicts or limits his self-interest?

[7] Benjamin Constant, *De la liberté des Anciens comparée à celle des Modernes* [*On the Liberty of the Ancients Compared to That of the Moderns*]
(1819).

[8] Ayn Rand, *The Virtue of Selfishness* (New York: New American Li-
brary, 1964).

modern needs. Consequently, one must never demand that it be sacrificed to establish political liberty."[9] Before him, John Locke declared that "A child is born a subject of no country or government," since once he becomes an adult, "He is a freeman, at liberty as to what government he will put himself under. He is free to choose the government under which he wants to live, what body politic he will unite himself to."[10]

The liberty to which liberalism appeals is an abstraction, tied to a "right" inherent in the human person which posits that the individual is justified in doing (and in demanding that he be able to do) what he wants with his own time, body, or money. Moreover, man is supposed to make choices only downstream from himself, without ever being conditioned or shaped by his heritage or belonging. Liberal freedom thus supposes that individuals can abstract from their origins, their environment, the context in which they live and in which their choices are made — i.e., from everything that makes them what they are and not otherwise. In other words, as John Rawls says, the individual is always prior to his ends. He is all the freer insofar as he is detached from all belonging, and he is supposed to construct his preferences just as he constructs himself: from nothing. But it cannot be demonstrated that the individual can apprehend himself as a subject free of all allegiance and determination. Nor does anything demonstrate that he will in all circumstances prefer his own liberty to every other good. By definition, such a conception ignores engagements and attachments that owe nothing to rational calculation. It is a purely formalist conception that does not allow any account to be taken of what a real person is.

From a liberal point of view, the individual has the right to do everything he wants so long as the use he makes of his freedom does not limit that of others. In other words, individual liberty must not be a burden to others, i.e., not be exercised to the detriment of the freedom of others. Liberal freedom "consists in being able to do anything that does not harm others" (Article 4

---

[9] Constant, *De la liberté des Anciens* (1819).

[10] John Locke, *Second Treatise of Government* (1689), Chapter 8.

of the Declaration of the Rights of Man and of the Citizen, August 1789), on pain of exposing himself to the punishments established by law. Since respect for the law has nothing to do with morality, all ethical preoccupations immediately disappear. Every desire is thus considered legitimate as long as it does not contradict the desires of another. With this one condition, all is possible and permitted. Liberty is then defined as the pure expression of a desire with no theoretical limit but the desire of someone else, the totality of these desires being mediated by commercial exchange. This is already what Grotius, the theoretician of natural right, affirmed in the seventeenth century: "It is not contrary to the nature of human society to work in one's own interest, provided one does so without damaging the rights of others."[11] From the start, all our desires are legitimate from the mere fact that they are ours!

This proposition obviously sins firstly by its irenic character: nearly all human acts are carried out in one way or another at the expense of the freedom of others. Moreover, it is nearly impossible to determine the moment at which the freedom of one individual can be considered as limiting that of others. Understood this way, liberal freedom is really defined in a purely negative fashion as the rejection of any external admixture ("freedom from" rather than "freedom for"). Moreover, and above all, it cannot involve any obligation to act for one's own good, nor even with a view to any good: one can even harm oneself provided this does not bother anyone. This is the radical abandonment of the idea of *telos*, or the search for intrinsic excellence. As Pierre Manent has put it, liberalism is first of all the renunciation of thinking about human life in terms of its good or its end.

In fact, the freedom of liberals is above all the freedom to possess. It resides not in being, but in having. Man is said to be free insofar as he is an owner, in the first instance, of himself; the fetishization of individual private property is merely a consequence of this. This idea that property in oneself fundamentally determines liberty will be taken up again by Marx.[12]

---

[11] Hugo Grotius, *On the Law of War and Peace* (1625).

[12] In certain respects, Marx himself adheres to a metaphysics of the

Alain Laurent defines self-realization as an "ontological insularity whose primary end lies in the search for one's own happiness."[13] For liberal authors, the "search for happiness" is defined as the free possibility of always seeking to maximize one's own best interest. But the problem instantly arises of what is to be understood by "interest," especially since those who follow the axiomatics of interest rarely concern themselves with describing its genesis or components, any more than they ask whether all social actors are fundamentally motivated by the same interests, or whether their interests are commensurable or mutually compatible. When cornered, they tend to give a trivial definition of the term: "interest" becomes for them a synonym for desire, intention, action directed toward a goal, etc. Everything becomes "interest," and even the most altruistic, most disinterested of actions can thus be defined as egoistic and self-interested since it corresponds to a voluntary intention (to a desire) of its author. But in reality, it is clear that, for liberals, interest is defined first

---

individual, something that led Michel Henry to see in him "one of the premiere Christian thinkers of the West" (*Marx* [Paris: Gallimard, 1976], vol. 2, 445). The thesis of Marxian individualism has been maintained by numerous authors, starting with Louis Dumont. Pierre Rosanvallon also writes: "The whole philosophy of Marx can be understood as an attempt to deepen modern individualism. The concept of class struggle itself only has meaning within the framework of an individualist image of society. In a traditional society, on the contrary, it has no meaning" (*Le libéralisme économique. Histoire de l'idée de marché* [*Economic Liberalism: History of the Idea of the Market*] [Paris: Seuil-Points, 1989], 188–89). Marx nonetheless rejects the fiction of the *Homo oeconomicus* that developed beginning in the eighteenth century, for he sees that the bourgeoisie uses it to alienate the real individual and chain him to an existence restricted to the sphere of self-interest. Now, for Marx, self-interest is merely the expression of a separation of the individual from his life. This is the basis of what is best in his work, viz., his critique of commodity fetishism, the "reification" of social relations. But he has no intention of substituting any common good for private interest. For him there is not even any class interest.

[13] Alain Laurent, *De l'individualisme. Enquête sur le retour de l'individu* [*On Individualism: Inquiry into the Return of the Individual*] (Paris: PUF, 1985), 16.

of all as a material advantage which, to be appreciated as such, must be susceptible to calculation and quantification, i.e., to being expressed within the horizon of that universal equalizer known as money.

Recognizing the individual's inalienable right to his freedom of choice automatically involves the equal social and legal acceptance of every conceivable manner of living. As Charles Robin has written: "In such a context, any reference to any sort of common morality or shared values can only appear fundamentally authoritarian and destructive to freedom, insofar as it continues to accord a meaning and philosophical legitimacy to *something beyond the individual.*"

From this point, one can hardly be surprised that the rise of liberal individualism has expressed itself first by a gradual dislocation of the organic structures of existence characteristic of holist societies, then by a general dissolution of the social bond, and finally by a situation of relative social anomie in which individuals find themselves to be increasingly strangers and potential enemies of one another, since all are caught up in that modern form of the "struggle of all against all" which is generalized competition. Such is the society described by Tocqueville in which each member, "withdrawn, is like a stranger to all the others." Liberal individualism tends everywhere to destroy direct sociability — which was long an obstacle to the emergence of the modern individual — and the collective identities associated with it. As Pierre Rosanvallon writes, "Liberalism somehow makes the depersonalization of the world the condition for progress and freedom."[14]

Liberalism must, however, recognize the fact of society. But instead of asking why the social realm exists, liberals are mainly preoccupied with understanding how society is able to establish itself, maintain itself, and function. Society, as we have seen, is for them nothing but the sum of its members (the whole is nothing but the sum of its parts). It is nothing but the contingent product of individual wills, a mere assemblage of individuals all

---

[14] Rosanvallon, *Le libéralisme économique*, vii.

seeking to defend and satisfy their particular interests. This society can be conceived either as the consequence of an initial rational voluntary act (the fiction of the "social contract") or as the result of the systematic interplay of all the actions produced by individual agents, an interplay regulated by the "invisible hand" of the market which "produces" the social realm as the unintentional result of human behavior. The liberal analysis of social reality thus rests upon either the contractual approach (Locke), or recourse to the "invisible hand" (Smith), or the idea of a spontaneous order not subordinate to any design (Hayek). The essential goal of society, according to liberals, is to regulate relations of exchange. In the end, it is a mere market.

All liberals develop the idea of a superiority of regulation by the market, which is supposedly the most effective, most rational, and therefore also most just way of harmonizing exchanges. At a first approach, then, the market presents itself as an "organizational technique" (in the words of Henri Lepage). From an economic point of view, it is both the real place where commodities are exchanged and the virtual entity where the conditions of exchange are formed in an optimal manner, i.e., the adjustment of supply and demand, as well as price levels. (From this point of view, there obviously cannot be any salary too high or too low, nor any abusive price, which permits the dismissal of any critique on this subject as "emotional.") As for the optimal functioning of the market, it involves nothing interfering with the free circulation of goods and services, men, and commodities, i.e., borders are considered non-existent. Whence the cosmopolitanism inherent in liberal capitalism, which is also the principle of free trade: "*Laissez faire, laissez passer!*" (This is also why employers have always ardently defended immigration, to which it has recourse all the more gladly in that it allows downward pressure on salaries.[15])

---

[15] It is not an accident that Laurence Parisot, then President of MEDEF [Mouvement des entreprises de France, France's largest employers' association], launched an appeal in *Le Monde* (April 17, 2011) for France to "remain an open country that profits from mixture." Jean-Claude Michéa writes: "Putting workers in competition with one an-

But liberals do not ask about the origin of the market, either. Just as man is supposedly "naturally" oriented toward the search for his best interest, commercial exchange is for them the "natural" model for all social relations. It follows that the market is also a "natural" entity, defining an order prior to any deliberation and decision. Constituting the form of exchange most conformable to human nature, the market was supposedly present from the dawn of humanity in all societies — which is obviously false, for in traditional societies the dominant logic is that of gift and counter-gift (defined by the triple obligation to give, to receive, and to pay back). For the physiocrats, Frédéric Bastiat, and Jean-Baptiste Say, for example, capitalism is an economic system born of the most natural human penchant, the market itself constituting the most "natural" form of exchange. (One wonders, then, why it did not appear earlier!) This is also what Alain Minc naïvely states: "Capitalism cannot collapse; it is the natural state of society. Democracy is not the natural state of society. The market is [*sic*]."[16] We find here the tendency of any ideology to "naturalize" its presupposition; in other words, to present itself not as what it is, a construction of the human mind, but as mere description, a simple transcription of the natural order.[17] With

---

other — of which the summoning of foreign workers is merely one form among others — has always constituted the most effective weapon at the capitalists' disposal (along with the formation of what Marx called 'the reserve industrial army'; in other words, a permanent brigade of the unemployed) for exercising a continual downward pressure on salaries, and thus increasing their own profits" (*Notre ennemi, le capital*, 151).

[16] Alain Minc, *Cambio 16*, December 5, 1994.

[17] This pretention has long been criticized. Cf. especially Karl Polanyi, *La grande transformation: Aux origines politiques et économiques de notre temps* [*The Great Transformation: The Political and Economic Origins of Our Time*] [1944] (Paris: Gallimard, 1983); and Réné Passet, *L'illusion néo-libérale* [*The Neoliberal Illusion*] [2000] (Paris: Flammarion-Champs, 2001). But there are disagreements on this point among liberal authors. Not all believe in the existence of a human nature, despite the difficulty of speaking of "rights of man" under such conditions, and Hayek interprets the market as literally *against nature*, which in his eyes is a reason for valuing it!

the state simultaneously rejected as artificial, the idea of a "natural" regulation of the social realm by way of the market is free to impose itself.

By understanding the nation as a market, Adam Smith carries out a fundamental dissociation of the concept of space from that of territory. Breaking with the mercantilist tradition that still identified political territory with economic space, he shows that the market cannot by nature be enclosed within specific geographic limits. The market in fact is not so much a space as a network. And this network is called upon to expand to the limits of the Earth, since in the end its only limit resides in the impossibility of exchange. Smith writes in a celebrated passage:

> A merchant . . . is not necessarily the citizen of any particular country. It is in a great measure indifferent to him from what country he carries on his trade; and a very trifling disgust will make him remove his capital, and, together with it, all its industry which it supports, from one country to another.[18]

These prophetic lines justify Pierre Rosanvallon's declaration that Adam Smith was the "first consistent internationalist." "Civil society conceived as a fluid market extends to all men and allows the divisions between countries and races to be overcome," he adds.

The principal advantage of the concept of the market is that it allows liberals to resolve the difficult question of the basis of obligation within the social contract. The market can in fact be considered as a law that regulates the social order without any legislator. Regulated by the action of an "invisible hand," itself naturally neutral since it is not incarnated in concrete individuals, it institutes an abstract form of social regulation founded on objective "laws" supposedly providing for the regulation of relations between individuals without any relationship of subordination or command between them. The economic order is thus called upon to realize the social order, with both being definable as

---

[18] Adam Smith, *An Inquiry into the Nature and Causes of the Wealth of Nations* (1776), Book III, chapter 4.

something that emerges without having been instituted. Since universal utility is no more than the aggregation of the utility of individuals, we simultaneously postulate the natural and spontaneous harmonization of interests. As Milton Friedman says, the economic order is "the unintended and unwilled consequence of the actions of a large number of persons moved only by their interests." This idea, which was extensively developed by Hayek, is inspired by Adam Ferguson's formula (1767) referring to social facts that "derive from the action of man, but not from his design."

Smith's metaphor of the invisible hand is well-known: in seeking "only his own gain, . . . he is . . . led by an invisible hand to promote an end that was no part of his intention."[19] This metaphor goes well beyond the banal observation that the results of men's actions are often very different from what they were counting on (what Max Weber called the "paradox of consequences"). In fact, Smith places his observation within a resolutely optimistic perspective, writing:

> Every individual is continually exerting himself to find out the most advantageous employment for whatever capital he can command. It is his own advantage, indeed, and not that of the society, which he has in view. But the study of his own advantage naturally, or rather necessarily, leads him to prefer that employment which is most advantageous to the society.[20]

---

[19] Smith, *Wealth of Nations*, Book IV, chapter 2.

[20] Free trade, as theorized in the last century by the Heckscher-Ohlin-Samuelson model (cf. Bertil Ohlin, *Interregional and International Trade* [Cambridge: Harvard University Press, 1933]), also rests on the belief in an "invisible hand," as well as on Ricardo's principle of an international division of labor and the postulate of the possibility of a "pure and perfect competition" (or "free and undistorted competition"). It has been shown many times that at the macro-economic level these beliefs are illusory and that the universalization of free trade ends in the ruin of political sovereignties; the dismantling of the state's capacity for action; the strengthening of the dominant positions and the widening of inequalities, dislocations, and the moving of industry to

This metaphor's theological connotations are obvious: the "invisible hand" is merely a secular avatar of Providence. But it must be specified that contrary to what is often believed, Adam Smith does not assimilate the very mechanism of the market to the action of the "invisible hand," for he only has the latter intervene to describe the end result of the totality of market exchanges. Moreover, Smith also admits the legitimacy of public intervention when individual actions alone do not succeed in realizing the public good. But this restriction will quickly disappear. Hayek forbids on principle any global approach by the society: no institution, no political authority may assign itself goals that might cause the beneficial functioning of "spontaneous order" to be questioned.

Under such conditions, the state cannot have any purpose proper to itself. The only role most liberals agree to attribute to it, apart from respect for the laws and individual rights, is to guarantee the necessary conditions for freedom of exchange, i.e., the free play of economic rationality at work in the market. From this point of view, the state must put itself at the service of the individual and his "freedom of choice," beginning with his right to act freely according to the calculation of his own private interests. It becomes the gendarme, manager, "night watchman," or arbiter of private interests, endowed not so much with functions as with responsibilities, and obliged to abstain from any intervention in economic and commercial affairs, it must remain neutral in all other domains and renounce proposing any model of the "good life" (Aristotle[21]), for that would amount to favoring the conceptions of some men to the detriment of others. Society

---

countries with low costs; and the universalization of social, fiscal, and environmental dumping; the concentration of wealth; the withering of food crops, etc. Cf. Arthur MacEwan, *Neo-Liberalism or Democracy? Economic Strategy, Markets, and Alternatives for the 21st Century* (New York: Zed Books, 1999).

[21] Concerning the role of the state, such is the most common liberal position today. Libertarians (also known as "anarcho-capitalists") go farther, since they reject even the "minimal state" proposed by Nozick. Not being a producer of capital, while it does consume labor, the state for them is necessarily a "thief."

must be ruled by principles that do not presuppose the superiority of any private conception of the common good, each individual being supposed to be free to live according to his own private definition of "happiness." (In the historical context where
liberalism emerged, this principle was considered a means of
doing away with wars of religion.)

The result is that with the arrival of the market, as Karl Polanyi writes, "Society [is run] as an adjunct to the market. Instead of economy being embedded in social relations, social relations are embedded in the economic system."[22] Commercial exchange, which was formerly only one mode of human activity
(and not considered especially important), becomes the foundation and general rule of civil society. Since *Homo oeconomicus* is in
the service of the economy and not the other way around, quality gives way to quantity ("you are what you have").

The consequences of the theory of the "invisible hand" are
decisive, especially on the moral level. From its first formula-
tions, liberalism makes everyone's prosperity rest upon the egoism of each, exhorting individuals not to respect a sense of proportion and limits, but to abandon themselves to *pleonexia*, the
unlimited thirst for having. Egoism thus becomes the best way
of serving others. As Adam Smith says: "By pursuing his own
interest, [man] frequently promotes that of the society more ef-
fectually than when he really intends to promote it." This is the
viewpoint developed by Bernard Mandeville in his celebrated
Fable of the Bees (1705): private vices, public benefits. In other
words, virtue proceeds from vice, good proceeds from evil; we
are already in the world of Orwell. (It should be noted, however,
that this Mandevillian idea that private vices are the cause of
public happiness amounts to thinking that the public action of
individuals is equivalent to their private action—the negation of
the distinction between public and private that liberalism claims
to maintain elsewhere.) Frédéric Bastiat sums up this viewpoint
in the formula: "Everyone, by working for himself, works for
all."[23]

---

[22] Polanyi, *The Great Transformation*, 60.
[23] Frédéric Bastiat, *Harmonies économiques* (1851).

From the moral point of view, this is a revolution. With this doctrine, liberalism rehabilitates the very forms of behavior that past ages had always condemned. By affirming that the interest of society is subordinate to the economic interest of individuals, and that by seeking to maximize our personal interest we are working without realizing it—and without even wanting to—in everyone's interest, it makes egoism the best way of serving others. Since the free confrontation of egoistic interests in the market allows "naturally, or rather necessarily" their harmonization by the play of the "invisible hand," which will make them work together toward the social ideal, there is nothing immoral in seeking one's own interest, above all, because in the end the egoistic action of each will contribute to the interest of all. Thus, in the end, egoism is nothing but altruism properly understood. And it is the actions of public authority that deserve to be denounced as immoral every time they (under the pretext of solidarity) contradict the right of individuals to act in view of their interests. What is called the axiomatics of interest is simply the translation into philosophical terms of this egoism that liberalism legitimates at the highest level. This is also the foundation of the metaphysics of subjectivity (Heidegger). It is a system that negates the common good in a double sense, since it rejects the concept of "the good" as well as of "the common," to say nothing of the bond between these two words.

Liberalism binds individualism and the market by declaring that the free functioning of the latter is also the guarantor of individual freedom. By assuring the most profitable result of exchanges, the market guarantees the independence of each agent. Ideally, if the proper functioning of the market is not hampered, this adjustment will be carried out in the optimal fashion, allowing the attainment of an ensemble of partial equilibria that defines the global equilibrium. Defined by Hayek as "catallaxy," the market constitutes a spontaneous and abstract order, the formal instrumental support of the exercise of private freedoms. Thus the market represents not only the satisfaction of an ideal of economic optimality, but the satisfaction of everything to which individuals (considered as generic subjects of freedom) aspire. Finally, the market blends with justice itself, which leads

Hayek to define it as a "game that increases the chances of all players," before adding that under these conditions the losers have no right to complain and have only themselves to blame. Finally, the market is supposedly intrinsically "pacifying," since it rests on "gentle commerce" that, substituting negotiation for conflict as a matter of principle, thereby neutralizes rivalry and envy.

We see here that for liberals the concept of the market goes well beyond the economic sphere. A mechanism for the optimal allocation of scarce resources and a system for regulating production and consumption cycles, the market is also and above all a sociological and "political" concept. Adam Smith himself, insofar as he designates the market as the commercial order's principal operator, is led to conceive relations between men on the model of economic relations, i.e., as relations with merchandise. The market economy thus naturally culminates in the market society. As Pierre Rosanvallon writes, "The market is first of all a way of representing and structuring social space; only secondarily is it a decentralized mechanism for regulating economic activities through the price system."[24]

For Adam Smith, generalized exchange is the direct consequence of the division of labor: "Every man thus lives by exchanging, or becomes, in some measure, a merchant, and the society itself grows to be what is properly a commercial society."[25] Thus the market is indeed, in the liberal view, the dominant paradigm in a society called upon to define itself in all its parts as a market society. Liberal society is merely a place of utilitarian exchanges participated in by individuals and groups motivated exclusively by the desire to maximize their own interest. A member of this society where anything can be bought or sold is either a tradesman, an owner, or a producer—and always a consumer. As Pierre Rosanvallon writes, "The superior rights of

---

[24] Rosanvallon, *Le libéralisme économique*, 124.

[25] Smith, *Wealth of Nations*, book I, ch. 4. Cf. e.g., Bertrand Lemennicier, *Le marché du mariage et de la famille* [*The Marriage and Family Market*] (Paris: PUF, 1988); *Privatisons la justice. Une solution radicale à une justice inefficace et injuste* [*Let's Privatize Justice: A Radical Solution to Ineffective and Unjust Justice*] (Nice: Ovadia, 2017).

consumers are to Smith what the general will is to Rousseau."

In the modern era, liberal economic analysis will be gradually extended to all social facts, as if analyzing a social fact economically (which is always possible) were enough to transform it into an economic fact. Privatized and deinstitutionalized, the family is assimilated into a small company, social relations into an interlacing of competing self-interested strategies, and politics into a market where voters sell their vote to the highest bidder. Man is perceived as capital, a child as a durable consumer good. Individuals are called upon to become managers of themselves in a thoroughly commercialized society. Economic logic is thus projected onto the whole of society in which it used to be embedded, with every form of human relation presumed to function under implicit conditions of contract and competition.[26]

As Gérald Berthoud writes, "Society can then be conceived on the basis of a formal theory of purposeful action. The cost-benefit ratio thus becomes the principle that makes the world go round."[27] Everything becomes a factor of production or consumption; everything is supposed to result from the spontaneous adjustment of supply and demand. Everything is worth its exchange value, as measured by its price. And at the same time, everything that cannot be expressed in quantifiable and calculable terms is considered either uninteresting or non-existent. Economic discourse thus proves itself deeply concretizing of social and cultural practices, and deeply foreign to any value not expressible in terms of price. Reducing all social facts to a universe of measurable things, it finally transforms men themselves into things—things interchangeable from the monetary point of view.

This strictly economic representation of society has considerable consequences. Finishing off the process of secularization and "disenchantment" of the world characteristic of modernity, it results in the dissolution of peoples and the systematic erosion

---

[26] Henry, *Marx*, vol. 1, 92.

[27] Gérald Berthoud, *Vers une anthropologie générale. Modernité et altérité* [*Towards a General Anthropology: Modernity and Otherness*] (Geneva: Droz, 1992), 57.

of their particularities. At the sociological level, the adoption of economic exchange leads the society to be divided into producers, owners, and sterile classes (such as the former aristocracy) at the end of an altogether revolutionary process. At the level of collective imagination, it ends in a complete reversal of values, raising to the highest level the commercial values that had always been considered inferior *par excellence*, since they arise from mere necessity. At the moral level, it rehabilitates the spirit of self-interested calculation, *hybris* (lack of measure), and egoistic behavior that traditional societies always condemned.

Considered intrinsically dangerous, insofar as it constitutes the locus where a power considered "irrational" is exercised, politics is reduced in this point of view to guaranteeing rights and the management of the social realm in terms of mere technical expertise. Carl Schmitt denied that there could be a liberal politics, since liberalism in his eyes is characterized—besides by the affirmation of the primacy of economics over politics and the private over the public—by an invincible tendency to "neutralize" political problems by depoliticizing them. What is called political liberalism is in fact merely a way of applying principles deduced from an economic and individualistic doctrine to political life, a doctrine that tends to limit the role of politics as much as possible, to rob it of its prerogatives by opposing the sovereignty of the market to the strictly political concept of sovereignty. The ideal of "axiological neutrality" itself implies the dismissal of politics insofar as the latter always consists in choosing between possibilities in order to obtain certain objectives determined according to certain values—even as it favors the rise of expertocracy, for which there is only one possible solution to problems, these themselves having been reduced to "technical" questions. "There is no alternative," as Margaret Thatcher used to say: an unpolitical statement *par excellence*. The result is to model the governance of men on the administration of things (or to replace the former by the latter). In the final analysis, relations between men themselves become like relations between things. This is the phantasm of the "transparent society," the vision of a society immediately coincident with itself, beyond any symbolic referent or concrete intervention. And this is also the deeper reason for the "reification" (*Verdinglichung*) of social relations so well studied by the young Lukács.

As Hervé Juvin rightly says: "The advent of the individual renders citizenship obsolete." In fact, it unbinds man from that which binds him to his fellows. Exclusively regulated by the anonymous and impersonal mechanisms of the market and the law, the social bond is reduced to legal contract and commercial exchange. From an anti-holist point of view in which society is merely an aggregate of individuals—"There's no such thing as society," as Margaret Thatcher put it—there can be no shared values or shared horizons.

If we want to continue speaking of "liberal politics," we can say it consists in accommodating social reproduction to capital reproduction by implementing the sociopolitical conditions for the extension of capital accumulation. This is the very definition of the "commercialization of the world."

In the long run, in a society entirely ruled by the market and founded upon the postulate of the self-sufficiency of "civil society," the state and its institutions are destined to wither away as surely as in the classless society imagined by Marxist authors. The logic of the market, as Alain Caillé has shown, is coextensive with a whole process of equalization; indeed, of making men interchangeable by way of a dynamic already observable in the modern use of money:

> Liberal ideology's sleight of hand lies in equating the rule of law with the commercial state, in reducing it to the role of an emanation of the market. From that point, the plea for the freedom of individuals to choose their own ends reverses itself into a real obligation to have only commercial ends.[28]

The paradox is that liberals constantly affirm that the market maximizes the chances of each individual to realize his own

---

[28] Alain Caillé, *Splendeurs et misères des sciences sociales. Esquisse d'une mythologie* [*Splendors and Miseries of the Social Sciences: Sketch of a Mythology*] (Geneva: Droz, 1986), 347.

ends even as they say these ends cannot be defined in advance, and that in the end no one can define them better than the individual himself. But how can you say that the market realizes the optimum when you do not know in what that optimum consists? You might even say the market multiplies the ends of individuals more than it gives them the means of obtaining them, increasing not their satisfaction but their dissatisfaction, in Tocqueville's sense of the word.

On the other hand, if the individual is always the best judge of his own interests, what can oblige him to respect even a norm of reciprocity—e.g., the "freedom of others?" As Alain Renaut writes, "In the ideal of autonomy, I remain dependent on norms and laws on the condition that I freely accept them." But why should I accept them? Liberal doctrine wants moral behavior to result no longer from any sense of duty or moral rules, but from self-interest properly understood. Gisèle Souchon writes, "It is because he thinks firstly of his personal interest that the individualist, just as he can unite with others when it appears useful to him, avoids harming them in order to avoid possible retaliation." By not infringing upon the freedom of others, I dissuade them from infringing upon mine. Fear of the police is supposed to do the rest. But if I can be certain that in breaking this rule I shall be at very little risk of punishment, and reciprocity is a matter of indifference to me, what can prevent me from violating this rule or the law by opposing the desires of others? What prevents me from defying the Kantian principle that the individual ought to be treated as an end, and not merely as a means? Nothing, obviously. On the contrary, taking only my own interest into account invites me to do so as often as I can.

In his *Theory of Moral Sentiments* (1759), Adam Smith writes,

> Though among the different members of the society there should be no mutual love and affection, the society, though less happy and agreeable, will not necessarily be dissolved. Society may subsist among different men, as among different merchants, from a sense of its utility, without any mutual love or affection; and though no man in it should owe any obligation, or be bound in gratitude

to any other, it may still be upheld by a mercenary exchange of good offices according to an agreed valuation.[29]

The meaning of this passage is clear. A society can very well
economize on—such is the correct term—any form of organic
sociality without thereby ceasing to be a society. It must only
become a society of merchants: the social bond will then be the
sentiment of "utility" and the "self-interested exchange of services." It is therefore enough to participate in commercial exchange, to make free use of your right to maximize your best
interest, in order to be human. Smith says that indeed, such a
society will be "less happy and less agreeable," but the nuance
will quickly be forgotten. One might even ask whether for certain liberals the only way to be fully human is not to behave like
a merchant, i.e., like those upon whom an inferior status was
once conferred, not because they were not regarded as useful
and even necessary, but precisely because they were merely useful—that their vision of the world was limited to the value of
utility. This obviously raises the status of those who do not behave in this way, whether because it is not to their taste or because they do not have the means to do so. Are they still human?

The logic of the market imposed itself only gradually starting
from the end of the Middle Ages, when long-distance trade and
local trade began to be unified within national markets at the
instigation of the nation-states then forming. These wanted to
monetarize formerly elusive non-commercial forms of exchange
within the community in order to raise tax revenue from them.
Far from being a universal fact, the market is thus a phenomenon strictly localized in space and time. And this phenomenon,
far from being "spontaneous," was instituted. Formerly, the
market was all the less "self-regulating" in that it was embedded
within the social realm and framed by the political and even religious realms. Especially in France, but also in Spain and several
other countries, the market was not constructed in opposition to
the nation-state but thanks to it. The state created the market just

---

[29] Adam Smith, *Theory of Moral Sentiments* (1759), Section II, ch. 3.

as it created money and the economic space that allowed for commercial transactions. The nation-state and the market were born together and proceeded in concert, the former constituting the latter at the same time as it instituted itself. As Alain Caillé writes:

> At the very least, we should not consider market and state as two radically different and antagonistic entities, but as two stages in the same process. Historically, national markets and nation-states were built in step with one another, and neither was possible without the other.[30]

In fact, both developed in the same direction. The market amplified the movement of the national state which, in order to solidify its authority, constantly and methodically destroyed all intermediate forms of socialization that in the feudal world constituted so many relatively autonomous organic structures (clans, village communities, brotherhoods, trade guilds, etc.). The bourgeois class, and nascent liberalism along with it, continued and aggravated this atomization of society insofar as the emancipation of the individual to which it aspires demands the destruction of all unchosen forms of solidarity or dependence, which represent so many obstacles to the extension of the market.

The new form of society that emerged after the end of the Middle Ages thus gradually constructed itself from the individual, from his ethical and political norms and interests, gradually breaking up the concurrence of political, economic, legal, and even linguistic spaces that the previous society tended to realize. In the seventeenth century, state and civil society nevertheless continued to coincide: the expression "civil society" was still synonymous with politically organized society. The distinction began to be made in the eighteenth century, especially with Locke, who redefined civil society as the sphere of property and exchange, the state of "political society" henceforward being dedicated to assuring the protection of merely economic interests.

---

[30] Caillé, *Splendeurs et misères des sciences sociales*, 333–34.

The distinction became more firmly established by making the sphere of production and exchange autonomous, and echoed the manner in which the modern state constructed itself, characterized by the specialization of roles and functions. The distinction led either to the valorization of a political society issuing from the social contract, as in Locke, or to the exaltation of a civil society based on the spontaneous adjustment of interests, as in Mandeville[31] or Smith. By becoming autonomous, civil society opened the way for the free deployment of the economic logic of interests. This is the meaning of the bourgeois revolution.

By the same token, society took on the form of an objective order distinct from the natural or cosmic order, which coincides with the universal reason to which the individual is supposed to have immediate access. Its historic objectification was first crystalized in the political doctrine of law, whose development can be followed from Jean Bodin to the Enlightenment. At the same time, political economy imposed itself as a new general science of society, the latter conceived as a process of dynamic development in the sense of "progress." Henceforward, society must be the object of a specific scientific form of knowledge. Insofar as it accedes to a supposedly rational form of existence in which all practices submit themselves to instrumental rationality as to their ultimate regulatory principle, the social world must follow a certain number of "laws." But from the very fact of this objectivization, the unity of society along with its integration in a symbolic dimension became highly problematic, insofar as the privatization of belonging and attachment was not slow to express itself in the fragmentation of the social body, by the multiplication of conflicting particular interests, and by the beginning of deinstitutionalization. New contradictions would soon appear, not between the society instituted by the bourgeois class and the vestiges of the *Ancien Régime*, but within the new society itself: e.g., the class struggle.

The distinction between public and private, the state and civil society, sharpened further in the nineteenth century, generalizing a twofold and contradictory apperception of social

---

[31] Bernard de Mandeville, *Fable of the Bees* (1714).

space. Liberalism, having extended its power, now promoted a "civil society" assimilated to the mere private sphere and denounced the "hegemonic" influence of the public sector, which led it to plead for the end of state monopolies on the satisfaction of collective needs and for extending intra-social commercial forms of regulation. "Civil society," defining itself less by its own nature than by its opposition to the state, as a vague representation of what is theoretically removed from the state, appeared as an ideological operator more than as a precise reality.

Beginning at the end of the nineteenth century, however, adjustments had to be made to the purely economic regulation and reproduction of society. These adjustments were not so much the result of conservative resistance as of the new social configuration's internal contradictions. Sociology itself was born from the resistance that real society opposed to political and institutional changes, alongside the appeal to a natural order on the part of those who denounced the new form of social regulation's formal and artificial character. Among the first sociologists, the rise of individualism gave birth to a double fear: fear of the "anomie" resulting from the disintegration of the social bond in someone like Durkheim, and fear of a "crowd" of atomized individuals suddenly united in an uncontrollable "mass" in others such as Le Bon or Gabriel Tarde (both of whom tend to lead the analysis of social fact back to a "psychology" or sociology of mores). The former would find an echo especially among the counter-revolutionary thinkers, while the latter would be mainly visible within a bourgeoisie concerned above all to protect itself against the "dangerous classes."

Although the market was born and instituted by the nation-state, the antagonism between liberalism and the "public sector" would grow from this point on. Liberals constantly thunder against the welfare state without realizing that it was the very extension of the market that made increased state intervention inevitable. The man whose labor power is abandoned to the play of the market alone is in fact vulnerable, for it can happen that his labor power does not find a taker on the market, or even that it is worthless. Modern individualism had by this time largely destroyed the organic relations of proximity that were above all relations of mutual assistance and reciprocal solidarity, simultaneously causing the disappearance of the old forms of social protection. Although it regulates supply and demand, the market does not regulate social relations, but disorganizes them, if only because it takes no account of the existence of an unmeetable demand. The rise of the welfare state then becomes a necessity, since it alone can correct the most flagrant disequilibria, in order to attenuate the most obvious distress. The welfare state was the response to the rise of individualism that gradually ruined older and more traditional forms of solidarity by seeking to limit social insecurity and compensate for certain inequalities — doing so at the threefold risk of aggravating social atomization further, transforming beneficiaries into dependents, and finding itself confronted with an insoluble problem of financing.

This is why, as Karl Polanyi has shown, each time liberalism seems to have won out, we have paradoxically witnessed an increase in state intervention made necessary by the damage done to the social tissue by the logic of the market. As Alain Caillé observes, "Without a relative peace brought about by the welfare state, the market order would simply have been swept away."[32] It is this synergy of market and state that long characterized the Fordist system. "Social protection is the necessary accompaniment of the self-regulating market," concludes Polanyi.[33]

Insofar as its interventions aim at compensating for the market's destructive effects, the welfare state hinders in a certain way the "commercialization" of social life. It cannot, however, be an integral substitute for the forms of communitarian protection that collapsed as an effect of industrial development, the rise of individualism, and the expansion of the market. Compared to these old forms of social protection, it displays characteristics that amount to so many limitations on the benefits it can bring. Whereas older forms of solidarity rested upon a mutual exchange of benefits that implied everyone's responsibility, the welfare state promotes lack of responsibility and transforms members of society into helpless dependents — leaving liberalism

---

[32] Caillé, *Splendeurs et misères des sciences sociales*, 332.
[33] Caillé, *Splendeurs et misères des sciences sociales*, 265.

free to denounce the rise of "dependency." Whereas the old forms of solidarity were embedded within a network of concrete relations, the welfare state presents itself as an abstract machinery, anonymous and distant, from which one expects everything while not feeling obliged to do anything. The substitution of an impersonal, external, and opaque solidarity for the old, immediate forms of solidarity is thus far from being satisfactory. On the contrary, it is the source of the welfare state's present crisis, which, by its very nature, seems destined only to be able to implement an economically inefficient and increasingly financially ruinous (because sociologically ill-adapted) sort of solidarity. As Bernard Enjolras writes, "Getting over the internal crisis of the welfare state depends upon rediscovering the conditions under which local solidarity may be produced," which are also "the conditions for reestablishing the economic bond in order to restore harmony between wealth production and social production."[34]

Péguy wrote, "All the degradation of the modern world — i.e., all the cheapening of the modern world — comes from that world which considers as negotiable those values that the ancient and Christian worlds considered non-negotiable."[35] Liberal ideology bears major responsibility for this degradation insofar as it is based on an unrealistic anthropology and deduces a series of erroneous consequences from this.

The idea that man acts freely and rationally in the market is merely a utopian hypothesis, for economic facts are never autonomous, but relative to a given social and cultural context. There is no economic rationality *per se*; such rationality is merely the product of a well-determined socio-historic progression. Commercial exchange is not the natural form of social relations, nor even of economic relations. The market is not a universal

---

[34] Bernard Enjolras, "Crise de l'Etat-Providence, lien social et associations: éléments pour une socio-économie critique" ["Crisis of the Welfare State, Social Bonds, and Associations: Elements for a Critical Socio-economy"], *Revue de MAUSS*, 1st semester 1998, 223.

[35] Charles Péguy, *Note conjointe sur M. Descartes* [*Joint Note on M. Descartes*] [1914] (Paris: Gallimard, 1969).

phenomenon but a local one. It never realizes the optimal adjustment of supply to demand, if only because it only takes effective demand into account. Society is always more than its individual components, just as a social class is always more than the elements that form it, since it is the class that constitutes them as such, and the class is thus logically and hierarchically distinct from those components, as Russell's theory of logical types demonstrates (a class cannot be a member of itself, any more than one of its members can constitute the class by itself). Finally, the abstract conception of a disinterested, "decontextualized" individual whose behavior rests upon strictly rational anticipation and who freely chooses his identity based on nothing is an absolutely untenable vision. Communitarian theoreticians, or those close to them (Alasdair MacIntyre, Michael Sandel), have shown the vital importance for individuals of having a community that necessarily constitutes their horizon, their *épistémè* — if only in order to develop a critical representation of it — both for the construction of their identity and for the satisfaction of their aims. The common good is the substantial doctrine that defines the way such a community lives, and thus its collective identity.

The entire contemporary crisis comes from the increasingly painful contradiction between the ideal of the universal abstract man, with its corollary of atomization and the depersonalization of social relations, and the reality of the concrete man, for whom the social bond continues to be based on affective bonds and relations of proximity, along with their corollaries of cohesion, consensus, confidence, and reciprocal obligation.

The economic dimension of liberal societies devotes them to "ever more," insofar as any quantity is always susceptible of increase. This "ever more" is then posited as a new regime of truth: more becomes synonymous with better, and ever more with ever better (this is also one basis of the ideology of progress). Economic growth is perceived as both natural and always desirable, meaning that every form of production deserves to be encouraged, however harmful or useless it may be. Humanity then lives on credit from a nature that is continually impoverished and degraded. Stimulated by the individual aspiration to satisfy any desire, this "ever more" finally results in generalized frustration, contributing to the "psychological pauperization" of a society composed of immature narcissists; this society of emptiness itself become "liquid" (in the words of Zygmunt Bauman) thanks to having rendered everything else liquid.

Marx rightly spoke of the "highly revolutionary role" played in the course of history by the bourgeoisie. He also saw that capitalism, far from being a "conservative" and "patriarchal" economic system—as an obsolete Left totally deluded as to its nature stubbornly persists in describing it—actually constitutes a permanent revolutionary force, to the point where "Never in the history of humanity has an economic and social system transformed so greatly and so quickly the entire face of the Earth *and the very substance of the human soul*" (Jean-Claude Michéa). For the logic of capital, anything that obstructs the indefinite extension of commercial exchange is a bar to be broken and a limit to be overcome, whether in political decision-making, territorial boundaries, moral judgment urging moderation, or cultural tradition favoring skepticism toward innovation. As Pasolini wrote, "From the anthropological point of view, the capitalist revolution demands men without any tie to the past." Whence the tragic inconsistency of those conservatives, or "national-liberals," who want to defend both the market system and the "traditional values" that this system continues to bulldoze.

Jean-Claude Michéa, as noted, has shown that the economic liberalism of the "Right" and the social liberalism of the "Left" are destined to join together, for they proceed from the same postulates: "Integral economic liberalism (officially defended by the Right) thus bears within itself a permanent revolution in mores (officially defended by the Left), just as the latter in turn demands the total liberation of the market."[36] Such slogans of May '68 as "enjoy without limits" and "it is forbidden to forbid" were typical liberal slogans. The Left today gives way all the more easily to social liberalism in that it has been fully converted to globalized economic liberalism.

Liberal authors believe in the possibility of a society entirely adapted to the values of individualism and the market. This is

---

[36] Michéa, *Le complexe d'Orphée*, 216.

an illusion. Individualism has never been the model for all social behavior and can never become so. Moreover, there are good reasons to think individualism can manifest itself in a society only insofar as it remains holist in some sense. As Louis Dumont writes:

> Individualism is incapable of completely replacing holism and reigning over all of society. . . . Moreover, it has never been able to function without holism contributing to its life in an unperceived and somehow clandestine manner.[37]

This is what confers upon liberal ideology its utopian dimension. So one would be wrong to see in holism only a legacy of the past destined to disappear. Even in the age of modern individualism, universal commercialization, the "atomization of the world," and the mutilation of human existence by the expedients of commercial prostitution and the machinery of profit, man remains a social animal. Holism reappears as soon as— faced with the liberal theory of a "natural harmony of interests"—we recognize the existence of a common good that takes precedence over particular interests.

---

[37] Dumont, *Homo aequalis*.

COMMUNITARIANS VS. LIBERALS

Liberal ideology has generally interpreted the fact of community in close relation to the emergence of modernity: the more the modern world becomes established, the more communal bonds are supposed to come undone, replaced by more voluntary, contractual forms of association, more individualistic and rational forms of behavior. From this perspective, community appears a residual phenomenon that institutional bureaucracies and global markets are called upon to eradicate and dissolve. Any stress laid on the value of community is interpreted either as a conservative "survival," testament to a vanished age, or as the product of romantic and utopian nostalgia (the dream of a "simple life" or "golden age"), or as an appeal to one form or other of "collectivism." A related theme is that in exchange for abandoning the old communities, members of society benefit from increased freedom and well-being, even destined to extend infinitely, and the very condition for which is the reorganization of society in a rationalized and atomized form. These themes are organized around the concepts of progress, reason, and the abstract individual.

Many are the authors who have studied social bonds with reference to the concept of community, most often opposing the latter to society. (Let us note here at the outset that the communities we are speaking of here have little in common with the "communitarianism" tied to immigration that has recently invaded public discourse in France.) Conceptualization of the terms *Gemeinschaft* (community) and *Gesellschaft* (society) is central to the new German sociology of the early twentieth century, beginning with the foundational work of Ferdinand Tönnies that appeared in 1887.[1] It is well-known that Tönnies relates these

---

[1] Ferdinand Tönnies, *Gemeinschaft und Gesellschaft* (Leipzig: Fues, 1887). *Cf.* also "Die Entstehung meiner Begriffe 'Gemeinschaft' und 'Gesellschaft'" ["The Emergence of my Terms 'Community' and 'Society'"], *Kölner Zeitschrift für Soziologie und Sozialpsychologie*, 1955, 7, 463–67.

two concepts to two distinct types of will, the *Wesenswille*, natural and spontaneous, and the *Kürwille*, rational and reflective. Qualifying this approach, Martin Buber introduces a new distinction between the old "blood community" (*Blutverwandschaft*) and the new "chosen community" (*Wahlverwandschaft*), while Max Weber makes use of the concept of communalization to describe the process of mutual orientation that occurs under the effects of communal sentiments between members of a given polity. The same dichotomy partly overlaps with Durkheim's conceptual opposition between mechanical and organic solidarity. It is prolonged in the work of Georg Simmel, Helmuth Plessner, Talcott Parsons, and even Louis Dumont with his holism-individualism pairing.[2] This contrast is usually drawn as part of a diachronic rather than synchronic approach. The decline of community, moreover, is a major theme in the thought of the conservative intellectuals who contributed to the founding of sociology in the nineteenth century.[3]

For some time now the three pillars of this critical and "historicist" approach to the concept of community have begun to show cracks. The ideology of progress seems the most affected, insofar as its promises have simply not been kept. The shock of twentieth-century totalitarianism, the concept of limits made fashionable by the spread of ecologism, the apparently irresistible growth in unemployment, the discontent resulting from the failure of the promised standard of living to match most people's hopes, and the inability of material well-being to give meaning to one's presence in the world — all these phenomena

---

[2] Louis Dumont, *Homo hierarchicus. Essai sur le système des castes* [*Homo hierarchicus: Essay on the Caste System*] (Paris: Gallimard, 1966); *Homo aequalis I. Genèse et épanouissement de l'idéologie économique* [*Homo aequalis I: The Genesis and Flourishing of Economic Ideology*] (Paris: Gallimard, 1955).

[3] *Cf.* Robert Nisbet, *The Quest for Community: A Study in the Ethics of Order and Freedom* (Oxford: Oxford University Press, 1953); *The Sociological Tradition* (New York: Basic Books, 1966). *Cf.* also Nicolas Kessler, *Robert A. Nisbet et la question de l'Etat* [*Robert A. Nisbet and the Question of the State*], Master's Thesis, Paris IV-Sorbonne, 1993–1994.

cause the future to inspire more worries than hopes.[4]

To this crisis of the ideology of progress is added another regarding pure reason and the abstract individual. Not only does the entire postmodern current contest the omnipotence of reason, but even Habermas himself rejects the idea of transcendental reason as conceived by the Enlightenment and tries to make it into a "thing of the world." The ideology of reason must then be redefined in relation to human finitude, which involves recognizing the historical nature of the knowing subject.[5] (His theory of communicative reason was born of this effort to "save" reason.) For his part, Derrida shows that reason is embedded in forms of life and the incommensurability of language games. Hans-Georg Gadamer is no less critical toward the rationalism of the Enlightenment and what he calls the "prejudice against prejudices." Rejecting both the subject-object dichotomy and the idea that self-reflection can transcend the socio-historical context, he simultaneously breaks with the classic opposition between reason and prejudice, reason and tradition, reason and authority, and affirms that the will to get rid of "prejudices" itself reflects a fundamental prejudice in which the very essence of the Enlightenment is found. Showing that reason cannot be understood as that by which man frees himself from his socio-historical context, he defines "legitimate" prejudices as those destined to facilitate hermeneutical understanding as a primordial mode of human presence in the world.[6]

---

[4] *Cf.* Christopher Lasch, *The True and Only Heaven: Progress and Its Critics* (New York: Norton, 1991).

[5] *Cf.* Jürgen Habermas, *The Philosophical Discourse of Modernity: Twelve Lectures* (Cambridge, Mass.: MIT Press, 1987).

[6] *Cf.* Hans George Gadamer, *Truth and Method.* On the impact of Gadamer's thought in the US, *cf.* Joel Weinsheimer, *Gadamer's Hermenueutics: A Reading of "Truth and Method"* (New Haven: Yale University Press, 1985); as well as the critical remarks of L. M. Palmer, "Gadamer and the Enlightenment's 'Prejudice Against All Prejudices,'" *Clio,* Summer 1993, 369–76. This discussion is reminiscent of the late-1940s debate between Michael Oakeshott and Karl Popper on the value of modernity and reason. In the tradition of Burke, Oakeshott saw in the hegemonic reign of modern reason the cause of contempt for experi-

So there is a historicity of belief, a contextuality of under-standing from which one cannot abstract. And in fact, a whole series of contemporary doctrines and philosophies emphasize the contextuality of knowledge and normativity, either from an explicitly anti-universalist point of view or in the name of a plu-ralist approach that sometimes veers toward relativism. This in-sistence on "context" is already present in the criticisms ad-dressed by Hegel (in the *Phenomenology of Spirit*) to Kant's moral philosophy, as well as in Dilthey's objections to the Hegelian philosophy of history. We find it in anthropologists such as Ev-ans-Pritchard and Malinowski, as well as in phenomenology with the Husserlian concept of *Lebenswelt*, in Searle's analytic philosophy with the concept of background, or in the role Witt-genstein attributes to "language games." A principle of the same sort is present in the philosophy of science with the concepts of "paradigm" (Kuhn), "*épistémè*" (Foucault), or "symbolic uni-verse" (Berger and Luckmann), as well as in sociolinguistics with that of "language community."

The dissolution of the old communities was accelerated by the birth of the nation-state, a "social" phenomenon (society as loss or disintegration of communal intimacy) that has with good reason been related to the emergence of the individual as a val-ue. Significantly, and to some degree logically, the crisis of the nation-state model is today bringing about a rebirth of the idea of community. But the idea is taking on a new significance. Communities no longer associate people on the basis of common origin or values theoretically shared by all. In a world where tribes, currents, and networks are multiplying, they constitute groups of the most various kinds. The best possible definition of the community might take inspiration from the definition of the nation offered by Otto Bauer, the leader of Austro-Marxism, who rejected both the metaphysical and reactionary conception of the nation and the "individualist-atomist conception of socie-

ence and traditions. *Cf.* Michael Oakeshott, "Rationalism in Politics," *Rationalism in Politics and Other Essays* (London: Methuen, 1962); Karl R. Popper, "Toward a Rational Theory of Tradition," in *Conjectures and Refutations* (New York: Harper & Row, 1968), 120–35.

ty": a "community of historical destiny" and a "never-finished product of an ever-ongoing process."[7]

At the same time, the concept of identity is returning to prominence in a way that could either nourish essentialist, xenophobic, and convulsive tensions, or else take the form of an open narratology of a fundamentally dialogic type. The question of community is taking on a new intensity with the prospect of a return to small units of collective life developing on the margins of the big institutional, bureaucratic, or governmental systems that are no longer succeeding in their former role as structures of integration. In this last regard, community (along with localism) appears the natural framework for a democracy of proximity — organic, direct, grass-roots democracy — based on more active participation and the creation of new public spaces, as well as a way of resolving the biggest challenge of our time: "How to make integration work and affirm one's identity without denying the diversity and specificity of its diverse components."[8]

Establishing itself as one of the possible forms for overcoming modernity, community also loses the "archaic" status long attributed to it by sociology. It appears less a "stage" of history supposedly abolished by modern times than as a permanent form of human association that gains or loses importance depending on the age. Max Weber had already seen in "community" and "society" ideal types coexisting in variable proportion within every polity. More recently, Jean-Luc Nancy has advanced the hypothesis according to which the very distinction between these two concepts is an effect of modernity. *Gesellschaft* did not so much succeed *Gemeinschaft* — which only continued to exist as a "vestige" — as it succeeded a social state anterior to the entire distinction, corresponding to that *universitas* which Michael Oakeshott opposed to *societas*.[9] Nancy writes:

---

[7] Otto Bauer, *Die Nationalitätenfrage und die Sozialdemokratie* [*The Nationalities Question and Social Democracy*] (Vienna: Marx Studien, 1907).

[8] Chantal Mouffe, "La citoyenneté et la critique de la raison libérale" ["Citizenship and the Critique of Liberal Reason"], in Jacques Poulain and Patrice Vermeren eds., *L'identité philosophique européenne* [*European Philosophical Identity*] (Paris: L'Harmattan-Association Descartes, 1993, 101.

[9] *Cf.* Michael Oakeshott, *On Human Conduct* (Oxford: Clarendon

Society was not constructed on the ruins of a community. It was constructed in the disappearance or conservation of something—tribes or empires—that perhaps had no more relation with what we call "community" than with what we call "society." So that community, far from being what society has broken up or lost, is what is happening to us— question, expectation, event, imperative—starting from society. So nothing has been lost, and for this reason nothing is lost.[10]

Farther on he writes:

Community is given to us with being and as being, well before all our projects, aims, and enterprises. It is fundamentally impossible for us to lose it. Society can be as uncommunitarian as possible, but it cannot cause community—tiny or inaccessible though it may be—to disappear from the social desert.[11]

It is within this framework, sketched here very roughly, that we must situate the appearance and development in North America beginning in the 1980s and '90s, of a "movement"—in fact a current of philosophical, moral, and political thought accompanied by a few concrete crystallizations—which has provoked countless debates on that side of the Atlantic, but which Europe, hitherto better informed about its competitors, the liberal (John Rawls, Ronald Dworkin) and libertarian (Robert Nozick, Murray Rothbard) currents, seems only to have discovered belatedly: viz., the communitarian "movement."[12]

Press, 1975).

[10] Jean-Luc Nancy, *La communauté désoeuvrée* [*The Idle Community*] (Paris: Christian Bourgois, 1986).

[11] Nancy, *La communauté désoeuvrée*, 87.

[12] It must be made clear here that the American term "community" does not refer to precisely the same thing known in French as *communauté*, nor to what is called *Gemeinschaft* in German. (Significantly, the Germans speak of *Kommunitarismus* when referring to the American communitarian current.) In the United States the term evokes both the

LIBERAL THEORY

This intellectual movement, far from constituting a unified whole, presents itself as a constellation of which its three principal representatives, the philosophers Alasdair MacIntyre,[13] Michael Sandel,[14] and Charles Taylor,[15] represent distinct poles.

---

political community in the global sense and cultural, religious, or ethnic "subcommunities" which the former may include. In its simplest sense, community is a collection of individuals in a state of social interdependence, bound to one another by moral habits, customs, and common existential situations, and who because of this are led to debate and decide in common. *Cf.* Robert Redfield, *The Little Community: Viewpoints for the Study of a Human Whole* (Chicago: University of Chicago Press, 1955); Paul and Percival Goodman, *Communities: Means of Livelihood and Ways of Life* (New York: Random House, 1960).

[13] Alasdair MacIntyre is professor of philosophy at the University of Notre Dame (Indiana) where he has held the McMahon/Hank chair since 1989. His two most celebrated works are *After Virtue: A Study in Moral Theory* (Notre Dame: University of Notre Dame Press, 1981) and *Whose Justice? Which Rationality?* (London: Duckworth, 1988). *Cf. Three Rival Versions of Moral Enquiry: Encyclopedia, Genealogy and Tradition* (Notre Dame: University of Notre Dame Press, 1990).

[14] Michael J. Sandel is professor of political philosophy at Harvard University. He is the author of *Liberalism and the Limits of Justice* (Cambridge: Cambridge University Press, 1982), and edited the collective volume *Liberalism and Its Critics* (New York: New York University Press, 1984). More recently he has published *Justice: What's the Right Thing to Do?* (New York: Farrar, Strauss & Giroux, 2009) and *What Money Can't Buy: The Moral Limits of the Market* (New York: Farrar, Strauss & Giroux, 2012). *Cf.* also Sayed Matar, *Michael Sandel. Repenser les fondements individualists du libéralisme* [*Michael Sandel: Rethinking the Individualist Foundations of Liberalism*] (Paris: L'Harmattan, 2018).

[15] Charles Taylor is a retired professor of philosophy and political science at McGill University in Montreal. His major publications include *Justice After Virtue* (Toronto: University of Toronto Press, 1987–1988); *Sources of the Self: The Making of the Modern Identity* (Cambridge: Cambridge University Press, 1989); *The Malaise of Modernity* (Toronto: Canadian Broadcasting Corp., 1991); "What's Wrong with Negative Liberty," in A. Ryan, ed., *The Idea of Freedom* (Oxford: Oxford University Press, 1979); "Atomism," in A. Kontos, ed., *Powers, Possessions and Freedom* (Toronto: University of Toronto Press, 1979); "Cross-Purposes:

Around or beside them we may situate a constellation of independent authors whose work deals with various aspects of the communitarian theme, including Roberto M. Unger, John Finnis, Mary Ann Glendon, or Amitai Etzioni.[16] In a third circle, finally, we can place authors such as Robert N. Bellah and his collaborators,[17] or Christopher Lasch[18] who, without directly appealing to communitarianism, share at least certain of its preoccupations (the critique of "narcissism" and progressivism in Christopher Lasch, and of the "tyranny of the market" in Bellah). Michael Walzer, who is sometimes associated with the communitarian viewpoint, seems to us best treated separately. On the other

---

The Liberal-Communitarian Debate," in Nancy Rosenblum, ed., *Liberalism and the Moral Life* (Cambridge, Mass.: Harvard University Press, 1989); and *La liberté des modernes* [*The Liberty of the Moderns*] (Paris: PUF, 1997).

[16] *Cf.* Roberto Mangabeira Unger, *Politics: A Work in Constructive Social Theory*, 3 vols. (Cambridge: Cambridge University Press, 1987); John Finnis, *Natural Law and Natural Rights* (Oxford: Clarendon Press, 1980); Mary Ann Glendon, *Rights Talk: The Impoverishment of Political Discourse* (New York: Free Press, 1993); Amitai Etzioni, *The Spirit of Community: Rights, Responsibilities and the Communitarian Agenda* (New York: Crown Publishers, 1993); and "Liberals and Communitarians," *Partisan Review*, Spring 1990.

[17] Robert N. Bellah is known mainly for his works on the American "civil religion" and for his critique of individualism and the invasion of instrumental rationality into all the domains of existence. Nonetheless, he maintains a certain distance from the debate between communitarians and liberals and prefers to reason in terms of "institutions" rather than community (letter to the author, November 28, 1993). *Cf.* Robert N. Bellah, Richard Madsen, William M. Sullivan, Ann Swidler, and Steven M. Tipton, *Habits of the Heart: Individualism and Commitment in American Life* (Berkeley-Los Angeles: University of California Press, 1985).

[18] Christopher Lasch (1932–1994), whom Jean-Claude Michéa has done much to make known in France, has tried to promote a Left-wing populism critical of the idea of progress and with communitarian accents: *The Culture of Narcissism: American Life in an Age of Diminished Expectations* (New York: Norton, 1979), *The Minimal Self: Psychic Survival in Troubled Times* (New York: Norton, 1984), and *The True and Only Heaven: Progress and Its Critics* (New York: Norton, 1991).

hand, we cannot dissociate from the work of the communitarians the numerous books and articles already devoted to them.[19]

"The central question of political philosophy—what principles of association is it just to establish?—is a moral question," writes Charles Larmore.[20] The aim of the communitarian movement is precisely to state a new theory closely combining moral and political philosophy. Although it will obviously have a much broader scope, this theory was first elaborated beginning in the early 1980s, firstly with reference to the peculiar situation of the United States, marked by a real inflation of the politics of "rights," the disintegration of social structures, the crisis of the welfare state, and the emergence of "political correctness" (i.e., in fact of ideological and linguistic conformity), and secondly as

---

[19] The literature on this subject is very extensive. Let us note especially Thomas Bender, *Community and Social Change in America* (New Brunswick: Rutgers University Press, 1978); Will Kymlicka, *Liberalism, Community, and Culture* (New York: Oxford University Press, 1989); Robert Booth Fowler, *The Dance with Community: The Contemporary Debate in American Thought* (Lawrence: University Press of Kansas, 1991), Shlomo Aveneri and Avner de-Shalit, ed., *Individualism and Communitarianism* (Oxford: Oxford University Press, 1992); and Elizabeth Frazer and Nicola Lacey, *The Politics of Community: A Feminist Critique of the Liberal-Communitarian Debate* (New York: Harvester Wheatsheaf, 1993). *Cf.* also William A. Galston, *Justice and the Human Good* (Chicago: University of Chicago Press, 1980); John Charvet, *A Critique of Freedom and Equality* (Cambridge: Cambridge University Press, 1981); Mimi Bick, *The Liberal-Communitarian Debate: A Defense of Holistic Individualism*, doctoral thesis, Oxford University, 1987; William A. Galston, *Liberal Purposes: Goods, Virtues, and Diversity in the Liberal State* (Cambridge: Cambridge University Press, 1991); and Marcello Veneziani, *Comunitari e liberali. Le prossima alternativa?* [*Communitarians and Liberals: The Next Alternative?*] (Roma-Bari: Laterza, 1999). In French, *cf.* especially André Berten, Pablo da Silveira and Hervé Pourtois, eds., *Libéraux et communautariens* [*Liberals and Communitarians*] (Paris: PUF, 1997) and Chantal Mouffe, "Le libéralisme américain et ses critiques" ["American Liberalism and its Critics"], *Esprit*, March 1987, 100–14.

[20] Charles Larmore, *Modernité et morale* [*Modernity and Morality*] (Paris: PUF, 1993), 20.

a reaction to liberal political theory[21] as reformulated in the course of the preceding decade by authors such as Ronald Dworkin, Bruce Ackerman, and especially John Rawls.[22]

This liberal theory first presents itself as a theory of rights based on an anthropology of the individualist type. As Serge-Christophe Kolm reminds us,

> Liberalism is a form of individualism. The freedom it demands is that of individuals. . . . Not only is the individual its explanatory point of reference, it is also from the individual that it explains individually given facts (e.g., preferences). So the individual is for liberalism the legitimate entity for both morality and science.[23]

Heir to a nominalism hostile to "universals," this individualism paradoxically posits itself as a form of universalism (individuo-universalism) by virtue of a postulate of equality resting on an abstract definition of agents. From the viewpoint of "possessive individualism" (Macpherson), each individual is considered an autonomous moral agent, "the absolute proprietor of his own capacities,"[24] which he uses to satisfy the desires expressed in his choices. The liberal hypothesis is that of a separate individual

---

[21] The word is obviously to be taken here in its Anglo-Saxon sense.

[22] Cf. John Rawls, A Theory of Justice (Cambridge, Mass.: Belknap Press of Harvard University, 1971); Ronald Dworkin, Taking Rights Seriously (Cambridge, Mass.: Harvard University Press, 1977); Law's Empire (Cambridge, Mass.: Harvard University Press, 1986); and Bruce Ackerman, Social Justice in the Liberal State (New Haven: Yale University Press, 1980). In the same vein cf. also Alan Gewirth, Reason and Morality (Chicago: University of Chicago Press, 1978); Amy Gutmann, Liberal Equality (Cambridge: Cambridge University Press, 1980); and Ian Shapiro, The Evolution of Rights in Liberal Theory (Cambridge: Cambridge University Press, 1986).

[23] Serge-Christophe Kolm, Le libéralisme modern. Analyse d'une raison économique [Modern Liberalism: Analysis of an Economic Reason] (Paris: PUF, 1984).

[24] Cf. C. B. Macpherson, Democratic Theory: Essays in Retrieval (Oxford: Clarendon Press, 1973), 199.

existing as a whole, complete in himself, who seeks to maximize his advantages by making free, voluntary, and rational choices that do not fundamentally result from influences, experiences, contingencies, and norms proper to the social and cultural context. Man thus defines himself as a consumer of utilities with unlimited needs.

Existing as wholes complete in themselves, individuals derive rights from their autonomous nature that liberal theory declares imprescriptible and inalienable. These are "prepolitical" rights for the protection of which individuals can decide contractually to leave the "state of nature," to "enter" into a society that is entirely their own work. So these rights are both prior to and independent of the fact of society. It follows that the interests and ends of individuals are somehow fixed "presocially," with reference only to their nature. From this viewpoint, obviously, no belonging can be constitutive of the individual on pain of infringing on his autonomy: only voluntary, contractual associations can exist, resulting from the will of agents to pursue their best interests. The inalienable character of rights can be supported in various ways: Kantian (Roger Pilon), Lockean (Friedrich A. Hayek), Hobbesian (Charles King, James M. Buchanan), "Thomist" (Ayn Rand, Douglas B. Rasmussen). Libertarians go so far as to speak of an "ontological priority" of rights over preferences, thereby indicating that rights cannot be alienated even if their holders consent to do so on the grounds that an increase in their well-being, happiness, or satisfaction would result. In every case, these rights are posited as "trumps" that prevail over every other consideration. From this it follows that there is no symmetry between liberal rights and duties, for rights derive from a human nature that has no need of others to exist: man has rights from the state of nature, duties only within the social state; rights are perfect in themselves, while duties are by definition imperfect. From this it can be deduced that moral obligation itself is purely contractual (it always remains posterior to the personal self-interest of the contracting party), and that society always has more duties to individuals (beginning with the duty to guarantee their rights) than they have toward it.

This importance attributed to rights explains the "imperative" and deontological (in the Kantian sense) character of liberal morality: liberal theory makes the right and the just prior to the good, deriving from the concept of justice a certain number of categorical obligations unconditionally binding upon all agents regardless of their commitments, belongings, or particular traits. For the Ancients, on the other hand, beginning with Plato and Aristotle, morality is "attractive" and teleological: it consists not in categorical duties but in the exercise of virtue. It forms part of a self-fulfillment toward which men feel drawn because of their *telos*. The good (the "good life") is thus prior, and just action is defined as that which is conformable to this good.

This debate over the priority of the right or the good is today central to American philosophical, political, and moral debate.[25] Referring to *The Methods of Ethics*, the famous work by Henry Sidgwick, one of the first to initiate the debate,[26] Charles Larmore make clear that:

> Ethical value may be defined either as what is binding or obligatory upon an agent, whatever may be his wants or desires, or as what an agent would in fact want if he were sufficiently informed about what he desires. In the first view, the notion of right is fundamental, in the second the notion of good. Each view, of course, makes use of the other notion as well, but it explains it in terms of its primary notion. If the right is fundamental, then the good is what an agent does or would want, so long as it conforms to the demands of obligation; it is the object of right desire. If the good is fundamental, then the right is what one ought to do in order to attain what one would indeed

---

[25] *Cf.* our article "Minima Moralia (2)" *Krisis*, April 1991, 16–25.

[26] Henry Sidgwick, *The Methods of Ethics* (London: Macmillan, 1874). A partisan of utilitarianism, Sidgwick is generally considered one of the most important representatives of Anglo-Saxon moral philosophy of the second half of the nineteenth century. Rawls himself cites him in the most laudatory manner. *Cf.* J. B. Schneewind, *Sidgwick's Ethics and Victorian Moral Philosophy* (Oxford: Clarendon Press, 1977) and Bart Schultz, ed., *Essays on Henry Sidgwick* (Cambridge: Cambridge University Press, 1992).

want if properly informed.[27]

Contested by Hume, Schopenhauer, Hegel (and more recently by Elizabeth Anscombe, Philippa Foot, and Alasdair MacIntyre), the priority of the just to the good appears clearly in John Stuart Mill and Kant, deriving from certain branches of Christian theology of the late Middle Ages, particularly the nominalism of William of Ockham. If justice is based on a particular conception of the good, this amounts (according to John Stuart Mill) in imposing certain preferences on certain citizens, which would interfere with the search for utility, and (according to Kant) subject individuals to irrationality, for no conception of the good can be the object of rational consensus. For Kant, the only thing that is unconditionally good is a good will, i.e., the disposition that drives us to act in accordance with moral principle independently of any idea of self-fulfillment.

Modern liberal theory takes up this idea of a priority of the right over the good. John Rawls, e.g., even as he seeks to detach the Kantian project from its idealistic background based on the transcendental conception of the subject (whence his recourse to the methodic fiction of the "original position"), defines justice as the first virtue of social institutions: the just constitutes itself under the effect of the will to justice, and not by way of conformity to any idea of the good (the good being nothing more than the "satisfaction of rational desire" manifested by the moral person). He adds: "The concept of justice is independent of the concept of the good and prior to it in the sense that its principles limit the conceptions of the good permitted."[28] We find the same idea in Robert Nozick, Bruce Ackerman, and Ronald Dworkin. The connection between the primacy of the just and the liberal conception of rights thus appears fairly obvious. Rights derive from

---

[27] Charles Larmore, *The Morals of Modernity* (Cambridge: Cambridge University Press, 1996), 20.

[28] Cf. *A Theory of Justice*, 92–93; "Justice as Fairness: Political Not Metaphysical," *Philosophy and Public Affairs*, Summer 1985, 223–51. Cf. also "The Priority of Justice and Ideas of the Good," *Philosophy and Public Affairs*, Fall 1988, 251–76.

the "nature" of agents, not from their merits or virtues, which are mere contingent aspects of their personality; they can only come from an abstract concept of justice, not a previous conception of the good or of the good life. With reference to these rights, justice is prior in two ways: in importance (individual rights can never be sacrificed to the common good) and from a conceptual point of view (the principles of justice that specify these rights cannot be based on a particular conception of the good). Thus, Rawls writes that "Each person possesses an inviolability founded on justice that even the welfare of society as a whole cannot override."[29] Individual dignity is an absolute that cannot be sacrificed for any presumed social advantages nor for any sort of general interest or common good. Similarly, Robert Nozick affirms that "There is no social entity with a good that undergoes some sacrifice for its own good. There are only individual people, different individual people with their own individual lives."[30] The critique of the concept of the common good is here tied to individualist anthropology: society is a mere aggregate of individuals, i.e., separate social atoms. As Michael J. Sandel sums up: "What justifies the rights is not that they maximize the general welfare or otherwise promote the good, but rather that they comprise a fair framework within which individuals and groups can choose their own values and ends, consistent with a similar liberty for others."[31]

The primacy of the just over the good appears directly related to the theory according to which the state must remain neutral regarding ends, a theory we find in different forms in most liberal authors—but also in republican "secularism." Thus, Bruce Douglass describes liberal society as one that "does not prejudge what its citizens must be, do, or believe."[32] Ronald Dworkin affirms that such a society does not adopt any particular positive

---

[29] Rawls, *A Theory of Justice*, 30. This is also the main argument that Rawls opposes to utilitarianism.

[30] Nozick, *Anarchy, State, and Utopia*, 32–33.

[31] Sandel, *Liberalism and Its Critics*, 4.

[32] Bruce Douglass, "Liberalism as a Threat to Democracy?" in Francis Canavan, ed., *The Ethical Dimensions of Political Life* (Durham: Duke University Press, 1983), 29.

view on the finality of existence."[33] Robert Nozick also favors a
government "scrupulously neutral between its citizens," while
Charles Larmore thinks this postulate of neutrality "is undoubtedly what best describes the minimal moral conception of liberalism."[34] The justification of this theory usually takes two different forms. Firstly, it is stated that no one knows better than the
individual himself wherein his best interests lie; secondly, existing social fragmentation is emphasized in order to draw the conclusion that members of society can never agree on a particular
conception of the good.

The first argument derives from the Kantian vision of autonomy as the basis of human dignity, i.e., of the equal capacity of
each person freely to determine his own ends: any particular
conception of the good life, i.e., any concrete way of life implying a specific structure of activities, meanings, and ends must be
regarded as purely contingent, for if it were constitutive of the
self, the individual could not freely make his choices by hoisting
himself above empirical circumstances. Here we find once again
the concept of the individual as a separate atom in which the self
is always prior to its ends. This priority of the self over its ends
means that I am never defined by my commitments or forms of
belonging, but that I can always distance myself from them to
make my choice freely, something impossible unless I am a separate being. It is this vision that finds expression in the idea of a
state conceived as a "neutral framework."[35] Michael J. Sandel
writes: "On the rights-based ethic, it is precisely because we are
essentially separate, independent selves that we need a neutral
framework, a framework of rights that refuses to choose among
competing purposes and ends. If the self is prior to its ends, then
the right must be prior to the good."[36]

---

[33] Dworkin, "Liberalism."

[34] Larmore, *The Morals of Modernity*, 165.

[35] The concept of "neutral political concern" seems to have been
coined by the liberal Joseph Raz, "Liberalism, Autonomy, and the Politics of Neutral Concern," *Midwest Studies in Philosophy*, 1982. Cf. also
Will Kymlicka, "Liberal Neutrality and Liberal Individualism," *Ethics*,
1989.

[36] Sandel, *Liberalism and Its Critics*, 5.

The second argument appeals to the concept of pluralism and is based on the idea that no rational agreement can be established that would allow us to decide between competing conceptions of the good. From this it is deduced that, in a pluralist society, a state that identifies with or privileges one conception of the good life over another discriminates between its citizens who adhere to this conception and the rest, and consequently is no longer able to treat all members of the society as equals. Just as it is impossible to say objectively and rationally what is the "best" concept of the good life, no liberal polity can base itself on a particular idea of the common good.[37] Conversely, no agreement on the nature of the good is required as long as the members of society agree on the priority of the right of each person to make his choice freely in a way compatible with the choices of others. So the role of the state is not to make its citizens virtuous, nor to promote particular ends, nor even to offer any substantial conception of the good life, but only to guarantee fundamental political and civil liberties (corresponding to Rawls's first principle, to which libertarians add the right to property) so that each can freely pursue the ends he has set with reference to his conception of the good, something only possible on the condition of adopting principles that do not presuppose any particular concept of the good.[38]

So the state must respect the multiplicity of "comprehensive" (global) doctrines and systems of values as long as these are compatible with its principles of justice,[39] and limit itself to

---

[37] Charles Larmore writes: "This ideal demands only that so long as some view about the good life remains disputed, no decision of the state can be justified on the basis of its supposed superiority or inferiority." *Patterns of Moral Complexity* (Cambridge: Cambridge University Press, 1987), 47.

[38] This idea that only a neutral political power can guarantee social peace between individuals considered as separate atoms, i.e., agents whose social character is merely an accidental form added to their nature, is already present in William of Ockham, along with the idea of an absolute but totally indeterminate divine power (*potentia absoluta*).

[39] This stipulation, which has given rise to debates we shall not examine here, is stated at length by John Rawls in his writings of the

applying moral rules derived from common reason without taking sides between competing conceptions of the good. Its values
must remain purely procedural in order to permit the competing
coexistence of these different conceptions while preventing the
use some make of their freedom from harming the equal capacity others must have to do the same. This procedural end, libertarians add, does not correspond to any determinate end, but
merely constitutes the framework within which individual
choices can be made.[40] As Sandel observes: "This liberalism says,
in other words, that what makes the just society just is not the
telos or purpose or end at which it aims, but precisely its refusal
to choose in advance among competing purposes and ends."[41]
The consequence of this theory of the "neutrality" of the state,
tied by definition to the idea of limited government and the distinction between the public and private sphere, is a purely instrumental vision of politics: politics is not the vehicle of any ethical dimension in the sense that we cannot demand (or even
promote) any conception of the common good in its name.

1980s and '90s (cf. *Justice et démocratie*, ed. Catherine Audard [Paris:
Seuil, 1993], especially chs. 5 and 7). It allows us to understand the limited and finally tautological character of the liberal theory which, while
declaring it remains neutral regarding conceptions of the good life, in
fact only allows those which do not call its own principles into question.

[40] *Cf.* Douglas J. Den Uyl, "Freedom and Virtue," in Tibor R. Machan, ed., *The Libertarian Reader* (Totowa, N.J.: Rowman & Littlefield,
1992), 211–55.

[41] Michael J. Sandel, "The Procedural Republic and the Unencum-
bered Self," *Political Theory*, February 1984, 82. On the problem of justice in its relations with liberal ideology, *cf.* also Serge-Christophe
Kolm, *Justice et équité* [*Justice and Equity*] (Paris: Editions du CNRS,
1972); *Le contrat liberal* [*The Liberal Contract*] (Paris: PUF, 1985); Ottfried
Höffe, *L'Etat et la justice* [*The State and Justice*] (Paris: J. Vrin, 1988); Jean-
Pierre Dupuy, *Le sacrifice et l'envie* [*Sacrifice and Envy*] (Paris: Calmann-
Lévy, 1992); Jean Ladrière and Philippe van Parijs, eds., *Fondements
d'une théorie de la justice* [*Foundations of a Theory of Justice*] (Louvain-la-
neuve: Peeters, 1984); Philippe van Parijs, *Qu'est-ce qu'une société juste?*
[*What Is Social Justice?*] (Paris: Seuil, 1991); and Salvatore Vecca, *La
società giusta* [*The Just Society*] (Milan: Il Saggiatore, 1982).

THE COMMUNITARIAN CRITIQUE

The point of departure for the communitarian critique of this theory is primarily sociological and empirical. Observing contemporary societies, communitarians notice the dissolution of the social bond, the eradication of collective identities, the rise of egoism, the disappearance of points of reference, and the generalized lack of meaning that results. These phenomena, they say, are so many effects of a political philosophy that provokes social atomization by legitimizing each individual's search for his own best interest, thus making him regard others as rivals if not potential enemies; which defends an unhistorical and disincarnate conception of the subject without seeing that agents' commitments and belonging are also constitutive of their selves; which by appealing to an abstract universalism causes a forgetting of traditions and erosion of common moral habits and differentiated ways of life; which, with Rawls, sees in society only a "cooperative enterprise based on mutual advantage" and denies the existence of the common good;[42] which, under color of neutrality, generalizes moral skepticism; and which—more generally, and because of its very principles—necessarily remains insensible to the concepts of belonging, common values, and shared destiny.

Following Allen E. Buchanan and Stephen Holmes, we can draw up a fairly precise list of the reproaches that communitarians address to liberalism, sometimes extended to a more general ("individualist") conception of man and society.[43] These reproaches are as follows.

Liberalism neglects communities and makes them disappear—a fundamental and irreplaceable element of human existence.

It devalues political life by considering political association a

---

[42] For liberals, writes Alasdair MacIntyre, society is "nothing more than an arena in which individuals seek to secure what is useful or agreeable to them," thus constituting "nothing but a collection of strangers, each pursuing his or her interests under minimal constraints" (*After Virtue*, 236, 251).

[43] Allen E. Buchanan, "Assessing the Communitarian Critique of Liberalism," *Ethics*, July 1989, 852–53; Stephen Holmes, *The Anatomy of Antiliberalism* (Cambridge, Mass.: Harvard University Press, 1993).

mere instrumental good, failing to see that citizen participation in the political community is an intrinsic good constitutive of the good life.

It is unable to account satisfactorily for, if it does not actually deny, a certain number of obligations and engagements such as those that do not result from a voluntary choice or a contractual obligation, such as family obligations, the necessity of serving one's country, or letting the common good override personal interest.

It propagates an erroneous conception of the self by refusing to admit that it is always embedded in a socio-historical context and constituted at least in part by values and engagements that are neither the objects of choice nor revocable at will.

It elicits an inflation of the politics of rights, which has little to do with right itself (demanding one's rights is not merely seeking to maximize one's interests to the detriment of others), but produces a new type of social being, the "dependent individualist" (Fred Siegel) as well as a new type of institutional system, the "procedural republic" (Michael J. Sandel).

It wrongly exalts justice as "the first virtue of social institutions" instead of seeing in it a palliative with a merely remedial virtue, and one that comes into play chiefly where communitarian virtues are lacking.[44]

Finally, because of its legal formalism, it fails to recognize the central role played by language, culture, moral habits, shared practices, and values as the base of a genuine "politics of recognition" of identities and collective rights.

---

[44] *Cf.* on this point Michael J. Sandel, *Liberalism and the Limits of Justice,* 31, 183. Liberal authors have reacted especially strongly to this criticism, which in fact can be broken down into two distinct propositions: the thesis of remedy (it is because communal values have collapsed that modern society is forced to give the first place to justice) and the thesis of proportionality (within a given polity, justice occupies a larger place in proportion to the weakening of communal sociality). It has been argued that there is no logical connection between these two positions, but that both amount to saying that justice has no intrinsic value since in an "ideal" situation it would not have to exist (*cf.* Allen E. Buchanan, "Assessing the Communitarian Critique of Liberalism," 877).

So for the communitarians, man is defined above all as a "political and social animal" (Aristotle). On that basis, "humanity" is defined not as what remains after taking away everything that attaches him to a given socio-historical context, but as the result of the free expression of identities situated and constituted within this context. Rights are not universal and abstract attributes, products of a "nature" distinct from the social state and forming an autonomous domain unto themselves, but the expression of values proper to differentiated collectivities or groups (an individual's right to speak his language is indissociable from the right of the group that speaks it to exist), as well as the reflection of a more general theory of moral action or virtue. Justice coincides with the adoption of a type of existence (the good life) directed toward the concepts of solidarity, reciprocity, and the common good. The "neutrality" of which the liberal state boasts is regarded either as disastrous in its consequences or more generally as illusory, since it implicitly appeals to a singular conception of the good that it does not acknowledge as such.

At the level of intellectual method, the communitarian viewpoint appears close to hermeneutics, inasmuch as the latter insists social facts are always "constructed" at the end of a process of interpretation, as well as to certain authors of the Frankfurt School (mainly Adorno), or even to the pragmatism of Richard Rorty because of its "social constructivism" and the importance he attaches to the concept of solidarity.[45] Taking inspiration from Hegel (Charles Taylor), the communitarians reject the primacy of the just over the good and the representation of individuals as autonomous moral agents. Taking inspiration from Aristotle (Alasdair MacIntyre), they affirm that we cannot organize a given polity without reference to common ends and objectives, and that we cannot conceive of ourselves without defining ourselves first as citizens.

We shall not examine further the different aspects of this critique here insofar as it refers to the question of rights and the

---

[45] Cf. Richard Rorty, "The Priority of Democracy to Philosophy," in Merrill D. Peterson and Robert C. Vaught, eds., *The Virginia Statue for Religious Freedom* (Cambridge: Cambridge University Press, 1988).

problem of "moral anarchy" (MacIntyre), to the "politics of recognition" and the question of identity (Taylor), or to the debate over state "neutrality" and the thesis of the priority of justice. But we will insist upon an important aspect of this critique that has hardly been studied in France: the theory of the self as we find it formulated especially in the work of Michael J. Sandel.

Communitarianism is clearly situated within a "holist" perspective, to use a term acclimated in France by Louis Dumont— whom Americans like to present as an "antimodern."[46] So its critique of the liberal philosophy of the subject bears above all on individualism. Liberalism as we have seen defines the individual as what remains of the subject once all his personal, cultural, social, and historical characteristics have been taken away, i.e., once he has been extracted from the community to which he belongs.[47] Moreover, it postulates the self-sufficiency of individuals with respect to society, and maintains that these individuals pursue their best interest by making free and rational choices without the socio-historical context in which they make them weighing on their capacity to exercise their "moral powers," i.e., to choose a particular conception of the good life. To support this conception of the subject, liberals are thus forced to regard as contingent or negligible everything of the order of belonging,

---

[46] *Cf.* J. G. Merquior, "For the Sake of the Whole," *Critical Review*, Summer 1990, 301–25.

[47] Jean-Luc Nancy writes:

The individual is merely the residue of the attempt to dissolve the community. By his nature—as his name indicates, he is an atom, indivisible—the individual reveals he is the abstract result of a process of decomposition. He is another and symmetrical figure of immanence: the for-itself absolutely detached, taken as origin and certainty. . . . One does not make a world from mere atoms. A swerve is necessary, an inclination of one toward another. . . . Individualism is an inconsistent atomism that forgets the stakes of the atom are those of a world. This is why the question of community is the great absence from the metaphysics of the subject, i.e. — individual or total State — from the metaphysics of the absolute for-itself. (*La communauté désoeuvrée*, 17)

social roles, cultural contexts, shared practices, and signification: when he "enters" into society, the individual never stakes the whole of his being, but only that part which expresses his rational will.

For communitarians, on the other hand, a presocial idea of the self is simply unthinkable: the individual always finds society already there—and it is society that prescribes his references, constitutes his manner of being in the world, and shapes his aims.[48] Sandel insists on the way liberals exaggerate the subject's capacity to distance himself from his roles. Charles Taylor also emphasizes that the self never confronts society as something external to himself, and that the subject's capacity to make choices can only develop within a given socio-cultural context.

From the liberal point of view, this "decontextualization" is the basis of freedom. Individuals have different desires, and any principle that derives from them can only be contingent. Now, the moral law demands a categorical, not a contingent, basis. Even a desire as universal as happiness cannot serve as a basis, for the idea people have of it is extremely varied. That is why Kant rests his entire system on the idea of freedom in relations between beings. The just, he says, has nothing to do with the end men have by nature, nor the means that allow him to attain it. So its basis must be sought prior to any empirical end, specifically in the subject capable of autonomous will: it is the rational being himself who is the basis of moral action, and this being is never a being *qua* particular person, but a being *qua* participant in pure practical reason, i.e., a transcendental subject. Sandel asks:

> Now what guarantees that I am a subject of this kind, exercising pure practical reason? Well, strictly speaking there

---

[48] The communitarian critique is here aiming especially at authors such as John Rawls. Friedrich A. Hayek willingly admits the priority of the social fact, but he draws radically different conclusions from it: it is the fact that society always goes beyond the individual, and that the latter cannot reshape it according to his wishes, which conditions his freedom. *Cf.* Brian L. Crowley, *The Self, the Individual, and the Community: Liberalism in the Political Thought of F. A. Hayek and Sidney and Beatrice Webb* (Oxford: Oxford University Press, 1987).

is no guarantee; the transcendental subject is only a possibility. But it is a possibility I must presuppose if I am to think of myself as a free moral agent. Were I a wholly empirical being, I would not be capable of freedom, for every exercise of will would be conditioned by the desire for some object. All choice would be heteronomous choice, governed by the pursuit of some end. My will could never be a first cause, only the effect of some prior cause, the instrument of one or another impulse or inclination. . . . And so the notion of a subject prior to and independent of experience, such as the Kantian ethic requires, appears not only possible but indispensable, a necessary presupposition of the possibility of freedom. . . . Only if my identity is never tied to the aims and interests I may have at any moment can I think of myself as a free and independent agent, capable of choice.[49]

For the communitarians, the problem is that this "modern" freedom—entirely negative as Isaiah Berlin says[50]—insofar as it presents itself as independent of any determination, might very well be not merely formal,[51] but empty of meaning. As Charles

---

[49] Sandel, "The Procedural Republic and the Unencumbered Self," 84–86.

[50] Isaiah Berlin, "Two Concepts of Liberty," reprinted in Michael J. Sandel, ed., *Liberalism and Its Critics,* 15–35. *Cf.* also Quentin Skinner, "The Idea of Negative Liberty: Philosophical and Historical Perspectives," in Richard Rorty, Jerome B. Schneewind, and Quentin Skinner, eds., *Philosophy in History: Essays on the Historiography of Philosophy* (Cambridge: Cambridge University Press, 1984).

[51] Against the libertarians, Philippe van Parijs emphasizes that a formal freedom, which is merely a right without power, cannot be a sufficient ethical value to found a society (*Qu'est-ce qu'une socété juste?*). He also writes: "If freedom really required the right to do as one desires with oneself and that of which one is the legitimate owner, it is not reduceable to this. It is not simply a question of the right to do as one desires in this sense. It is also a question of the means" ("Quelle réponse cohérente au néoliberalisme?" ["What Coherent Response to Neoliberalism?], *Economie et humanisme* [*Economy and Humanism*], March–April 1989), reprinted in *Problèmes économiques* [*Economic Prob-*

Taylor writes: "Complete freedom would be a void in which nothing would be worth doing, nothing would deserve to count for anything."[52] Any will to subordinate the totality of the pre-suppositions of our social situation to our power of rational self-determination comes up against the indeterminacy of the demand for free self-determination itself: it "cannot specify any content to our actions outside of a situation which sets goals for us, which thus imparts a shape to rationality and provides an inspiration for creativity."[53] Sandel concludes: "To imagine a person incapable of constitutive attachments . . . is not to conceive an ideally free and rational agent, but to imagine a person wholly without character, without moral depth."[54]

The liberal conception of the self also supposes a world empty of meaning. As Sandel writes:

Bound up with the notion of an independent self is a vi-

---

lems], January 4, 1990, 25). Andrew Bard Schmookler, for his part, shows how the idea of a freedom of choice within a market society reveals itself upon closer examination as a deceitful illusion insofar as agents can only maximize their choices in such a society insofar as they conform to its principles. He writes:

The market is exquisitely sensitive to the needs we have as "social atoms," and it disregards the needs we have as a social community. . . . Theory says we are autonomous entities, separate except at those points at which we choose to come together for exchange. The system makes it hard for us to be anything else. . . . The market creates a society rich in its fragmented parts but poor in its organic wholeness. (*The Illusion of Choice: How the Market Economy Shapes Our Destiny* [Albany: State University of New York Press, 1993], 62–63.)

On the paradoxes of the logic of individual interest, *cf.* also Richard H. Thaler, *The Winner's Curse: Paradoxes and Anomalies of Economic Life* (New York: Free Press-Macmillan, 1992).

[52] Charles Taylor, *Hegel and Modern Society* (Cambridge: Cambridge University Press, 1979), 157.

[53] Taylor, *Hegel and Modern Society*.

[54] Sandel, "The Procedural Republic and the Unencumbered Self," 90.

sion of the moral universe this self must inhabit. Unlike classical Greek and medieval Christian conceptions, the universe of the deontological ethic is a place devoid of inherent meaning, a world "disenchanted" in Max Weber's phrase, a world without an objective moral order. Only in a universe empty of *telos*, such as a seventeenth-century science and philosophy affirmed, is it possible to conceive a subject apart from and prior to its ends. . . . Where neither nature nor cosmos supplies a meaningful order to be grasped or apprehended, it falls to human subjects to constitute meaning on their own.[55]

Rawls' "original position" also presupposes this "unencumbered" image of a self stripped of all its contingent attributes and endowed with a kind of supra-empirical status. Moreover, it rests on the idea of a permanent distance between the values I have and the person I am.

In the liberal conception of the self, explains Sandel, to say that I possess this or that characteristic means firstly that the characteristic is mine and not that of another, of course, but also that there nevertheless exists a certain distance between it and me: it is mine, but it is not me. It follows that if I lose this characteristic, I nonetheless remain the same person. From this viewpoint, "rational" behavior will be precisely that which leads me to reason without taking account of all the characteristics that I have but that are not me.

This is what John Rawls means when he says the self is prior to the ends it assigns itself: the relation between the self and its ends is determined solely by the choice of ends the individual makes:

No role or commitment could define me so completely that I could not understand myself without it. No project could be so essential that turning away from it would call into question the person I am. For the unencumbered self,

[55] Sandel, "Justice and the Good," in Michael J. Sandel, ed., *Liberalism and Its Critics*, 168–69.

what matters above all, what is most essential to our personhood, are not the ends we choose but our capacity to choose them.[56]

By the same token, the subject is denied any possibility of being bound to a community by commitments prior to his choice: "He cannot belong to any community where the self *itself* could be at stake. Such a community—call it constitutive as against merely cooperative—would engage the identity as well as the interests of the participants."[57]

But Sandel maintains that such a conception contradicts our perception of ourselves. If the self pre-existed its own ends, we should be able to perceive it apart from those ends by introspection. But we never perceive ourselves as a pure abstraction. We only do so in relation to motivations and projects we know to be constitutive of ourselves. And it is when the self is "disencumbered," by contrast, that there "is nothing left of it that could reflect on itself."

The liberal conception of the subject finally renders impossible any true knowledge or comprehension of oneself. If the limits of the self are predetermined, the self cannot learn anything more of itself by attaining the ends it has fixed for itself by its own choices. The self itself is situated beyond the reach of experience and in the end becomes a stranger to itself.

To this instrumental conception of the self, Sandel opposes a constitutive conception in which the self, far from being prior to the ends it gives itself, is itself constituted by ends that are only partly objects of its choices. The distance between the characteristics I possess and the person I am is at once abolished: I am everything that constitutes me, and I can only make use of my reason within the framework of what I am.

The self, in other words, is always involved in a context from which we cannot abstract it. It is concretely situated and incarnated. If we accept this, community is no mere means for the

---

[56] Sandel, "The Procedural Republic and the Unencumbered Self," 86.
[57] Sandel, "The Procedural Republic and the Unencumbered Self," 87. *Cf.* also Sandel, *Liberalism and the Limits of Justice,* 55–64.

individual to realize his ends, nor any mere framework for the efforts he devotes to seeking his best advantage. It is at the very basis of the choices he makes, insofar as it also contributes to the basis of his identity: institutions, social facts, churches, the family, political and educational systems constitute the person from infancy. From this viewpoint, writes Sandel, individuals must be considered "less as individuated subjects with certain things in common, and more as members of a wider (but still determinate) subjectivity."[58]

It follows from this that a socio-historical way of life is inseparable from identity, just as belonging to a community is inseparable from self-knowledge, and that it is impossible to appreciate the value of a way of life justly if we do not acknowledge that the influence it exercises is itself constitutive of the identity of agents. This means not simply that it is from a given way of life that individuals can make choices (including choices opposed to this way of life), but also that it is this way of life that constitutes as values or non-values what individuals consider valid or not. So, Sandel says, if I belong to a practicing Jewish community, then my eating choices will be predetermined by the rules of Kashrut. Charles Larmore adds: "Such ways of life (shared customs, ties of place and language, and religious orthodoxies) shape the sense of value on the basis of which we make the choices we do. They have become ours not because we have chosen them, but rather because they make up the traditions to which we belong."[59]

If our roles, our forms of belonging, and our commitments are constitutive of the persons we are, adds Michael J. Sandel, "If we are partly defined by the communities we inhabit, then we must also be implicated in the purposes and ends characteristic of those communities."[60]

This idea is also found in Alasdair MacIntyre, who proposes a narrative conception of personality where the self is "embedded"

---

[58] Sandel, *Liberalism and the Limits of Justice*, 143.

[59] Rawls, "Political Liberalism," *Political Theory*, August 1990, 339–60.

[60] Sandel, *Liberalism and Its Critics*, 6.

in a life history ordered toward a particular *telos* indissociable from a specific form of belonging. This narrative conception, an open conception, implies that an agents' good always stands in some relation to the good of the communities whose history he shares.

> We all approach our own circumstances as bearers of a particular social identity. I am someone's son or daughter, someone else's cousin or uncle; I am a citizen of this or that city, a member of this or that guild or profession. I belong to this clan, that tribe, this nation. Hence what is good for me has to be the good for one who inhabits these roles.[61]

Sandel continues: "Open-ended though it be, the story of my life is always embedded in the story of those communities from which I derive my identity — whether family or city, tribe or nation, party or cause. On the communitarian view, these stories make a moral difference, not only a psychological one."[62]

Sandel clearly distinguishes this "constitutive" communitarianism from "instrumental" or "sentimental" communitarianism. Instrumental communitarianism limits itself to emphasizing the importance of altruism in social relations. Sentimental communitarianism adds the idea that altruistic practices best allow the maximization of average utility. But these two attitudes are not incompatible with liberal theory.

"Constitutive" communitarianism, on the other hand, does not have an optional character, but rests on the idea that it is simply impossible to conceive of the individual outside of his community or the values and practices expressed therein, for it is these values and practices that constitute him as a person. The fundamental idea then becomes that the self is discovered more than it is chosen, for by definition we cannot choose what is already given. Consequently, self-understanding amounts to gradually discovering what our identity and nature consist in.

---

[61] MacIntyre, *After Virtue*, 255.
[62] Sandel, *Liberalism and Its Critics*, 6.

The essential question is not: "What should I be, what kind of life should I live?," but: "Who am I?"[63]

Sandel also says individuals are not so much beings of need or desire in themselves, but integral to communities that are themselves "systems of desires" (and needs) hierarchically arranged. He writes: "Communities of various sorts could count as distinct 'systems of desires'" in the sense that they define "an order or structure of shared values partly constitutive of a common identity or form of life."[64]

Communitarians thus affirm that every human being is embedded in a network of natural and social circumstances that constitute his individuality and at least in part determine his conception of the good life. This conception, they add, is valid for the individual not insofar as it results from a "free choice," but because it expresses attachments and engagements constitutive of his being. Such allegiances, explains Sandel,

> go beyond the values from which I could maintain a certain distance. They go beyond the obligations I voluntarily contract and the 'natural duties' I owe to human beings as such. They are such that I sometimes owe them more than justice demands, or even than it authorizes, not because of the commitments I have contracted, nor because of the demands of reason, but in virtue of these very bonds and more or less durable commitments which, taken together, in part constitute the person I am.[65]

From this perspective, no one chooses from a position of sovereign freedom, but all exercise their freedom on the basis of what binds them to others.[66]

In this critique we clearly run into the classic distinction between Hegelian *Sittlichkeit* and Kantian *Moralität*. *Sittlichkeit*

---

[63] Sandel, *Liberalism and Its Critics*, 168–69.

[64] Sandel, *Liberalism and the Limits of Justice*, 167.

[65] Sandel, "The Procedural Republic and the Unencumbered Self," 91.

[66] *Cf.* Sandel, *Liberalism and the Limits of Justice*, 150.

refers to the moral obligations we have toward the community to which we belong, and which are based on the moral habits, customs, and norms prevailing in that community; *Moralität* refers to my categorical obligations not as a member of a given community, but as an individual endowed with a rational will. In the former case, there is obviously no opposition between what is and what ought to be, whereas that opposition arises instantly in the latter, since categorical obligation imposes upon me the duty to realize a moral action not founded on any empirical contingency. Hegel posits the primacy of *Sittlichkeit*, which he treats as going back to ancient Greek ethics (the same ethics contested by Socrates): freedom and happiness flourish when the norms and ends expressed in public life allow the members of the city to attain their *telos*. Whence the definition of community as "ethical substance" and source of spiritual life, to which Hegel adds the idea that these norms and ends at work in public life also express the ontological (or at least ontic) structure of things.[67]

An authentic community is no more a mere grouping or addition of individuals than is society as a whole. Its members *qua* members have ends in common; they are bound by shared values or experiences, and not merely by more or less congruent private interests. These ends are proper to the community as such, and not particular objectives that happen to be the same for all or most of its members. In a mere association, individuals regard their interests as independent and potentially divergent from one another. So the relations between these interests do not constitute an intrinsic good, but merely a means of obtaining the particular goods sought by each. Community on the other hand constitutes an intrinsic good for all those who are parts of it, an affirmation that communitarians present either as a descriptive

---

[67] On this subject, *cf.* Charles Taylor, *Hegel and Modern Society*; "Hegel: History and Politics," in Michael J. Sandel, ed., *Liberalism and Its Critics*, 177–99. Peter Berger ("On the Obsolescence of the Concept of Honor," *European Journal of Sociology*, 1970, 339–47), shows that the concept of honor implies that identity be fundamentally associated with subjects' social roles, while that of dignity on the contrary involves an identity radically distinct from those roles.

psychological generalization (human beings have a need to belong to a community), or as a normative generalization (community is an objective good for human beings).[68] As Roberto
Unger writes:

> There are two distinct ways to conceive of a sharing of
> values. On one view, it is a coincidence of individual pref-
> erences, which, even when combined, retain the character-
> istics of individuality and subjectivity. On another view, it
> refers to group values that are neither individual nor sub-
> jective. If we start from the premises of liberal political
> thought, we must treat every sharing of values as a precar-
> ious alliance of ends that simply reveals the subjective
> preferences of the allies.[69]

For his part, Michael Walzer observes:

> Membership is important because of what the members of
> a political community owe to one another and to no one
> else, or to no one else in the same degree. And the first
> thing they owe is the communal provision of security and
> welfare. This claim might be reversed: communal provi-
> sion is important because it teaches us the value of mem-
> bership. If we did not provide for one another, if we rec-
> ognized no distinction between members and strangers,
> we would have no reason to form and maintain political
> communities.[70]

For communitarians there can be no doubt that if modern man is
constantly in search of himself, it is because his identity is no

---

[68] The second thesis, by contrast with the first, implies a theory of
the good in the proper philosophical sense: the community would continue to be good even if men did not sense the need for it.

[69] Roberto M. Unger, *Knowledge and Politics* (New York: Free Press,
1975), 102.

[70] Michael Walzer, *Spheres of Justice: A Defense of Pluralism and Equality* (New York: Basic Books, 1983), partly reprinted as "Welfare, Membership and Need" in Sandel, ed., *Liberalism and Its Critics*, 200.

longer constituted by anything.

In the nearly unanimous opinion of all who have studied it, the communitarian "movement" remains difficult to classify politically. In some of its aspects, such as the importance it attaches to "premodern" norms and to traditions, it appears close to a certain republican conservatism. On the other hand, it shares a number of the political aspirations of classical socialism, and its prioritizing of social factors over individual determinations explains why the works of its representatives have sometimes been likened to the writings of the young Marx.[71] Paul Piccone thinks that

> Communitarianism as a project of social reconstruction is tied neither to the Left nor to the Right. In the 1930s it was a Leftist project culminating in the New Deal, while in the 1980s it was successfully appropriated by the Right and translated into the electoral successes of "Reagan's revolution." Today both major political parties appeal to it, or to its substantive values, to anchor their respective programs.[72]

Michael Walzer has similarly remarked that "The communitarian correction of liberalism can strengthen the old inequalities of traditionalist ways of life or it can counteract the new inequalities of the liberal market and the bureaucratic state."[73]

---

[71] For Will Kymlicka, on the contrary, Marx's point of view remains closer to the liberal point of view than to the communitarian critique precisely because communism is supposed to emancipate humanity from these same social allegiances that the communitarians regard as constitutive of the identity of agents, while liberals consider them so many limitations upon "freedom" (cf. *Liberalism, Community, and Culture,* "Marxism and the Critique of Justice," 100–31). Cf. also A. Buchanan, *Marx and Justice: The Radical Critique of Liberalism* (London: Methuen, 1982).

[72] Ken Anderson, Paul Piccone, Fred Siegel, and Michael Taves, "Roundtable on Communitarianism," *Telos* no. 76, Summer 1988.

[73] Michael Walzer, "The Communitarian Critique of Liberalism," *Political Theory,* February 1990, 23.

The same ambivalence is found at the level of men. Alasdair MacIntyre is a conservative of Aristotelian-Thomist inspiration, Roberto M. Unger an "anarchist" influenced by Nietzsche, Charles Taylor has a past on the radical Left, while Amitai Etzioni, a former advisor to Jimmy Carter, likes to call himself a "neo-progressive." In 1988, Michael Sandel exhorted Democratic party candidate Michael Dukakis to make the idea of community one of the principal themes of his presidential campaign.[74] Later on, President Clinton's wife, Hillary Rodham Clinton, spoke out in favor of a "politics of meaning," a theme launched by Michael Lerner, editor of the progressive Jewish journal *Tikkun*, from which communitarian themes are not absent.[75]

At the sociological level, we must also take into account the strong resonance that the communitarian point of view has in certain feminist milieus, as well as in the ecological movement, as the privileged locus of resistance to the practices of institutional bureaucracies and the extension of global markets.[76]

Some points of convergence are clear, however. Nearly all communitarians dispute the idea of economic citizenship that transforms members of society into "spectators who vote" and consumers ever desirous of improving their condition within the market. Nearly all criticize centralism, the state bureaucracy, and preach various forms of participative democracy. The basis of their message is that if we cannot breathe life once again into organic communities ordered around the idea of the common good and shared values, society will have no alternative but authoritarianism or disintegration. If some propose revitalizing traditions while others emphasize the importance of public goods and collective equipment, many appeal to a republican tradition going back to antiquity (Titus Livius) that knew its apogee in the Italian republics of the late Middle Ages before playing a role in the French and American revolutions. In the United

---

[74] *Cf.* Michael J. Sandel, "Democrats and Community."

[75] *Cf.* Michael Lerner, "The Politics of Meaning," *Tikkun*, September– October 1993, 19–26 and 87–88.

[76] *Cf.* Tim Luke, "Community and Ecology," *Telos*, Summer 1991, 69–79.

States, this tradition borrows as much from Machiavelli, James Harrington (*Oceana*, 1656), and Hannah Arendt as from Thomas Jefferson, Patrick Henry, and John Dewey.[77] The concept of renewing an active citizenry constitutes its center, along with a redefinition of democratic life centered on the idea of participation,[78] recognition, and the common good. Thus, Charles Taylor writes: "The central notion of civic humanism is that men find their good in the public life of a citizen republic." Communitarianism thus seems to issue in a questioning of the nation-state and a certain renewal of the federalist and localist idea.[79]

For her part, Chantal Mouffe affirms that the critique of liberal reason, "For all those who refuse to believe that 'really existing' liberal democratic capitalist societies represent the end of history, constitutes the *conditio sine qua non* of any democratic progress."[80]

---

[77] *Cf.* J. G. A. Pocock, *The Machiavellian Moment: Florentine Political Thought and the Atlantic Republican Tradition* (Princeton: Princeton University Press, 1975) and Gordon Wood, *The Creation of the American Republic, 1776–1787* (New York: W. W. Norton, 1969).

[78] *Cf.* Benjamin R. Barber, *Strong Democracy: Participatory Politics for a New Age* (Berkeley: University of California Press, 1984).

[79] Marcel Gauchet was able to speak of "that intrinsically non-communitarian space that is the nation" ("Le mal démocratique" ["The Democratic Evil"], *Esprit*, October 1993, 82). *Cf.* also Paul Piccone, "The Crisis of Liberalism and the Emergence of Federal Populism," *Telos*, Fall 1991, 7–44, who declares himself in favor of creating "small autonomous organic communities" to allow the institution of a true participative democracy within a federal framework.

[80] "La citoyenneté et la critique de la raison libérale," 102.

LIBERALISM & IDENTITY

Beginning in the seventeenth and (especially) eighteenth centuries, the concept of freedom merged with the idea of the independence of the subject, henceforth free to assign itself its own ends. Each individual was supposed to determine his own good freely by means of nothing more than his will and reason. This emergence of the individual occured within a double context: the devaluation of forms of belonging prior to the subject, and the rise of the ideology of Sameness.

Emerging modernity constantly combatted organic communities, which were regularly denounced as structures that prevented human emancipation, since they suffered the weight of traditions and the past. From this point of view, the ideal of "autonomy," hastily transposed into an ideal of independence, implied the rejection of every root as well as every inherited social bond. As Zygmunt Bauman writes: "Beginning with the Enlightenment, it has been considered a common-sense truth that the emancipation of man, the liberation of true human potential, demanded breaking the bonds of community and freeing individuals from the circumstances of their birth."[1] Thus, modernity was constructed upon the radical devaluing of the past in the name of an optimistic vision of the future intended to represent a radical break with what proceeded it (the ideology of progress). The dominant model was that of a man who must emancipate himself from all his forms of belonging not merely because they dangerously limit his "freedom," but also and above all because they are posited as not constitutive of his self.

But that same individual, thus extracted from the context of his belonging, was also posited as fundamentally like every other, which is one of the conditions of his full insertion into the market, which was then in the process of formation. Because progress was

---

[1] Zygmunt Bauman, *La vie en miettes. Expérience postmoderne et moralité* [*Life in Fragments: Postmodern Experience and Morality*] (Arles: Le Rouergue/Chambon, 2003), 372.

supposed to bring about the disappearance of communities, human emancipation occurred not by recognizing singular identities but by assimilating everyone to a dominant model. Finally, the nation-state increasingly assumed a monopoly in producing the social bond. As Patrick Savidan writes, in the modern vision of the world:

> The other is posited above all as the same. This means that the other is a person like me, a subject, and because of this we must be endowed with the same rights. In other words, we are equals, i.e., the human being *qua* human being appears as my similar. In view of this, a kind of reduction of difference and promotion of resemblance gets carried out.[2]

So the modern liberal dynamic tears man from his natural communitarian bonds by abstracting from his embeddedness in a particular form of humanity. The liberal dynamic is the vehicle of a new anthropology in which it is man's task, in order to acquire his freedom, to tear himself away from ancestral customs and organic bonds, this tearing from "nature" being regarded (in a very Kantian manner) as characteristic of that which is properly human. The ideal is no longer, as in classical thought, to conform to the natural order; on the contrary, it resides in the

---

[2] Patrick Savidan, "La reconnaissance des identités culturelles comme enjeu démocratique" ["The Recognition of Cultural Identities as a Democratic Issue"] in Roman le Coadic, ed., *Identités et démocratie. Diversité culturelle et mondialisation: repenser la démocratie* [*Identities and Democracy. Cultural Diversity and Globalization: Rethinking Democracy*] (Rennes: Presses universitaires de Rennes, 2003), 234. Axel Honneth also observes that "The intermingling of legal recognition and the hierarchical order of values — which more or less corresponds to the moral foundation of all traditional societies — broke down with the arrival of capitalism and the normative transformation of legal relations under the pressure of expanding markets and the simultaneous impact of post-traditional ways of thinking" ("La reconnaissance: une piste pour la théorie sociale contemporaine" ["Recognition: A Path for Contemporary Social Theory"], *Identités et démocratie*, 216–17).

capacity to free oneself from that order.[3] The modern liberal perspective rests on an atomistic conception of society as the addition of fundamentally free and rational individuals who are supposed to act like disengaged beings exempt from any *a priori* determination and freely able to choose their ends and the values guiding their actions. As Justine Lacroix writes: "Whatever their divergences, all liberal theories share a universalistic postulate in the sense that they tend to abstract from any empirical element in order to rise to the transcendental conditions of possibility of a just society, valid for any reasonable community."[4]

Alain Renault confirms this: "A liberal conception situates man's humanity not in the ends he chooses but in his capacity to choose them."[5] This amounts to saying that man possesses his ends without ever being possessed or determined by them, that the self is always irreducible to what it decides to be, that the subject is always independent of the choices he makes, that he always remains at a distance from his particular situation: in short, that he is a being who chooses his ends rather than discovers them. Liberal modernity thus posits the priority of the self both in reference to its ends and to any inherited form of belonging. This is what leads it to support the priority of the just over the good as well. As Michael J. Sandel emphasizes,

> While the morality of the just corresponds to the limits of the self and refers to what distinguishes us, the morality of the good corresponds to the unity of persons and refers to what binds us. In a deontological ethics where the just is prior to the good, this means that what separates

---

[3] *Cf.* Robert Legros, *L'idée d'humanité. Introduction à la phénoménologie* [*The Idea of Humanity: Introduction to Phenomenology*] (Paris: Grasset, 1990).

[4] Justine Lacroix, *Communitarisme versus libéralisme. Quelle modèle d'intégration politique?* [*Communitarianism Versus Liberalism: Which Model of Political Integration?*] (Brussels: Editions de l'Université de Bruxelles, 2003), 79.

[5] Alain Renaut, *Libéralisme politique et pluralisme culturel* [*Political Liberalism and Cultural Pluralism*] (Nantes: Pleins Feux, 1999), 36.

us is in an important sense prior to what binds us, and this priority is both epistemological and moral.[6]

In this new ideological landscape, identity comes down to liberal bourgeois individuality. At the same time, modernity disconnects singular from collective identity to place the latter in a domain of indistinction. Bernard Lamizet observes:

> It is the recognition of an indistinction of rights that has made historically possible the recognition of this fundamental difference between singular identity, otherwise based on filiation and origin, and indistinct collective identity, otherwise founded on belonging and forms of representation of sociability. . . . In this sense, the universality of law represents a radical questioning of the problematic of identity.[7]

Filiation is then driven back into the private sphere: "From the moment the institutional model is founded on the recognition of indistinction, filiation ceases to have a meaning within the structuring of the political identities that structure public space."[8]

First attacking traditions and beliefs, which it secularizes at best, modernity tears the identitarian question away from any "naturalness" in order to place it in the social and institutional field of political and economic practices that henceforth structure public space differently. It fundamentally separates the biological order of existence from the institutional order. Modern public space is one of indistinction, i.e., one where natural distinctions of belonging and affiliation are considered insignificant. In public space we exist not as persons, but as citizens with interchangeable political capacities. This public space is

[6] Michael J. Sandel, *Liberalism and the Limits of Justice* (Cambridge: Cambridge University Press, 1982).

[7] Bernard Lamizet, *Politique et identité* [*Politics and Identity*] (Lyon: Presses universitaires de Lyon, 2002), 302–304.

[8] Lamizet, *Politique et identité*, 109.

governed by law. To conform to the law is to assume the socially indistinct part of our identity. (We note nevertheless that this indistinction is still only relative, since it is limited by the borders within which citizenship is exercised. By distinguishing one polity from another, political life also distinguishes between spaces of belonging and sociability.)

As soon as public space is governed by indistinction, identity can only put on a symbolic character. As Bernard Lamizet observes once again:

> If we place ourselves in the field of history, politics, and social facts, identity can only be symbolic, since individualities there are merged in indistinction. . . . While in private space we only represent the forms and practices constitutive of our affiliation, in public space we let the forms and representations of our belonging and sociability appear, which forms thereby acquire a symbolic consistency and significance. . . . As soon as it falls within a symbolic dimension, identity in the public space is established as mediation: it does not provide a basis for the singularity of the subject, but for its dialectical consistency as a subject of belonging and sociability.[9]

For Hegel, the essence of man resides in self-consciousness. It follows, as Karl Marx observed in 1844, that any alienation of human conscience is merely an alienation of self-consciousness. This is another way of saying that alienation first of all affects identity: whoever has no identity cannot be conscious of himself. However, the great modern ideologies have rarely attributed importance to this problem of identity.

Marx, for example, scarcely takes account of the strictly normative dimension of social struggles, since he remains attached to an anthropology that leads him to conceive of social classes as above all vehicles of a collective project. For him, as Axel Honneth observes, "The subjects of a society are not fundamentally conceived as moral actors, bearers of a series of

---

[9] Lamizet, *Politique et identité*, 11–12.

normative demands to which correspond *loci* where wrongs are inflicted on them, but as actors endowed with a rational finality to which certain interests should be attributed."[10] Freud always displayed hostility to any global apprehension of the individual life of the mind. His theory is elaborated around the concept of a *symptom,* which is constructed in the unconscious and thus foreign to the self. The Freudian ego has no personal identitarian specificity. Freud is not interested in identity but in identifications, which he interprets as transfer or projection. Identification for him is above all an attempt to realize desires one cannot admit, especially at the stage of infancy and adolescence.[11]

From this viewpoint, liberalism is directly antagonistic to the affirmation of collective identities. In fact, a collective identity cannot be analyzed in a reductionist manner as the mere sum of characteristics possessed by individuals gathered within it. Such an identity requires that the members of this collectivity be clearly aware that their membership includes or exceeds their individual being, i.e., that their common identity results from an effect of composition. It also implies recognition that there exist within a given ensemble emergent properties distinct from the characteristics of the singular individuals that compose it. Now, liberalism denies the existence of these emergent properties — those which make a forest more than a sum of trees, a people more than a sum of individuals. Insofar as it is based on individualism, moreover, liberalism tends to break all social bonds that go beyond the individual. As for the optimal functioning of the market, it involves nothing hindering the free circulation of men, capital, and commodities, which further contributes to the dissolution of structures, specific ways of life, and shared values. (This does not mean, of course, that liberals have never been able to defend collective identities. But they can do so only by contradicting the principles they proclaim.)

---

[10] Axel Honneth, "La reconnaissance."

[11] We note that *Vocabulaire de la psychanalyse* [*Vocabulary of Psychoanalysis*] by Jean Leplanche and Jean-Bertrand Pontalis (Paris: PUF, 1967), significantly, contains no entry for the word "identity."

So modernity is characterized not merely by the banishing of organic relations and hierarchic values, with the corollary of replacing honor with dignity. Nor is it limited to discrediting membership in traditional communities, which it interprets as archaic vestiges or irrational annoyances, nor to banishing differences to the private sphere, where they cannot flourish since the locus of recognition is the public sphere. It is also constructed upon the exclusion of third parties and the reduction of diversity. Suppression of castes and statuses with the Revolution, the homogenization of the rules of language and law, the gradual eradication of specific ways of life tied to habitat, profession, social milieu, or faith, increasing lack of distinction between feminine and masculine roles along with gender theory: the entire history of modernity can be read as a continual unfolding of the ideology of Sameness. In all domains, including (recently) within the very domain of filiation itself, we see a rise in indistinction, a process that will reach its apogee with globalization. Modernity has everywhere made differentiated ways of life disappear. Old organic bonds have dissolved. The difference between the sexes has been devalued or denied. Roles within the family have themselves been overturned. Only quantitative inequalities persist—in purchasing power—with reference to the possibility of acceding to the dominant way of life. The result is as Marcel Gauchet describes: "Collective belonging . . . is tending to become unimaginable to individuals in their will to be individuals, whereas they depend upon such belonging more than ever."[12] Who am I? Who are we? These are the fundamental questions that liberal modernity constantly obscured or made more difficult to answer.

But of course, this rise of indistinction has led to reactions. Differentiation between subjects and objects inevitably structures perceptual space; the *indistinct society* produces unease because it is perceived as chaotic and devoid of meaning. Just as globalization, even as it homogenizes cultures, also brings about hitherto unseen forms of fragmentation, so the rise of the

---

[12] Marcel Gauchet, *La démocratie contre elle-même* [*Democracy Against Itself*] (Paris: Gallimard-Tel, 2002), xxi.

ideology of Sameness has brought about and constantly stimulated identitarian questioning. Over the course of the last two
centuries, this questioning has taken on different forms, beginning in the age of romanticism with the "expressivist" revolution, which gave rise to a search for "authenticity." But we
must also mention the way modern social and national belonging have been able to respond to this questioning.

The higher value attributed to work — originally supported
by the bourgeoisie as a reaction against a nobility stigmatized
as committed to the values of gratuitousness and therefore
"unproductive" — furnished a first substitute for identity. Individual accomplishment within the framework of an industrial-
ly organized division of labor will in fact become the object of a
desire for recognition founded especially on having employment and taking pride in "work well done."[13] But the new form
of social division will also transform social class into a substitute for collective identity. In the nineteenth century, the class
struggle played a frequently underestimated identitarian role.
Belonging to a class served as a *status* (status being a subject's
identity as it results from an institution), and the classes endowed themselves with a specific culture. The class struggle
allowed new identities to crystallize, inasmuch as class was not
defined solely by socio-economic activity, but also by an anthropological reference to the natural bases of society. As Bernard Lamizet says: "The existence of classes recognizes the con-
flictual and dialectic character of the difference between forms

---

[13] Axel Honneth writes:

> The individualistic principle of accomplishment is in fact the on-
> ly normative resource that bourgeois, capitalist society has for
> morally justifying an extremely unequal division of life oppor-
> tunities and goods. Because the fact of belonging to a certain sta-
> tus no longer regulates the amount of esteem one enjoys and the
> scope of legal and economic privileges from which one benefits,
> the concomitant ethno-religious valorization of work and of the
> establishment of a capitalist market suggest the dependence of
> such esteem upon individual accomplishment. (Honneth, "La
> reconnaissance," 220)

of belonging in the public sphere."[14]

Whether or not it is grafted upon the class struggle, political life also allows individuals to acquire a substitute identity — this time as citizens. Political identities, at first, gave birth to specific cultures, which were maintained within certain sociological families. The institution of universal suffrage itself responds to an identitarian demand: "Being able to vote is merely being able to give a consistency to the political identity one bears."[15] As for political struggles and conflicts, they have a clearly identitarian dimension, "for they put the identity of social actors to the test of the public sphere."[16]

But class identities, like political and ideological identities, are merely sectorial identities in competition with one another. Beside and above them, more comprehensive collective identities will form: national identities. Observing that the evolution of capitalism had brought with it a massification that has provoked a "crisis of collective identity," Jean-Pierre Chevènement recently suggested that "Social being has a need to incarnate itself just as the person has need of a body."[17] In the nineteenth century, this need for "incarnation" would give birth to the nationalities movement and all modern forms of nationalism, based on the idea that "Political unity and national unity ought to be congruent" (Ernest Gellner). Because of this, nationalism appears as one of the typical fruits of modernity.

But nationalism is not merely a political phenomenon. It is nourished by an imagination in which history, culture, religion, popular legends, and much else are mixed. All these factors are

---

[14] Honneth, "La reconnaissance," 13.

[15] Honneth, "La reconnaissance," 205.

[16] Honneth, "La reconnaissance," 192.

[17] Jean-Pierre Chevènement, *Le vieux, la crise, le neuf* [*The Old, the Crisis, the New*] (Paris: Flammarion, 1974), 210. The future minister of national defense added at the time that "The nation-state in France constituted itself over the course of centuries by a series of cultural genocides on a scale we are only now beginning to appreciate," and that "National demands, far from having to be regarded as obsolete, are eminently popular" (210), a position rather different from those he would later assume . . .

revisited, idealized, and transfigured in order to arrive at a coherent narrative of legitimation.[18] As Chantal Delsol has written, "each people identifies itself historically with characteristic values or models. If these values or models collapse, identity itself is threatened."[19] So values and models will play a role as dispensers of identity, alongside the "grand narratives" we saw developed in the age of "disciplinary societies" (Michel Foucault): the narrative of the nation-state, the narrative of the emancipation of working people, the narrative of the religion of progress, etc.

The classic distinction between "civic nations" and "ethnic nations" — or, to use Friedrich Meinecke's terms, between "political" and "cultural" nations — appears in this respect rather artificial, not only because most national societies blend the two principles in various proportions, but also because the state is most of all society's concern, and all human societies are cultural societies.[20] Moreover, whatever its political character, no nationality has ever failed to have recourse to national myths. Under the monarchy, the French successively believed, or wanted to believe, themselves heirs of the Trojans, the Franks, and the Gauls. After the Revolution, when the nation defined itself in purely political terms, ignoring every pre-political aspect prior to the civic contract, the beliefs that were the basis of national identity conserved all their power. In the era of secularization, they constituted a compensation for the weakening of purely religious beliefs, sometimes giving rise to genuine secular religions.[21] Contemporary "nationalism" can base itself all it likes on the political ideal of the state and citizenship — it would still be a mistake to think abstract political

---

[18] *Cf.* Ernest Gellner, *Nations and Nationalism* (Ithaca: Cornell University Press, 1983).

[19] Chantal Delsol, *La République. Une question française* [*The Republic: A French Question*] (Paris: PUF, 2002), 98.

[20] *Cf.* Alain Dieckhoff, *La nation dans tous ses Etats. Les identités nationales en movement* [*The Nation in All its States: National Identities on the Move*] (Paris: Flammarion, 2000), 41–43.

[21] On this subject, *cf.* Anthony D. Smith, *Chosen Peoples: Sacred Sources of National Identity* (Oxford: Oxford University Press, 2003).

values suffice to form a common identity and, above all, to think they suffice for demanding from the members of the society the sacrifices to which they must sometimes agree. Such demands cannot be formulated unless the bonds of citizenship are felt as a true "immediate common good" based on an identification with a historical community itself founded on certain values.[22] The "national romances," the myths, legends, epics, foundational stories always play the same role, constituting so many symbolic mediations that base sociability on the transmission of a common "knowledge" or shared belief.

This "common knowledge" includes, of course, a large measure of fantasy. Most often, it engrafts favorable interpretations and arbitrary idealistic projections onto incontestable historical realities.[23] The strongest fantasy is that of origin, which is also a fantasy of purity: at the origin, everything was clear and simple, not yet loaded down with all the complexity of actual history. A fantasy of a golden age. The same hermeneutic similarly transfigures events or heroes considered foundational. Arminius and Vercingetorix, Charles Martel, Clovis or Joan of Arc, to cite just a few, obviously never really had the central role or decisive importance the modern imagination has attributed to them. The battles of Poitiers, Bouvines, or Valmy were not great battles that changed the course of history, but this has never prevented them from being considered "foundational."

---

[22] *Cf.* Wayne Norman, "Les paradoxes du nationalisme civique" ["The Paradoxes of Civic Nationalism"] in Guy Laforest and Philippe de Lara, eds., *Charles Taylor et l'interprétation de l'identité moderne* [*Charles Taylor and Modern Identity*] (Paris: Cerf, 1998), 155–70. *Cf.* also Clause Nicolet, *La fabrique d'une nation. La France entre Rome et les Germains* [*The Making of a Nation: France Between Rome and the Germans*] (Paris: Perrin, 2003).

[23] *Cf.* especially Benedict Anderson, *Imagined Communities: Reflections on the Origin and Spread of Nationalism* (London: Verso, 1983); Wolfgang Bialas, ed., *Die nationale Identität der Deutschen: Philosophische Imaginationen und historischen Mentalitäten* [*The National Identity of the Germans: Philosophical Imagination and Historical Mentalities*] (Bern-Frankfurt/M.: Peter Lang, 2002).

Under these conditions, it is all very well for critics of national identity to want to "reestablish the historical truth": their mistake lies in failing to see that although national identity is often a product of the imagination, such an imagination is indispensable to the life of the group. Another mistake is thinking they can extinguish identitarian feeling by demonstrating fantasy's share in it. The "fantasy" in question should rather be compared to *myth*. Myth is active, not despite being mere myth, but because of this. The belief may well be "false" as regards its object, it still becomes "true" through what it arouses in the individual or the group, or because of what it does for them. This is the error of someone like Marcel Detienne when he mocks the pretense of autochthony in a book that, while taking shots at Ferdinand Braudel, tries to present the Ancient Greeks as disciples of Barrès *avant la lettre*.[24] Detienne has an easy time showing how the Greeks, by means of complex myths and scabrous stories, invented an imaginary ancestry for themselves. But he is wrong to think he has demonstrated something. For while it is true that no one can be regarded as autochthonous if you go back far enough, it remains no less true that the conviction of being or not being autochthonous can structure consciousness and provide norms for behavior. As Leszek Kolakowski notes, "If the Greeks, the Italians, the Indians, the Copts of the Chinese today sincerely feel they belong to the same ethnic community as their most distant ancestors, no one can convince them otherwise."[25]

Durkheim was one of the first to speak of a "collective consciousness." Fourier referred to "putting the passions in common." More recently, the role of imagination in self-representation within a group has been studied by Gilbert Durand (mythopoesis and structural anthropology) as well as by certain psychoanalysts of the English school, disciples of Melanie

---

[24] Marcel Detienne, *Comment être autochtone. Du pur Athénien au Français raciné* [*How to Be Indigenous: From the Pure Athenian to the Rooted Frenchman*] (Paris: Seuil, 2003).

[25] Leszek Kolakowski, "On Collective Identity," *Partisan Review*, Winter 2002–2003, 10.

Klein.[26] The collective imagination is a reality: the group structures itself by means of common representations and images. All peoples, all nations have at their disposal a certain number of beliefs relative to their origins or history. Whether these beliefs refer to an objective reality, an idealized reality, or a "myth" is of no importance. It is enough that they evoke or represent an *exordium temporis*, a founding moment. The Catholic church as well has always legitimated itself as a mystical body, and it is this legitimation that has allowed it to traverse the centuries independent of the moral quality of its representatives or the evolution of its dogmas.

In the nineteenth and twentieth centuries, the dialectic between national belonging and class belonging was especially complex. During the war of 1914–1918, as is well-known, the former prevailed over the latter. Men of the Right generally saw in this a proof that the nation had a deeper, more substantial reality than class. But we cannot ignore that national identity has been — along with the right to vote, the welfare state, and the Fordist system — one of the methods that Form-Capital (specifically the masters of the capitalist economic world) has used to domesticate the "dangerous classes." Exalting national solidarity was one way of putting the brakes on the class struggle (or "transcending" it, as the various forms of fascism wanted to do, imagining it was possible to put the bourgeoisie at the service of the nation). It is true that in those days capital-

---

[26] *Cf.* Didier Anzieu, *Le groupe et l'inconscient. L'imaginaire groupal* [*The Group and the Unconscious: The Group Imagination*] (Paris: Dunod, 1984). On the role of myth in politics, we must of course cite Georges Sorel and Carl Schmitt. There exists, moreover, a certain relation between historical "fantasy" and stereotype. The latter is an abusive generalization but, like the (favorable or unfavorable) prejudices to which it gives rise, it also plays a useful role in constituting an ideal type to which it may be good to refer at least provisionally. "Stereotyping amounts to categorizing, and categorization is indispensable to thought. The stereotype is just as indispensable to social interaction as the cliché is to literature" (Jacques-Philippe Leyens, Paola Maria Paladino, and Stéphanie Demoulin, "Nous et les autres" ["We and Others"], *Sciences humaines* [*Human Sciences*], May 1999, 28.

ism still had a national dimension, and that liberalism, in principle hostile to the state, was itself not the least to contribute to the construction of a national spirit. At the beginning, let us recall, the nation was not a category prized by conservatives; it was rejected by internationalist socialism as well. "The liberals alone saw in the nation an appropriate expression of the sum of individual wills," writes Immanuel Wallerstein.[27] It was only later that first conservatives, then socialists, rallied to this new political form.

---

[27] Immanuel Wallerstein, *L'après-libéralisme. Essai sur un système-monde à réinventer* [*Post-Liberalism: Essay on a World-System to Reinvent*] (La Tour-d'Aigues: L'Aube, 1999), 57.

THE FIGURE OF THE BOURGEOIS

Mocked, denounced, derided for centuries, today the bourgeois seems no longer questioned. Not many defend him, but
not many directly attack him either.[1] On the Right as well as
the Left, people seem to think there is something antiquated or
merely conventional about critically assessing the bourgeois.
"There is no longer any reviled template of the bourgeois,
whereas the very word was still clearly pejorative barely ten
years ago," observes the sociologist Béatrix Le Wita; "now
there is something reassuring about it."[2] However, far from
being a class on the road to disappearing, as Adeline Daumard
has imprudently suggested, the bourgeoisie seems rather to
correspond to a *mentality* that has invaded everything.[3] If it has

---

[1] René Johannet, with his *Eloge du bourgeois français* [*Praise of the
French Bourgeois*] (Parid: Grasset, 1924) did not have many successors.
At present, the defense of liberalism has taken the baton. Let us mention, e.g., Félix Colmet-Daâge's essay *La classe bourgeoise. Ses origines,
ses lois d'existence et son rôle social* [*The Bourgeois Class: Its Origins, its
Laws of Existence, and Its Social Role*] (Paris: Nouvelles Editions latines,
1959) where we learn among other things, "that there has never been
any great civilization in the world that was not bourgeois and capitalist" (11)! In Italy, Domenico Settembrini, in his *Storia dell'idea anti-
borghese in Italia, 1860–1989* [*History of the Anti-Bourgeois Idea in Italia,
1860–1989*] (Bari-Roma: Laterza, 1991), reproaches the intelligentsia
with having impeded Italian society's march toward capitalist felicity.
A similar thesis has been supported by the neo-enlightenment writer
Francesco Alberoni. On the critical side, cf. Robert Poulet, *J'accuse la
bourgeoisie* [*I Accuse the Bourgeoisie*] (Paris: Copernic, 1978).

[2] Cited in *Le Point*, May 22, 1993, 59.

[3] Adeline Daumard, *Les bourgeois et la bourgeoisie en France depuis
1815* [*The Bourgeois and the Bourgeoisie in France Since 1815*] (Paris:
Aubier-Montaigne, 1987), 2nd ed. (Paris: Flammarion, 1991). *Cf.* also
Régine Pernoud, *Histoire de la bourgeoisie en France* [*History of the Bourgeoisie in France*], 2 vols. (Paris: Seuil, 1960), 2nd ed. (Paris: Seuil-
Points, 1981). The famous trilogy by Emmanuel Berl, *Mort de la morale
bourgeoise* [*Death of Bourgeois Morality*] (Paris: Gallimard, 1929), *Mort
de la pensée bourgeoise* [*Death of Bourgeois Thought*] (Paris: Grasset, 1929)

lost its visibility, this is because it can scarcely be localized any longer. "The bourgeois has literally *disappeared*, we have heard since the end of the last century, he no longer exists, he is Man himself, and the word is only employed by a few dinosaurs who will eventually get killed off by ridicule."[4] In other words, the term has no content because it has too much. And yet, as Jacques Ellul remarked: "To pose the simple question 'Who is the bourgeois?' provokes such excesses among the most reasonable persons that I cannot believe it dormant and without danger."[5] So let us try to pose the question afresh, firstly by describing in general terms the history of its formation and the rise of the bourgeois class.

In France, the rise of the bourgeoisie owes everything to the Capetian dynasty, which allied with it to liquidate the feudal order. Over the course of the twelfth and thirteenth centuries, the communal movement gained strength: the communes, which were "bourgeois" town associations,[6] perceived the feudal system as a threat to their material interests. Almost everywhere, the bourgeois—who were neither nobles nor serfs, yet

---

and *Frère bourgeois, mourez-vous?* [*Bourgeois Brother, are You Dying?*] (Paris: Grasset, 1938) has aged rather badly by now.

[4] *Chronique en onze lettres* [*Chronicle in Eleven Letters*] (L'Antenne, 1989), 8.

[5] Jacques Ellul, *Métamorphose du bourgeois* [*Metamorphosis of the Bourgeois*] (Paris: Calmann-Lévy, 1967), 10.

[6] Originally, as is widely known, the "bourgeois" was the inhabitant of a *bourg*, a small, fortified town (*cf.* the German *Burg*, "fortified castle"). Fundamentally, he is a citizen as opposed to the peasant or country-dweller. As Félix Colmet-Daâge writes: "Freedom by means of money and security, or money in freedom or security, form the essence of the bourgeois. It was only normal that they were first found in towns" (*La classe bourgeoise*, 31). The word "bourgeois" appears about 1080 by way of opposition both to noble and to the man of the people, *villein* or peasant. The word "bourgeoisie" (in the form "bourgesie") is attested as early as 1240. Many modern words for "citizen" go back to the bourgeois of the towns: in German, *Bürger* means both "bourgeois" and "citizen" (a mayor is a Bürgermeister).

were independent[7] — demanded to come under the king's authority so as not to be subject to their lords. In revolt against the
aristocracy, they acknowledged the king and disavowed their
lord, i.e., they asked the king to give them *lettres de bourgeoisie*
freeing them from their former obligations. The Capetian monarchy, rivals of the feudal lords, supported this movement and
created a class of "king's bourgeois." Beginning in the twelfth
century, it maintained a right of appeal to the royal courts from
sentences handed down by feudal lords. It also forbade the nobility to raise taxes. At the same time, it established a more
homogeneous jurisdiction based on rational law and derived
from Roman law at the expense of customary law. Elsewhere in
Europe, where the "mercantile revolution" was most intense,
merchants did not hesitate to rise up against local authorities
who restricted their prerogatives (e.g., Cologne in 1074, or
Bruges in 1127).

If the bourgeois bet on the then-emergent state, it was obviously because it appeared most likely to favor his own rise.
Moreover, being more distant, it constituted a more abstract,
more impersonal authority. Thanks to it, the bourgeois reinforced their interests by obtaining commercial and professional
franchises that allowed them to escape religious or political
constraints to some degree. Referring to the constitution of
these bourgeois associations, Max Weber did not hesitate to
write that, from the legal point of view, it already amounted to
a "revolutionary usurpation." The state for its part mainly expected financial benefits from the bourgeoisie. But while assuring the bourgeoisie's promotion, it also sought to destroy the
feudal bonds that presented an obstacle to its own power. This
movement accelerated remarkably at the time of the Hundred
Years War (1346–1452). To take part in war, the lords had to

---

[7] The communal movement is not properly speaking a popular
movement. The idea of communal magistracies elected by the mass of
the people is today recognized as a myth that flourished mainly
among the historians of the Restoration. In Italy, the *popolani* who
eliminated the *grandi* from the administration of Florence in 1292 represented exclusively the mercantile fraction of the town.

alienate rights to their property even more than to their persons. The bourgeoisie profited from this. Thus, beside the seigneurial economy was created a new economic sector free of feudal constraints, which was to evolve toward a precocious form of capitalism. It was by relying on the bourgeoisie that the Capetian monarchy created at once the kingdom and the market, beginning a process of unifying France that would essentially be completed by the end of the fifteenth century. Pierre Lucius emphasizes: "Without the cooperation the bourgeoisie freely gave the monarchy, the latter would have been unable to proceed with gathering in the lands that today constitute France."[8]

The feudal system definitively collapsed at the beginning of the fifteenth century. At the same time, the arrival of artillery robbed fortified castles of their military usefulness. As the old, landed aristocracy began to be impoverished, the osmosis between the bourgeoisie and the Capetian dynasty grew stronger. Royalty recruited its councilors from the bourgeois class: e.g., Jacques Coeur became Charles VII's minister of finance. In the following century, in 1522, François I instituted the venality of offices on the advice of the financier Paulet. By payment of a tax, the office became hereditary. Lucius writes: "The venality of offices would assure the triumph of the bourgeoisie which had attained affluence in commerce and industry. While the nobility was decimated by war or languished idle at court or on its estates, the wealthy bourgeoisie made itself masters of the state."[9]

At the same time, the state tried by every means to maximize its financial and tax revenues to put its political power on a firm basis. From the thirteenth century, its economic activity began to be based on rationalization and excessive intervention. Descended from several generations of merchants, Colbert would say: "Everyone, I think, would agree that the greatness and power of a state is measured exclusively by the amount of

---

[8] Pierre Lucius, *Déchéance des bourgeoisies d'argent* [*Decline of the Bourgeoisies of Money*] (Paris: Flammarion, 1936), 27.

[9] Lucius, *Déchéance des bourgeoisies d'argent*, 65–66.

money it possesses."[10] To this end, the state developed large-
scale commerce and extended the market into a "defeudalized"
space already made homogenous by the standardization of legal norms. Since noncommercial intracommunal exchanges
based on ties of mutual personal dependence could not be fis-
cally exploited, it seeked to minimize them. As Pierre Rosanvallon observes: "The state is vitally interested in the development of the market economy and the reduction of noncommercial exchanges. Its political and fiscal ambitions are thus joined,
binding its fate to that of the market."[11] So the modern market
did not result from a natural expansion of local markets, but
from "extremely artificial stimulants" (Polanyi) given by public
power. Karl Polanyi writes:

> Economic history reveals that national markets did not at
> all appear because of the gradual and spontaneous
> emancipation of the economic sphere from governmental
> control. On the contrary, the market was the consequence
> of a conscious and often violent intervention by the state
> which imposed market organization on society for non-
> economic reasons.[12]

But the formation of the market, made possible by the dismantling of the feudal system, also implied the generalization of
the system of exchange within which the individual was increasingly led to seek nothing but his private interest. So by
working to institute "industrial freedom," the monarchy was
attacking traditional organic forms of solidarity. Henceforth, it
exercised power over subjects and no longer over autonomous
groups. So it was already detaching the individual from his

---

[10] P. Clément, ed., *Lettres, instructions, etc. de Colbert*, vol. 2, Second
Part, ccvii.

[11] Pierre Rosanvallon, *Le Libéralisme économique. Histoire de l'idée de
marché* [*Economic Liberalism: History of the Idea of the Market*](Paris:
Seuil-Points, 1989), 117–19.

[12] Karl Polanyi, *La grande transformation. Aux origines politiques et
économiques de notre temps* [*The Great Transformation: The Political and
Economic Origins of Our Time*] (Paris: Gallimard, 1983), 321.

neighbors, beginning a process that the Revolution would merely radicalize. The nation-state constructed itself simultaneously with the market, while the bourgeoisie pursued its irresistible rise. As Durkheim would say: "Individualism and statism march in step."

Many authors have focused on this close relation between individualism, the nation-state, and the advent of the market. As Pierre Rosanvallon notes:

The market is firstly a way of representing and structuring social space. In this respect, the nation-state and the market refer to a single form of socializing individuals. They are only imaginable within the framework of an atomized society where the individual is conceived as autonomous. So there can be no nation-state or market, in the sociological and economic sense of these terms, in places where society is developed as a global social being.[13]

It is in this context that we must situate the action of the Capetian monarchy to dissolve the social relations inherited from feudalism with the help of the bourgeoisie.

[The state] will constantly and methodically destroy all kinds of intermediary socialization formed within the feudal world that constitute natural communities large enough to be relatively self-sufficient: families and clans, village communities (which play for peasants the role of lineage for nobles), brotherhoods, trades, parties, etc. . . . The state can only conceive society as truly its own territory if it dissolves all these *loci* in order to make the individual "a son of civil society" (Hegel). By participating in the liberation of the individual from his previous forms of dependence and solidarity, it promotes the atomization of society which it needs in order to exist.[14]

---

[13] Rosanvallon, *Le libéralisme économique*, 124.
[14] Rosanvallon, *Le libéralisme économique*, 115.

We find the same observation in Gilles Lipovetsky: "It is the conjoined action of the modern state and the market which allowed the great fracture that now separates us permanently from traditional societies, the advent of a kind of society in which the individual man takes himself for the ultimate end and only exists for himself."[15] Thus we may posit the equivalence of these three terms: bourgeoisie, capitalism, modernity.[16] To ask about the formation of the bourgeois class is to bring to light the roots of modernity.

In the sixteenth century, the great discoveries freed Europe of dependence on the Orient as a source of precious metals and gave the Atlantic decisive importance. Above all, they seemed to open up the possibility of an infinite extension of appropriable wealth. Economic activity was deterritorialized, and great commercial companies legally acquired genuine powers of brigandage (the exchange of commodities with the indigenous peoples amounted to an imposed form of commerce). The passion for gold joined forces with the spirit of enterprise. Large-scale capitalism began its ascent. Commodity markets began opening everywhere. The one in Antwerp, founded in 1531, had inscribed on its pediment: "To the merchants of all nations."

Karl Polanyi explains:

In the fifteenth and sixteenth centuries, deliberate state action imposed the commercial system upon the fierce protectionism of the towns and principalities. Mercantilism destroyed the obsolete particularism of local and

---

[15] Gilles Lipovetsky, *L'ère du vide. Essais sur l'individualisme contemporain* [*The Era of the Void: Essays on Contemporary Individualism*] (Paris: Gallimard, 1983), 216.

[16] This equivalence has also been emphasized by Werner Sombart among others. Péguy for his part writes: "We too often forget that the modern world, from another point of view, is the bourgeois world, the capitalist world. It is even an amusing spectacle to see how our socialists . . . careless of contradiction, glorify the same world under the name modern which they castigate under the names bourgeois and capitalist."

intermunicipal commerce by destroying the barriers that separated these two kinds of noncompetitive commerce, thus leaving the field open for a national market that increasingly ignored the distinction between town and countryside as well as between various towns and provinces.[17]

But it was in fact during the fifteenth century that money began to play a truly essential role. Erasmus (*"Pecuniae obedient omnia"* [18]) lamented it, as did Hans Sachs (*"Gelt is auff erden der irdisch gott"* [19]). Feudal society was entirely ordered according to the concept of the common good: the corporations had solemnly to swear to submit to its demands. The right of property was recognized not as intrinsic or absolute, but for practical and contingent reasons (since wealth could be better managed by particular people than by collectivities), and always within certain limits. Economic calculation at that time was merely a makeshift. Moreover, exactness was not aimed at: "It is a specifically modern idea that accounts have to be exact" (Sombart). Finally, money existed only to be spent: *"Usus pecuniae est in emissione ipsius"* [20] (Thomas Aquinas).

The pursuit of profit for the sake of profit, *lucrum in infinitum*,[21] speculation, and the manipulation of money were condemned as a shameful passion. The Middle Ages were severe in their judgment of buying and selling at a profit things whose practical value had not been increased by labor. It seemed to people then that the profit was not justified by any service the seller had rendered to the buyer. It was by virtue of the same principle that the church condemned lending at interest.[22]

---

[17] Polanyi, *La grande transformation*, 98-99.

[18] "Money obeys everything" — Trans.

[19] "On earth, money is the earthly God." — Trans.

[20] "The use of money is to spend it." — Trans.

[21] "Profit to infinity" — Trans.

[22] Lucius, *Déchéance des bourgeoisies d'argent*, 22–23.

As the bourgeoisie became established, we witness a true reversal of values. Accounting becomes fundamental; greed passes for a virtue.[23] In his *Treatise on Political Economy* dedicated to Louis XIII, Antoine de Montchrestien proclaims that enrichment is an end in itself: "Man's happiness consists principally in wealth."

The nature of economic activity then changed. It was empirical; it became rational. Formerly it had to satisfy human ends; then men had to submit to its laws. Formerly it was essentially an economy of demand and custom; then it became an economy of supply and exchange. Moreover, the more the market spread, the greater was the need felt for economic intermediaries, increasing the role of the merchant, i.e., element of the economic class interested especially in the quantitative aspect of production. Werner Sombart emphasizes:

> Commerce has in fact habituated man to orienting his mind toward quantity, concentrating his attention and interest on the quantitative side of things. . . . The merchant soon renounces purely qualitative evaluation, and for the simple reason that no organic bond connects him to the objects or goods he buys or sells. . . . The merchant adopts a purely external and disinterested attitude toward the objects of his commerce. . . . He sees in them only objects of exchange, another reason (this one positive) for his purely quantitative evaluation of things: an object of exchange is an amount, and it is this amount alone that interests the merchant.[24]

The Reformation marked a turning point of the greatest importance. While Luther fought hard against emerging capitalism,

---

[23] If we are to believe the tone of chronicles reaching back to the ninth century, which frequently criticize priests for loving money above all else, this greed first appeared in the ranks of the clergy.

[24] Werner Sombart, *Le Bourgeois. Contribution à l'histoire morale et intellectuelle de l'homme économique moderne* [*The Bourgeois: Contribution to the Moral and Intellectual History of Modern Economic Man*] (Paris: Payot, 1926), 403–404.

Calvin was busy trying to reconcile it with Christian morality: the Puritans of England and the Netherlands, then America, would see in abundant profits a sign of divine election. But the Catholic church, despite its refusal to attribute an intrinsic value to money, also contributed to the rise of capitalism. First, it developed a certain idea of labor-value (man is in the world to work, and to work ever more): denouncing "inactivity" (*otium*), it thereby supported non-inactivity, i.e., *neg-otium*, or "business." Its whole morality, moreover, is based on an idea of rationalizing behavior: within the order of human activities, sin is everything in opposition to the requirements of reason. This is why Thomas Aquinas condemns, along with idleness (*otiositas*), everything that involves passion. As Sombart writes:

> If one wants to get an accurate idea of the role the Catholic religion was able to play in the formation and development of the capitalist spirit, one must consider that the fundamental idea of rationalization was already of a sort to favor the capitalist mentality that, as we know, is entirely rational and teleological. The idea of profit and economic rationalization in the end means nothing more than the application to economic life of rules that religion proposed for life in general. For capitalism to flourish, natural, impulsive man had to disappear, and the spontaneous and original side of life had to give way to a specifically rational psychic mechanism: in short, one condition for the flourishing of capitalism was a reversal, a transmutation of all values. It was from this reversal, this transmutation of values that the artificial and ingenious being known as *Homo oeconomicus* was born.[25]

---

[25] Sombart, *Le Bourgeois*, 288–89. Sombart goes so far as to say that the church's proscription of lending at interest aimed mainly at forbidding "idleness" (the lender does not work; his money works for him), or even at favoring capital formation. We find similar ideas in Georges Sorel (*cf.* his 1894 articles "The Old and the New Metaphysics" and "The End of Paganism," reprinted, respectively, in *La ruine du monde antique* [*The Ruin of the Ancient World*] [Paris: G. Jacques, 1902] and *D'Aristote à Marx* [*From Aristotle to Marx*] [Paris: M. Rivière,

It was in this new climate that the Medieval image of the world collapsed. Succeeding nominalism, Cartesianism introduced a radically transformed relation to the sensible world. Spirit and matter were divorced, as were the divine and the world, thought and action. The basis of reality became discontinuous. The henceforth "disenchanted" world transformed itself into an object of which one could take possession by rational action, "rationalize," i.e., subject to reason. From that point on, the world was merely a thing filled with things. And all these things could be evaluated and calculated. They had a price, i.e., an exchange value, once we considered supply and the demand as determined by scarcity.

Formerly, the personality was formed against a background of belonging: in aiming at excellence, the individual sought to illustrate and simultaneously continue what had preceded him. His way of conceiving the world thus involved a certain valorization of origin. Henceforth, the *novum* took on an intrinsic value. The developing spirit of enterprise involved an orientation toward the future as well as a certain freedom in relation to present constraints that result from the past. Moreover, economic activity was itself posited as unlimited: every capitalist economy must work beyond needs to stimulate ever-new needs. So the world had to be *changed* by creating constant novelty. The optimum then became synonymous with the maximum; the best became indistinguishable from the most: an obsession with work, change, setting in motion. We had to transform the world by *doing*, whether financial, industrial, or technical. From this time, as Jacques Ellul writes,

> What characterizes the bourgeoisie much more than private property is the enormous commotion it imposes on society. A whole world was set to work, a succession of revolutions aimed at imposing or perfecting an ideal political regime. It was the overturning of economic structure and, within an astonishingly brief time, the establishment

1935]). *Cf.* also Bernhard Groethuysen, *L'Eglise et la bourgeoisie* [*The Church and the Bourgeoisie*], 2 vols. (Paris: Gallimard, 1977).

of new structures, the conquest of the entire world.[26]

In the seventeenth and eighteenth centuries, the bourgeois invented the idea that we are on earth to be "happy." This idea would soon appear the most *natural* in the world.[27] The rise of industries and techniques led to the thought that happiness is within reach, that suppressing the last hinderances inherited from the past is sufficient for attaining it. Humanity was thus engaged in an irresistible march forward. As for happiness, it was conceived primarily as material well-being (comfort and security), depending on external conditions one can act upon. So we will be happier when society is "better." The ideology of happiness thereby rejoined that of progress, which in turn supported it.

Progress principally means continuous economic development and all it is supposed to bring. Development was no longer a process of maturing tending towards plenitude, nor the accomplishment of a norm or finality. It became an unending addition of finite quantities. Development aimed at "reaching a state defined by nothing except the capacity to reach new states" (Cornelius Castoriadis). The bourgeoisie, in other words, reintegrated infinity into the world: yesterday's best is merely a lesser thing in comparison with the greater to come. But at the same time, by placing the infinite in the material world, the bourgeoisie (in spite of its formal reference to religion) creates the conditions for a spiritual form of closure. This is something Nikolai Berdyaev saw well:

> The bourgeois, in the metaphysical sense of the term, is a man who only believes in the world of visible and palpable things, and who seeks to occupy an assured and stable position within this world. . . . He is scarcely aware of the vanity and nullity of the goods of the world. He takes only economic power seriously. . . . The bourgeois lives within the finite, fearing infinite extensions. The only infinity he

---

[26] Ellul, *Métamorphose du bourgeois*, 99.

[27] Ellul, *Métamorphose du bourgeois*, 77.

recognizes is that of economic development. . . . He recognizes the infinity of increasing well-being, and he does
not see limits to the organization of life, but all this increasingly imprisons him within the finite.

Berdyaev concludes: "It is the bourgeois who creates the kingdom of things, but it is things that govern and dominate
him."[28] In a world transformed into an object, man is himself
called upon to become a thing.

The bourgeoisie long found its alliance with the monarchy
advantageous. However, this alliance was not without its tensions over the course of history. Very early on, the bourgeoisie
was not satisfied simply to have the favor of the state; it sought
to assume control of it, as during the insurrection of Étienne
Marcel (1358) and under Louis XI, then again under François I
and Louis XIV. However, at these times the bourgeoisie did not
yet have any means equal to its ambitions. It was only in the
eighteenth century that it acquired enough strength to appropriate sovereignty for its own benefit.

We can distinguish three phases in its relations with the
state. At first, the bourgeoisie pursued its rise within the terms
set by political power, which favored it, and which alone had
the administrative means necessary for constructing the market. During a second phase, thanks to the positions it had attained, it created a power proper to itself, an economic power
of a private type. In the final phase, it called upon political
power to submit to its ends. Beginning around 1750 the bourgeois class—rich, powerful, and won over to the ideas of the
Enlightenment—had no further need of the king, who was by
then an obstacle to its projects. The monarchy, for its part,
slipped into absolutism. The bourgeoisie, which had already
assumed power in England in 1688,[29] took over in France in

---

[28] Nikolai Berdyaev, *De l'esclavage et de la liberté de l'homme* [*Slavery and Human Freedom*] (Paris: Desclée de Brouwer, 1990), 232–34.

[29] The gap between the aristocracy and the bourgeoisie was
bridged early and more fully in England than in France, so much so
that English political power very early on rested on its navy, which

1789. The Revolution would overturn everything.

In its demand for perfect freedom to do and to produce, the bourgeoisie supported itself with the conviction that the permanent search for maximum profit is so legitimate that it prevails over any other aspiration. So it sought to destroy anything that appeared to be of a nature to limit economic activity: political power, traditions, corporations are for it merely so many rivets to be burst. In fact, the emergence of modernity would destroy all the counterweights that previously made glory more than a mere temporal datum, as Péguy would say:

> When the modern age arrived, a great number of strong material powers—most of them, even—fell; but far from their fall benefiting the powers of the spirit in any way, or leaving the way free for them, the suppression of other powers profited hardly any power but that of money. It did little more than clear the way for the money power.

It is well-known that all the essential protagonists of the Revolution were bourgeois. But the bourgeoisie did not carry out the Revolution in its own name: it also appealed to the "rights of man." In other words, it dissimulated its interests under the mask of the "universal," even as it let it be understood (and no doubt itself believed sincerely) that its particular qualities were human virtues in general, those which allowed every abstract individual to be invested with a fundamental dignity.

Thus emerges the idea that property is a "natural right," because man first of all owns himself, and because the normal behavior of any human being consists of seeking one's own best interest on all occasions, the public interest being at best no more than an effect of composition resulting from the mutual adjustment of individual strategies and the adding up of the utilities maximized by agents.

---

largely depended on commerce and industry, rather than upon its land army. English colonial expansion would be mostly the work of the middle class.

With this redefinition of justice the idea also triumphs that
the essential goal of life is the search for what is good for each
individual taken in isolation. In fact, the result will be that observed by Emmanuel Mounier: "By reducing man to an abstract individuality with no vocation, no responsibility, no resistance, bourgeois individualism is the quartermaster responsible for the reign of money, i.e., as the common expression
puts it so well, of the anonymous society[30] of impersonal forces."[31]

Just as it was able to rid itself of the monarchy when it no
longer needed it, the bourgeoisie would try to rid itself of the
people once absolutism was overthrown. To do so, it invented
the notion of the "nation," an abstract entity that allowed them
to take back from the people the sovereignty previously solemnly attributed to them. In theory, the people is "sovereign."
In reality, sovereignty only belongs to the nation, which is supposed to represent the people, but which only expresses itself
on the basis of its legal and constitutional status. And since the
constitution reserves the right to vote to "active" electors, i.e.,
the affluent, while the assembly alone is invested with the
power of will and of legislating in the nation's name, only the
representatives of the bourgeoisie really decide, with property
qualifications for voting allowing the electorate to be reduced to
a suitable proportion.[32] Parliamentary sovereignty was already

---

[30] The "common expression" is "*société anonyme,*" the French term
for a limited liability company. — Trans.

[31] Emmanuel Mounier, *Manifeste au service du personnalisme* [*Manifeste in the Service of Personalism*] (Paris: Ferndand Aubier, 1936), 27.

[32] On this subject, one may consult the exhaustive study by Patrice
Gueniffey, *Le nombre et la raison. La Révolution française et les élections*
[*Number and Reason: The French Revolution and Elections*] (Paris: Editions de l'Ecole des hautes études en sciences sociales, 1993). In the
preface to this book, François Furet writes: "To the very end, the men
of the Revolution refused to make electors, even of the second degree,
the arbiters of the devolution of power" (xi). *Cf.* also Bernard Chan-
tebout, *De l'Etat. Une tentative de démythification de l'univers politique,*
[*The State: A Tentative Demystification of the Political Universe*] (Paris:
Consortium de la librairie et de l'édition, 1975), 107–13; and Pierre

winning out over popular sovereignty.

The bourgeoisie needed several more decades to establish its power, but it would rapidly pass through these stages. Under the Restoration and the July Monarchy, aristocratic families were removed from positions they had traditionally occupied (diplomacy, the judiciary, the administration of the royal domains) to the benefit of the bourgeoisie. Louis XVIII accepted a constitution on the English model. Bourgeois prosperity increased under Charles X and especially Louis-Philippe, as a policy of colonial conquest was introduced. Guizot, whose essay *Moyens de gouvernement et d'opposition dans l'état actuel de la France* (*Means of Government and Opposition in the Current State of France*, 1821) declared that the future belonged to the "shop," advised the commercial bourgeoisie to enrich itself, and openly proclaimed: "Nations only govern themselves well when they are hungry." On May 3, 1837, in the Chamber of Deputies, he made it his political program to work toward the "political preponderance of the middle classes in France."

After the Revolution of 1848 and the Second Empire, there opened for liberal capitalism an unprecedented phase of expansion, with a counterpart in the formation of an ever more numerous proletariat. In 1875, the establishment of the Third Republic consecrated the results of the wealthy bourgeoisie's efforts. The year 1900 was that of the Universal Exposition, the Grande Roue,[33] the Moulin Rouge, and President Loubet. Despite opposition from the reactionaries ["ultras"] and the workers' movement, the Belle Époque was indeed that of the triumphant bourgeoisie.

A similar development could be observed in England, where the tension between the rising industrial bourgeoisie and the landed aristocracy resulted in the Poor Law Amendment Act of 1834, which abolished the principle of domicile and the law

---

Rosanvallon, *Le sacre du citoyen. Histoire du suffrage universel en France* [*The Coronation of the Citizen: History of Universal Suffrage in France*] (Paris: Gallimard, 1992).

[33] The Grande Roue was an early Ferris wheel built for the Universal Exposition in Paris. — Trans.

regarding the right to a minimal income: industry had need of a labor force divisible and displaceable at will. Already in 1796, William Pitt stated in the House of Commons that "The law of domicile prevents the laborer from going wherever he can sell his labor most favorably." Rootlessness became universal in order to obey the demands of the economy. The result was the formation of a mobile proletariat cut off from all its attachments, forced to sell its labor at a low price in order not to die of hunger. While in France worker's coalitions were forbidden, in England "Chartists" were thrown in prison. The people only saw itself given the right to vote once its docility toward the system in place was certain. The market society was aborning.

The nineteenth-century bourgeois was defined by his status, rank, wealth, and relations. He was the man who "kept a salon" (Charles Seignobos), who "had financial reserves" (André Siegfried), or even who "owned a piano." Whether he belonged to the petty, middle, or grand bourgeoisie, the business bourgeoisie, the entrepreneurial bourgeoisie, the *rentier* bourgeoisie, or the "intellectual and liberal" bourgeoisie, both his customs and matrimonial choices attested to his respect for appearances, conventions, and the established order.[34]

This is the era of that "bourgeois Christianity" attacked by Bloy, Péguy, and Bernanos, and which led Proudhon to accuse the church of being "stationed like a maid in the service of the most crassly conservative bourgeoisie."[35]

This is also the Age when "progress" triumphed in the form of the scientistic ideology: the bourgeois believed in science as he believed in railroads, omnibuses, and gas lighting.

But above all it was the age of the grotesque bourgeois mocked by romantics, artists, bohemians, and dilettantes. The

---

[34] *Cf.* Marguerit Perrot, *Le mode de vie des familles bourgeoises* [*The Way of Life of Bourgeois Families*] (Paris: Armand Colin, 1961).

[35] For a critique of "bourgeoisism" from a Christian point of view, *cf.* Bernard Dumont, "La tentation bourgeoise" ["The Bourgeoisie Temptation"], *Catholica*, April 1991, 8–22. *Cf.* also the very well documented survey by Emile Poulat, *Eglise contre bourgeoisie. Introduction au devenir du catholicisme actuel* [*The Church Contra the Bourgeoisie: Introduction to the Future of Current Catholicism*] (Paris: Casterman, 1977).

tradition of the ridiculous, tricked, cuckolded bourgeois grey-beard goes back to Molière, it is true, if not to the fabliaux of the Middle Ages, but henceforth it blossoms as never before. Like Scrooge and Gradgrind in Dickens, the characters of Perrichon, Fenouillard, Bouvard and Pécuchet, Monsieur Poirier, Prud'homme, César Birotteau were the natural successors of the *Bourgeois gentilhomme* and Bonhomme Chrysale. They inspired popular novels and theatrical comedy (Labiche, Clément Vautel, Jules Sandeau, Émile Augier). They stimulated the eloquence of Baudelaire or Balzac, the sketches of Daumier, and the cartoons of *L'Assiette au beurre* [*The Butter Dish*]. Flaubert, who claimed the only way to be a good bourgeois was to cease to be one, launched his celebrated *mot*: "I call bourgeois anyone who thinks basely."

In an extraordinarily violent passage, Huysmans writes:

> More villainous, more vile than the despoiled nobility and the fallen clergy, the bourgeoisie borrows from them their frivolous ostentation, their obsolete boastfulness, which it degrades with its own lack of breeding, stealing their faults which it converts into hypocritical vices; and at once authoritarian and sneaky, base and cowardly, it mercilessly machine-guns its eternal and necessary dupe, the common people, whom it itself unmuzzled and put in a position to jump at the throat of the old castes! . . . Once its work is done, the populace was bled white as a matter of public hygiene; the bourgeois, reassured, jovially sat enthroned on the strength of its money and the contagiousness of its folly. The result of its arrival was the crushing of all intelligence, the negation of all probity, the death of all art. . . . It was the great prison of America transported to our continent; finally, it was the enormous, profound, incomparable boorishness of the financier and the parvenu, radiating like some abject sun upon the idolatrous town which spewed forth filthy canticles before the impious temple of the banks![36]

---

[36] Joris-Karl Huysmans, *À rebours* [*Against the Grain*] (Paris: G.

Accused of every fault, the bourgeois seemed a Proteus. He was blamed for his worship of money, taste for security, reactionary spirit, intellectual conformism, lack of taste. He was called a philistine, selfish, mediocre. He was portrayed as an exploiter of the people, an undistinguished parvenu, a conspicuous consumer, a self-satisfied cretin. These often contradictory criticisms undoubtedly fed into facile caricature, but they become clearer when we consider the very different milieus from which they arose, and above all the ideal types to which the bourgeois wass opposed. The bourgeoisie was often held in contempt by the antiliberal Right for aesthetic reasons and in the name of "aristocratic" values (the world of the bourgeois was ugly and pretentious, its values mediocre), whereas the Left was angry at him in the name of "popular" moral values (he represented the "privileged"). This double critique is clearly revealing. It shows that the bourgeois was perceived at once as "exploiter," antihero, elite and pseudo-elite, the successor to the aristocracy and at the same time a caricature of it.

Mobilized against the bourgeoisie, the workers' movement was divided on what strategy to adopt. The rising socialist movement split into opportunists and revolutionaries, "revisionists" and "collectivists." Its reformist wing would finally decide to play the game of parliamentary democracy. Revolutionary syndicalism, on the other hand, would hold that the bourgeoisie could not be fought on its own ground, preaching direct action and denouncing the "representatives" who prevented the working class from making its own demands. Sorel and Lagardelle were among those who condemned most forcefully the conversion of socialism to the rules prevailing in bourgeois society and its long-term evolution toward social democracy.

Marx's attitude was notably ambiguous. On the one hand, he condemned the bourgeoisie in words that have remained famous:

The bourgeoisie, wherever it has got the upper hand, has

Charpentier et Cie, 1884), 332.

put an end to all feudal, patriarchal, idyllic relations. It has pitilessly torn asunder the motley feudal ties that bound man to his "natural superiors" and has left remaining no other nexus between man and man than naked self-interest, than callous "cash payment." It has drowned the most heavenly ecstasies of religious fervor, of chivalrous enthusiasm, of philistine sentimentalism, in the icy water of egotistical calculation. It has resolved personal worth into exchange value, and in place of the numberless indefeasible chartered freedoms, has set up that single, unconscionable freedom — Free Trade. . . . The bourgeoisie has stripped of its halo every occupation hitherto honored and looked up to with reverent awe. It has converted the physician, the lawyer, the priest, the poet, the man of science into its paid wage laborers. The bourgeoisie has torn away from the family its sentimental veil and has reduced the family relation to a mere money relation.

But at the same time, Marx is pleased to note that the bourgeoisie has "subjected the country to the rule of the towns" and killed off the reciprocal relations that characterized feudal society. He emphasizes its "eminently revolutionary" character and the role it played in the development of productive forces:

The bourgeoisie cannot exist without constantly revolutionizing the instruments of production, and thereby the relations of production, and with them the whole relations of society. . . . All fixed, fast-frozen relations, with their train of ancient and venerable prejudices and opinions, are swept away, all new-formed ones become antiquated before they can ossify. All that is solid melts into air, all that is holy is profaned, and man is at last compelled to face with sober senses his real conditions of life, and his relations with his kind. The need of a constantly expanding market for its products chases the bourgeoisie over the entire surface of the globe. It must nestle everywhere, settle everywhere, establish connections everywhere. The bourgeoisie has through its exploitation of the world market given a cosmopolitan character to production and consumption in every country. To the great chagrin of Reactionists, it has drawn from under the feet of industry the national ground on which it stood. All old-established national industries have been destroyed or are daily being destroyed. . . . It compels all nations, on pain of extinction, to adopt the bourgeois mode of pro-duction; it compels them to introduce what it calls civili-zation into their midst, i.e., to become bourgeois them-selves. In one word, it creates a world after its own im-age. . . . The bourgeoisie keeps more and more doing away with the scattered state of the population, of the means of production, and of property. It has agglomerat-ed population, centralized the means of production, and concentrated property in a few hands. The necessary consequence of this was political centralization. Inde-pendent, or but loosely connected provinces, with sepa-rate interests, laws, governments, and systems of taxa-tion, became lumped together into one nation, with one government, one code of laws, one national class-interest, one frontier, and one customs-tariff.[37]

In fact, Marx never really explained what he means by the "bourgeois class" except to say that it is the class which holds capital. Concerning its historical and sociological origins, he was nearly silent. This was because he did not see that the bourgeois is first of all *economic man*. And insofar as he himself accorded the economy decisive importance, he could only criticize the bourgeoisie within a framework that continued to be his own as well. In other words, his economism prevented him from mak-ing a radical critique of bourgeois values. Moreover, it is obvious that these values fascinated him. Wasn't the bourgeoisie, after all, the first to want to change the world instead of merely un-derstanding it? While calling for an end to the exploitation for

---

[37] Karl Marx and Friedrich Engles, *Manifesto of the Communist Par-ty*, 1848.

which the bourgeoisie was responsible, he remained very much behindhand as regards bourgeois values: the classless society was in many respects a bourgeoisie that includes everyone.[38]

The various forms of fascism would be no less equivocal. Theoretically hostile to liberalism, wanting in principle to be "neither Right nor Left," they usually limit themselves to radicalizing a "national" conservative clientele already largely won over to bourgeois values. A large share of their electorate was constituted by the middle classes frightened by the economic crisis and threatened by modernization, which contributed to make them more bourgeois. Fond of opposing "industrial and productive capitalism" to "speculative and financial capitalism," they limited themselves to denunciations of the "fat cats," representatives of the "bourgeois dynasties,"[39] without inquiring further into the logic of capital. They would champion the moral order to which that petty bourgeoisie described by Péguy as "the most unhappy social class"[40] always remained so attached.

René Johannet, author of a famous *Panegyric on the French Bourgeoisie*, also had sympathies for Mussolini's fascism. And when we reread today the "Manifesto of the Young Right"

---

[38] It is in this sense we can paradoxically say that while the soviet system collapsed in the East, "Marxism" was largely realized in the West, as has been maintained notably by the Italian Catholic philosopher Augusto Del Noce. From a similar point of view, Alain Badiou observes that today, "The 'death of communism,' the lapsing of all Marxist politics, is expressed from within its only real triumph, that of the 'vulgar' positivist Marxism which affirms the absolute primacy of the economy" (*D'un désastre obscure. Droit, Etat, Politique* [*On an Obscure Disaster: Law, State, Politics*] [La Tour-d'Aigues: L'Aube, 1991], 28).

[39] *Cf.* Emmanuel Beau de Loménie, *Les responsabilités des dynasties bourgeoises* [*The Responsibilities of Bourgeois Dynasties*] 5 vol., Paris: Denoël, 1963–1978 (1st edition of the first two volumes: Paris: Denoël, 1943–1947).

[40] Mounier said, no doubt more correctly: "In the end, the only real bourgeois is the petty bourgeois. Every grand bourgeois is going in that direction, which can be sensed in his manners" (*Révolution personnaliste et communautaire* [*Personalist and Communitarian Revolution*] [Paris: Ferdinand Aubier, 1935], 355).

published by Drieu La Rochelle in the *Revue hebdomadaire* [*Weekly Review*] of January 16, 1926, we observe that this text proudly proclaims that the Young Right considers itself "bourgeois": "It frankly states as a matter of principle that its leaders are bourgeois and that the bourgeois—those who become bourgeois or remain so from one generation to another by means of their work and their talents—must know how to maintain authority with responsibility!"[41]

On top of this we find the ideology of work, productivism, the doctrine of "the struggle for life" (sometimes transposed into racial terms, or at least into social Darwinism): all concepts with roots in the liberal bourgeois conception of competitive efficiency.

Moreover, fascist movements, and fascist regimes even more, will make large concessions to nationalism. In other words, as Mounier writes, they "combat within their borders an individualism that they fiercely support at the level of the nation."[42] But the bourgeoisie has never failed to defend the nation, the fatherland, the established order whenever doing so could safeguard its own interests.[43]

In sum, it is undoubtedly among the "nonconformists of the 1930s" that we find the most radical critique of the bourgeoisie and bourgeois values in the twentieth century.[44] And

---

[41] Emmanuel Berl writes, not without humor: "Drieu La Rochelle, who invented the strange theory that the petty bourgeois has the most contacts with the most diverse parts of the nation, is himself so little bourgeois that he cannot even distinguish the bourgeois from the adventurer" (*Frère bourgeois, mourez-vous?*, 46).

[42] Mounier, *Manifeste au service du personalisme*, 26.

[43] On the equivocal relations between fascism and the bourgeoisie, *cf.* also Julius Evola's two articles published in 1940 (for the collective volume edited by Edgardo Sulis, *Processo alla borghesia* [*Trial of the Bourgeoisie*] (Rome: Roma, 1940), "Procès de la bourgeoisie" ["Trial of the Bourgeoisie"] and "Mythe et réalité dans la lutte antibourgeoise" ["Myth and Reality in the Anti-Bourgeois Struggle"] translated in *Essais politiques* [*Political Essays*] (Puiseaux: Pardès, 1988), 201–17 and 219–29.

[44] *Cf.* especially Thierry Maulnier, "Contre la culture bourgeoise"

also, before them, in Charles Péguy, according to whom the modern world suffers above all from "bourgeois and capitalist sabotage":

> It cannot be said too often: the evil has come entirely from the bourgeoisie. The entire aberration, the entire crime. It is the capitalist bourgeoisie that has infected the people. And it has infected them precisely with the bourgeois, capitalist spirit. . . . It cannot be said too often, it was the bourgeoisie who began the sabotage, and all the sabotage originated with the bourgeoisie. It is because the bourgeoisie took to treating man's work as a value on the labor market that the worker himself has taken to treating his own work as a market value. It is because the bourgeoisie has taken to making a killing speculating on human labor that the worker himself, by way of imitation, by collusion and opposition, one could almost say by agreement, has taken to constantly making a killing from speculating on his own labor.[45]

The bourgeois has always been analyzed both as a class and as the representative of a specific mentality, a human type ordered according to a certain set of values. Thus, for Max Scheler, the bourgeois is defined first of all as a "biopsychic type" driven by its lack of vitality to resentment and calculating selfishness. The bourgeois, he says, never asks himself whether things have a value in themselves; he limits himself to asking: "Is this good for me?"[46] Eduard Spranger distinguishes six ideal personality types among which the bourgeois corresponds to "economic man" — he who only takes the usefulness of things

["Against Bourgeois Culture"], *Combat*, October 1936 and February 1937.

[45] Charles Péguy, *L'argent* [*Money*], III, 1913, reprinted in *La République. Notre royaume de France* [*The Republic: Our Kingdom of France*] (Paris: Gallimard, 1948), 286–87.

[46] Max Scheler, *Vom Umsturz der Werte* [*On the Overthrow of Values*] (Leipzig: Der Neue Geist, 1919).

into account.[47] For Nikolai Berdyayev, "bourgeoisism" is essentially a "spiritual category." The bourgeois spirit is not to be automatically conflated with the bourgeois class. "Whoever has been able to take on the moral habits of the bourgeoisie is bourgeois," said Edmond Goblot.[48] And André Gide:

> I do not care much about social classes; there can be bourgeois among the nobility as well as among the working class and the poor. I recognize the bourgeois not from his clothing or his social rank, but from the level of his thoughts. The bourgeois hates the non-commercial, the disinterested. He hates everything he cannot raise himself high enough to understand.

Sombart also sees in the bourgeois a psychological type, unevenly distributed among the European nations at first, but given the opportunity by capitalism to acquire a dominant position. Of course, he also recognizes the bond between the spirit of capitalism and capitalism itself. However, positing the principle that psychic or spiritual factors enter into economic life as much as that life determines such factors, and recalling that since organizations are human creations, the producer necessarily precedes the product, he asserts that the capitalist spirit somehow preexisted capitalism, i.e., that emerging capitalism was first produced by temperaments predisposed to certain types of behavior: introverted, concentrated temperaments more given to saving than spending, contracted rather than expansive, repressed rather than luxuriant.[49] According to him, this capitalism appeared in the mercantile republics of Northern Italy, especially

---

[47] Eduard Spranger, *Lebensformen* [*Forms of Life*, 1914] (Halle: Max Niemeyer, 1925).

[48] Edmond Goblot, *La barrière et le niveau. Etude sociologique sur la bourgeoisie française moderne* [*The Barrier and the Level: Sociological Study of the Modern French Bourgeoisie*, 1925] (Paris: PUF, 1967), 6.

[49] Sombart, *Le Bourgeois*. Sombart speaks of "Naturen mit kapitalistischer Veranlagung" ["natures with a capitalist disposition"], among which the bourgeois spirit germinated.

in Florence, toward the end of the thirteenth century.[50]

The perfect bourgeois type is already found in Leon Battista Alberti, author of a famous treatise written between 1434 and 1441 and entitled *Del governo della famiglia* [*Of the Government of the Family*]. In it, Alberti praises what he calls the "sacred spirit of order" (*sancta cosa la masserizia*), characterized by the spirit of saving and the rationalization of economic behavior. Not only must one not spend more than one has, but it is better to spend less than one has, i.e., to save, for one does not only get rich by earning much, but by spending little. Sombart writes: "The doctrine of the bourgeois virtues has not developed much since the Quattrocento. What the following centuries have taught successive generations of bourgeois can be reduced to what Alberti sought to inculcate in his disciples."[51]

These are in fact the same precepts we find beginning in the seventeenth century in the great treatises of bourgeois "morality," such as *Le parfait négociant* [*The Perfect Trader*] by Jacques Savary (1675), who develops the idea of the fundamentally peaceful nature of the commercial relation, or *The Complete English Tradesman* written by Daniel Defoe around 1725, a work in which the author of *Robinson Crusoe*, making a plea for the autonomy of economic activity, defends puritan morals and condemns aristocratic ways in the following terms: "When I see young shopkeepers keep horses, ride a-hunting, learn dog-language, and keep the sportsmen's brogue upon their tongues, . . . I am always afraid for them." The same ideas (the critique of frivolity, useless expense) are also present in Locke as well as Benjamin Franklin.

It was in the Anglo-Saxon world, stimulated by Calvinism and Puritanism, that the old-style bourgeois virtues—hard work, saving, frugality, temperance, the spirit of order and calculation—would proliferate most freely. These virtues aim above all at eliminating fantasy, chance, passion, gratuitousness, creating everywhere laws and regulations, weighing the value of things, evaluating the practical interest of every daily

---

[50] This thesis has, of course, been disputed.
[51] Sombart, *Le Bourgeois*, 141.

activity. Franklin justifies virtue by saying it is first of all *useful*. For the bourgeois, every action must breathe "economic prudence" (Sombart).

Thus, what the old bourgeois virtues most fundamentally oppose is the old seigneurial way of life made up of gifts, prodigality, uncounted expense, predation as well as generosity, gratuitousness in every sense of the word. Sombart has described this opposition of temperaments in striking terms:

> These two basic types, the man who spends and the man who saves, the seigneurial and the bourgeois temperament, clearly oppose one another in all circumstances, in all life situations. Each appreciates the world and life in a manner totally unlike the other. . . . One is sufficient unto himself; the other gregarious; one represents a personality, the other a mere unity; one is aesthetic and an aesthete, the other moralistic. . . . One sings and resounds; the other has no resonance; one is resplendently colorful, the other entirely colorless. . . . One is artistic (by predisposition, not necessarily by profession); the other is utilitarian. One is made of silk, the other of linen.[52]

La Fontaine's fable "The Grasshopper and the Ant" already presents a complete reversal of values in a comic vein. "What meant decadence for the aristocracy becomes an ideal for the bourgeois" (Evola). All qualities connected with honor (the "point of honor") are particularly devalorized. Benjamin Franklin writes: "Do not take offences too much to heart. They are never what they first appear." For a form of moral reasoning based on honor, a concept implying a personal identity inseparable from the social roles that constitute it, is gradually opposed a form of reasoning based on dignity, which involves an abstract identity independent of these roles.[53]

---

[52] Sombart, *Le Bourgeois*, 244–45.

[53] *Cf.* Peter Berger, "On the Obsolescence of the Concept of Honor," *European Journal of Sociology*, 1970, 339–47 (reprinted in Stanley Hauerwas and Alasdair MacIntyre, eds., *Revisions: Changing Perspec-*

For the philosophers' concern for self, for the *amour de soi-même* celebrated by Rousseau (by way of opposition to *amour-propre*), for the aristocratic ethic directed toward the search for glory is substituted the calculus of mere individual interests. Henceforth glory must not be sought, nor honor, nor heroism. In all things one must be practical, economical, measured. The bourgeois cares about reputation, which involves respecting conventions, more than about renown, which is sometimes only acquired by trampling on conventions. Practical intelligence and wisdom thus give way to the spirit of caution, love and charity to mere affection, honor and duty to "integrity," pride in service and in being what one is to pride in entrepreneurship, magnanimity and benevolence to respect.

The aristocratic ideal, but also the popular ideal, was rooted in values posited from the beginning as nonnegotiable, since negotiating (or justifying oneself) was perceived as a kind of lowering of oneself. The bourgeois, who negotiates every day, thinks one can always "explain oneself." He explains his own reasons and tries to understand those of others. Practical rationality triumphs, and from that point on quality gets reduced to merit, which does not necessarily proceed in tandem with grandeur. As Georges Sorel said, "sublimity is dead in the bourgeoisie."

Sombart also uncovers a radical opposition between the bourgeois temperament and the "erotic temperament."

Just as foreign to the erotic temperament are the nonsensual and sensual temperaments, both perfectly compatible

---

tives in Moral Philosophy [Notre Dame: University of Notre Dame Press, 1983], 172–81). The author, who directly relates the emergence of modernity and the growing importance of individual dignity, shows the place occupied in this process by the "bourgeoisification of honor" as described by Norbert Elias (*Der Prozess der Zivilisation* [*The Process of Civilization*] [Bern: Francke, 1969]). He writes: "By contrast with honor, dignity is always related to an intrinsic humanity freed of any norm or any socially imposed role." Already in Montesquieu we read: "The nature of honor is to demand preferences and distinctions" (*De l'esprit des lois* [*The Spirit of the Laws*], book III, chapter 7, [Paris: Flammarion, 1979], 149).

with the bourgeois temperament. There exists a deep opposition between sensuality and eroticism, an unbridge-
able abyss. . . . We can say in general that between a good
head of the household, i.e., a good bourgeois, and an
erotic temperament of whatever degree there exists an irreducible opposition. Either one considers economic interest (in the broadest sense of the term) the principal
value in life, or erotic interest; one lives either for economy or for love. To live for economy is to save; to live for
love is to spend.[54]

Sombart also emphasizes the importance of the resentment
aristocracy inspires in the bourgeois, who feels himself excluded, and which it invariably caricatures every time it seeks to
replace it.[55] Finally, he observes that the bourgeois capitalist
has typically infantile character traits: like a child, he loves concrete grandeur, rapid movement, novelty for its own sake, the
feeling of power he gets from the possession of objects.
    Emmanuel Berl remarks quite correctly that in the aristocracy
the son tries to resemble, if not his father, at least the image attached in his mind to the name he bears, whereas "the bourgeois

[54] Sombart, *Le Bourgeois*, 246–47.
[55] "They were men of bourgeois extraction . . . jealous of lords and
their way of living, at bottom loving the seigneurial way of life but
finding themselves excluded from it for internal or external reasons,
who went about proclaiming everywhere that there was nothing
more vicious than this way of life and preaching a real crusade
against it" (Sombart, *Le Bourgeois*, 411). We sense the influence of Nietzsche here. The importance of resentment in the bourgeois class is
also emphasized by Max Scheler. *Cf.* also Maria Ossowsak, *Bourgeois
Morality* (London: Routledge & Kegan Paul, 1986), chapter 6: "Resentment as a petty bourgeois trait." In a more lapidary style, Raouol
Vaneigem writes: "We know in what contempt the aristocratic class
holds the work that guarantees its own survival. From economic matter, in which feudalism did not want to see anything but the excrement of the gods, the bourgeois nourishes himself, demonstrating
that he was the real excrement, whether of religion or the economy"
(*Le livre des plaisirs* [*The Book of Pleasures*, 1979] [Brussels: Labor, 1993],
24).

ideal involved a certain progress on the part of the son over the father and an accumulation of merits corresponding to the accumulation of money and honors toward which the family is striving."[56] We see here the orientation towards the future. Children should "succeed" better than their parents, and the first thing expected of a school is that it should help them do so. It is in fact a deeply bourgeois idea that the educational system must above all permit one to acquire a trade, and that because of this the most useful disciplines are also the best.[57]

For the old-style bourgeois, then, every superfluous expense must be suppressed. And to this end one must ceaselessly count. But what is "superfluous?" Precisely whatever cannot be counted, that has no calculable utility, that cannot be reduced to an evaluation in terms of individual advantage and profitability. As Cornélius Castoriadis writes:

> The emergence of the bourgeoisie, its expansion, and its final victory march in step with the emergence, expansion, and final victory of a new "idea," viz., that the unlimited growth of production and productive forces is *in fact* the central goal of human life. This "idea" is what I call an *imaginary social signification*. New attitudes, values, and norms correspond to it, a new social definition of reality and being, of what *counts* and what *does not count*. To put it briefly, what counts henceforward is what can be counted.[58]

What characterizes the bourgeois spirit is thus not merely the rationalization of economic activity, but the extension of this rationalization to all domains of life, with economic activity being implicitly treated as paradigmatic for all social facts.

---

[56] Berl, *Frère bourgeois, mourez-vous?*, 92.

[57] Jacques Ellul: "All reproaches currently directed toward education are a function of the primacy of money" (*Métamorphose du bourgeois*, 59).

[58] Cornélius Castoriadis, *Domaines de l'homme. Les carrefours du labyrinthe II* [*Domains of Man: The Crossroads of the Labyrinth II*] (Paris : Seuil, 1986), 140.

Aristotle held that virtue could not be acquired by external means or goods, but external goods are obtained by virtue. Similarly, Cicero expressed the truth of his time by declaring: "What is important is not the usefulness one represents, but what one is."[59] From the bourgeois point of view, the reverse is true: proof of value is provided by material success; one is no more than one has.[60] And since what one has must be measurable objectively, money quite naturally becomes the universal standard. The proverb is well-known: "A poor idiot is an idiot; a rich idiot is a rich man."

Money, explains Sombart, is "a remarkably convenient means for transforming all naturally imponderable, immeasurable values into quantities, and thus bringing them within the competence of our value judgments. Nothing is valuable unless it costs a lot of money."[61] At the limit, the idea of equality is no longer conceived as equality in law but as numerical equality (1=1), as the interchangeability of (almost) any human activity with (almost) any other, the model here no longer being merchandise but money.[62] Social relations end by only unfolding in conformity with the model of the market, i.e., a system of objects divided into possessing objects and possessed objects. No one has better described this reification of the social realm than Karl Marx, who showed that individuals pursuing their best interests unavoidably end up transforming themselves into things.[63]

Time itself becomes a kind of merchandise. The Catholic church, it is true, was the first to present time as a rare and

---

[59] Cicero, *Brutus*, 257.

[60] "Having is a degraded substitute for being," emphasizes Emmanuel Mounier. "One has what one cannot be, but one only has it in a human sense insofar as one tries to be with it, i.e., to love it. The bourgeois sickness is to want to have in order to avoid being" (*Révolution personnaliste et communitaire*, 210).

[61] Sombart, *Le Bourgeois*, 210.

[62] *Chronique en onze lettres*, 15.

[63] "When it is a question of interest, the bourgeois who reflects always slips a third term between himself and his life" (Karl Marx and Friedrich Engels, *The German Ideology* [1845]).

irreplaceable commodity that must not be "squandered."[64] Since then, the measurement and calculation of time have not ceased to improve in step with the conviction, proclaimed by Franklin, that "time is money." Calculating the divisions of time is in fact something of the same order as calculating monetary quantities: no more than wasted money, one never gets lost time back!

Besides the paradoxes that result from this in everyday life,[65] this statement opens up a revolutionary perspective. To say that time is a rare commodity amounts to saying it is a *limited quantity*. Now, if time is a matter of quantity, each period of time is henceforward equivalent, and the *quality* of its content is no longer the most important consideration. The length of one's existence, e.g., becomes intrinsically valuable, allowing one not to care so much about its quality or intensity. Once again, the best gets reduced to the most. Time becomes homogeneous. Bourgeois society has a merely quantitative relation to time.

So the bourgeois wants to have and to seem, not to be. His whole life is directed toward "happiness," i.e., to material well-being, this happiness itself being related to property defined as the totality of what one possesses, without the slightest reservation, and of which one can dispose as one likes. Hence the bourgeois propensity to make property the first of "natural rights." Whence also the importance the bourgeois ascribes to "security," which is both indispensable to the protection of what he already has and to the rational pursuit of his future interest: security is first of all a comfort to the mind, guaranteeing the maintenance of what has been acquired and allowing calculation of what may yet be added.

Bourgeois politics is a direct reflection of these aspirations.

---

[64] *Cf.* Thomas Aquinas, *Summa Theologiae*, II, 9, 2, §2.

[65] "Consumption in fact takes time, and the more there is to consume, the more time becomes a scarce good. . . . The result is that people spend more and more time trying to save time" (Jean-Pierre Dupuy, *Ordres et désordres. Enquête sur un nouveau paradigm* [*Orders and Disorders: Investigation into a New Paradigm*] [Paris: Seuil, 1982], 85–86).

Distrustful of politics, the bourgeois expects from the public powers merely the institution of a security that allows him to enjoy his goods without risk. The ideal government for him is one too weak to prevail over commercial activity, but strong enough to guarantee its proper functioning. We recognize here the liberal state: the gendarme or "night watchman" state.

In the eighteenth century, the doctrine of separation of powers aimed to restrict politics' field of operations and allow the bourgeoisie to exercise legislative power within representative assemblies based on elections with property qualifications. Naturally, this state action is conceived as essentially formal.

Just as he does not like scandal, which makes situations more difficult to master, nor risk when it cannot be calculated, the bourgeois also dislikes using force, authority, or decisiveness. He thinks everything can be arranged by compromise, discussion, publicity, debates, "dialogue," and appeals to reason. If he wants to make politics subordinate to law (the "rule of law"), this is because he thinks he can in this manner forego initiatives not determined by pre-established norms. And this is why, as Carl Schmitt has shown, he is always helpless in emergency situations and states of exception. Legal norms are for him a way of conjuring away chance, reducing the unpredictable to what is already known.

Political activity is thus a calque upon economic activity: to the merchant, who is an intermediary between the producer and the consumer, corresponds the representative, who is an intermediary between the voter and the state; to contractual negotiation corresponds discussion as a source of compromise allowing decision-making to be economized upon. The liberal Orléaniste Right would long incarnate this model in exemplary fashion.[66] It was with reference to this faction that Donoso Cortés would define the bourgeois class as the "discussing class," and Nietzsche in 1887 would denounce the "preeminence of merchants and intermediaries, even in the intellectual do-

---

[66] Péguy: "Everything from which we are suffering is fundamentally a form of Orléanism" (*L'Argent*, III, 386).

main."[67] Soon, Orléanism would even contaminate the Left. And Péguy was able to write:

> The bourgeois has knowingly forged the intermediary: they are these "bourgeois intellectual" politicians, in no way socialists, in no way of the common people, automatic distributors of propaganda, clad in the same spirit, artisans with the same methods as the adversary they combat. It is through them that the bourgeois spirit descends by gradual layers all the way to the world of the working class and kills off the people, the old organic people, to substitute for it this amorphous, brutal, mediocre mass forgetful of its race and its private virtues: a public, the crowd filled with hatred.[68]

In fact, the bourgeoisie does not like overly strong convictions, nor (especially) unforeseeable behavior. It likes neither enthusiasm nor faith. This is why it thinks that "ideology is always antibourgeois" (Emmanuel Berl) and likes to proclaim the "end of ideologies" — without seeing that this end merely coincides with the arrival of its own. In short, the bourgeoisie does not like the infinite that exceeds material things, the only ones over which it has a grasp. Emmanuel Mounier, who saw in the bourgeois spirit the "perfect antipode to any form of spirituality," wrote: "The bourgeois is the man who has lost the sense of Being, who moves only among things, useful things robbed of their mystery."[69] Bernanos wrote: "The only strength of this petty ambitious character is not to admire anything."

It is in this light that we must analyze "bourgeois morality," for example the puritan ethic from which the old-style bour-

---

[67] Quoted by Pierre-André Tagiueff, "The traditionalist paradigm: horror of modernity and antiliberalism. Nietzsche in reactionary rhetoric," in Luc Ferry and Alain Renaut, eds., *Pourquoi nous ne sommes pas nietzschéens* [*Why We Are Not Nietzscheans*] (Paris : Grasset, 1991), 224.

[68] Péguy, *L'Argent*, III.

[69] Mounier, *Manifeste au service du personnalisme*, 20. *Cf.* also *Révolution personnaliste et communitaire*, 352.

geois virtues arose, and which is always based on utility. Thus, commercial honesty, which is one of the cardinal virtues, has no other justification than that it is profitable. A dishonest merchant will lose his customers, so it is in his own interest not to cheat them ("Honesty is the best policy").

The same merchant, however, will not hesitate to demand the right to aggressive competition, which is nothing more than the right to take from those in the same business the customer base they have built up.[70] And if through certain promotional or advertising practices he can lower his prices to the detriment of the quality of the product he offers while knowing that he can hide this from his customers, he will not hesitate to do so. As Sombart writes, "The economy is organized exclusively with a view to the goods exchanged. Profit, as high as possible, being the only rational goal of capitalist enterprise, the criterion and measure for the production of goods is not the nature and quality of the products, but only their possible sales volume."[71]

The old-style bourgeois is not so much moral as moralistic. As Mounier has seen, he only adheres to morality from an instrumental point of view. Moral principles are for him expedients that allow him to protect himself from those above, the political authorities (whose decisions can also be delegitimized through moral argument) or—especially—from those below, the people (the "dangerous classes") who must be dissuaded from revolting against their destiny. Like religion, morality becomes an auxiliary of the police. It allows the maintenance of order and the elimination of dissidents who do not respect the rules of the social game and challenge the "established disorder."

---

[70] It is well-known that this right to aggressive competition has been judged immoral for most of history. At the beginning of the nineteenth century, certain companies refused to have recourse to advertising, judging that the quality of their products should be sufficient to assure them of customers. On the difference between acting morally and acting in conformance with morality but with a view to maximizing an interest or profit, cf. Immanuel Kant, *Foundations of the Metaphysics of Morals*.

[71] Sombart, *Le bourgeois*, 217.

Where does this leave us today? Since the beginning of the twentieth century, an amalgamation of professional origin has tended increasingly to confound the bourgeois class with the middle class. Since then, the middle classes have continued to grow. Donald McCloskey was able to write in a libertarian journal: "The bourgeois has won. . . . The twenty-first century will be the age of the universal middle class."[72] But in his own time Péguy was already able to state: "A godly man in our days is necessarily a bourgeois. And today everyone is bourgeois." This last remark could serve as a leitmotif of the sociology of late modernity.

Especially since the period of the "Thirty Glorious Years" we have been able to observe the *embourgeoisement* of French society in every sense: individual conduct and social behavior have become uniform and are changing deeply, particularly under the influence of television and advertising, while rural France is visibly shrinking. Jean-François de Vulpillières has hastily but convincingly sketched this process which affects the Right as well as the Left, institutions and doctrines, political and labor union life, the family, leisure and professional activity, and which is reflected in phenomena as different as the obsession with performance and competition, the rehabilitation of money, the spread of incivility, the rise in abstention from voting, the fashion for "consensus," the adaptation of school to the needs of business, the critique of "ideologies" and even the decline in birth rates, one of the principal causes of which is the idea that children represent an obstacle to material freedom and social mobility. He writes: "Everything related to popular tradition is in decline; everything inspired by bourgeois habits sets the tone. This goes much farther than behavior and fashion: bourgeois values are inundating people's minds."[73]

This change is even accelerating. A study that appeared in *Le Point* in 1993 already proclaimed a "return of the bourgeois spirit," of which the Prime Minister at that time, Édouard Bal-

---

[72] Donald McCloskey, "Bourgeois Blues," *Reason*, May 1993, 47.

[73] Jean-François de Vulpillières, *Le printemps bourgeois* [*Bourgeois Spring*] (Paris: Table ronde, 1990), 13.

ladur, might be considered the living embodiment:

> The French are seeking security and comfort more than
> ever. . . . Bourgeois values are in fact reassuring. Once rid
> of their "social class" dimension, they have become the
> insurance contract, the charter of consensus, the great
> common denominator of an anxious community. . . . The
> whole trend of society is towards cohabitation between
> the undeniable contributions of consumer society and the
> rediscovery of the bourgeois heritage. . . . The famous un-
> fettered enjoyment of May 1968 has indeed been assimi-
> lated. Neo-bourgeois culture has simply transformed it
> into comfort.[74]

Schools of opinion, political parties, social groups no longer
compete over anything but who can best realize the promise of
these bourgeois "values," since they have even become the ideal of the "victims of progress." People are as bourgeois as their
finances allow them to be, and the rapid rise of the "caviar
Left" shows that Orléanism is the main thing (fashionable) society has in common. Those we might call the "new bourgeois"
(both men and women) are merely those who, in a world entirely modelled on the bourgeois mentality, seek to distinguish
themselves by creating a separate superidentity by caricaturing
old aristocratic habits (of which they retain only the most
pointless and conventional). Ordinary French women with
their abortions and birth control pills, divorced and remarried
like everyone else, are no less bourgeois than American "career
women" and the stylish young women one meets with at political protests.[75]

---

[74] Christian Makarian, "Le retour de l'esprit bourgeois" ["The Return of the Bourgeois Spirit"], *Le Point*, May 22, 1993, 59–61.

[75] *Cf.* Marie-Laure de Léotard and Valérie Hanotel, "Nous, les
bourgeoises . . ." ["We the Bourgeois"], *L'Express*, April 4, 1991. *Cf.*
also Christian Baudelot, *La petite bourgeoisie en France* [*The Petite Bourgeoisie in France*] (Paris: Découverte, 1981); Michel Pinçon, *Voyage en
grande bourgeoisie. Journal d'enquête* [*Journey to the Grand Bourgeoisie:
Journal of an Inquiry*] (Paris: PUF, 1998); and Michel Pinçon and
Monique Pinçon-Charlot, *Sociologie de la bourgeoisie* [*Sociology of the*

At first sight, the modern bourgeois appears to have changed greatly. We can no longer recognize in him the old-fashioned bourgeois like Benjamin Franklin, frugal and hard-working. Nor does he resemble the nineteenth century bourgeois, well-fed, self-satisfied, and stuffed to the gills with convention. He likes to consider himself dynamic, sporty, pleasure-loving, and even bohemian. Far from avoiding superfluous expenses, he seems a febrile consumer who seeks out all the latest gadgets. Far from trying to practice self-restraint, his way of life, centered on the cult of the self, is "entirely devoted to pleasure, so to speak" (Péguy). Celebrities [*le* people] have replaced the people [*les peuple*], and the bourgeois have become "bobos." At the same time, the retreat into private life has also strengthened: "cocooning," the Internet, smart-phones, Internet commerce, home delivery, interactive systems, etc., allowing one to remain in contact with the world without participating in it, remaining within a domestic bubble as airtight as possible where everyone becomes more or less the continuation of his computer terminal or TV remote. It is the world of screens, whose primary characteristic is to screen people off.

Another phenomenon essential to this development is the generalization of credit that allows us to use commodified time in a new way: not only is time money, but this money can be spent in advance, i.e., by way of anticipating the value of time to come. Thanks to credit, every individual can live financially a little longer than he really lives. The old-fashioned bourgeois preached self-control in matters of expenditure. Credit invites us, at the risk of drowning in debt, to spend more than we have, whence this remark of Daniel Bell:

> The Protestant ethic was undermined not by modernism but by capitalism itself. The greatest single engine in the destruction of the Protestant ethic was the invention of

Bourgeoisie] (Paris: Découverte, 2000). A neo-Marxist point of view: Isabelle Garo, Anne-Catherine Wagner, Pierre-Paul Zalio *et al.*, *La bourgeoisie, classe dirigeante d'un nouveau capitalisme* [*The Bourgeoisie, Ruling Class of a New Capitalism*] (Paris: Syllepse, 2001).

the installment plan, or instant credit. Previously, one had to save in order to buy. But with credit cards, one could indulge in instant gratification.[76]

This means that the bourgeois has created his world, and that in this world the old virtues do not need to be incarnated in exemplary fashion by individuals simply because they have been transferred to society as a whole. It is this relation to society that allows us to understand the evolution of the modern bourgeois. Henceforth, it is society itself that must be managed in a rational, cautious, economically and commercially reliable fashion. Werner Sombart demonstrated this in the case of business enterprises: modern capitalism conserves all the bourgeois virtues, but it removes them from persons to transfer them to companies, at which point these virtues cease "to be qualities inherent in living men to become objective principles of economic behavior."[77] It is no longer necessary for the bourgeois to be trustworthy because the firm is so for him. Today, nations themselves are no more than giant firms directed by experts and management technicians. The same goes for "morality"—individual members of society have less need to obey moral principles individually because political life consults moral authorities and respects the "rights of man" in order to create a "more just" society. Immorality can thus spread undisguised within a society that otherwise affirms itself as eminently "moral" in its overall aspirations. So the bourgeoisie has only disappeared as a class to give way to a society in which the bourgeois spirit and *action* cause everyone to share the same enthusiasms and aversions.

But in reality the bourgeois has not changed all that much. Beneath the various shapes he has assumed, certain constants can be identified. The law of least effort seems to contradict the denunciation of "idleness," but if we reflect carefully, it proceeds from the same spirit of economy. In today's hedonism as in yesterday's thrift, the spirit of calculation and the search for

[76] Daniel Bell, *The Cultural Contradictions of Capitalism* (New York: Basic Books, 1976), 21.
[77] Sombart, *Le Bourgeois*, 223.

one's own best interests are always present. We spend more but calculate just as much. We waste but are no more inclined than before to value the truly gratuitous, that which cannot be bought. In short, we always seek utility above all. In all things we adopt the behavior of the merchant in the market. We try to maximize our profit. We still champion the individual as owner of himself, the primacy of practical reason, the cult of novelty and profitability. Even if fashion has taken the place of conventions, public notoriety that of respect, and if the press book has sometimes replaced commercial patents, the bourgeois continues more than ever to live for appearance and having. More than ever, the bourgeois is the one who constantly seeks his own advantage and who, in order to legitimate his conduct, has undertaken to persuade humanity that his way of being is the most natural and normal of all. More than ever, he is the exception that poses as the rule, the particular who presents himself as universal. Radically foreign to him, more than ever, are the taste for useless things, genuine gratuitousness, the sense of honor, a taste for gift giving—in short, everything that could give our presence in the world a significance beyond mere individual existence.

Werner Sombart writes:

What characterizes the bourgeois in our day is his complete indifference to the problem of man's destiny. Man is almost totally eliminated from the table of economic values and the field of economic interests: the only thing we still take an interest in is the process of either production or transportation or price determination, etc. *Fiat productio et pereat homo!*[78]

To which we might add these prophetic words of Emmanuel Berl: "This is the time of the last men Nietzsche feared. American imperialism will triumph without a battle. The *embour-*

---

[78] Sombart, *Le Bourgeois*, 400. "Let there be production, and let man perish!" — Trans.

geoisement of the proletariat will resolve the class struggle."[79]

We can ask ourselves, however, what aspect of postmodernity might presage the end of the Bourgeois Age,[80] as well as about the contradictions that today affect a social domain whose homogeneity conceals (ever more poorly) obvious deep fractures. One important point is that we are already seeing the disconnect between a large fraction of the middle class and the financial *grande bourgeoisie*, a disconnect that actualizes the breakup of that "hegemonic bloc" which for decades has associated the fate of the petty bourgeoisie with the rise of a now-disappearing "national" capitalism. The globalization of the economy, the development and increasing concentration of technological and media networks, the very speed of this development in a context marked by unemployment and the threat of a general recession, cause the middle classes to live once again in anxiety and insecurity, in fear for the future, indeed, in a feeling of panic confronted with the risk of downward social mobility, which this development might involve for them. The result is that an increasing fraction of the middle class feels overwhelmed and "proletarianized," so much so that what until recently constituted a guarantee of social order is becoming a factor contributing to social fragility.

Over the course of its history, the bourgeoisie has been criticized from above as well as from below: by the aristocracy as well as by the people. As others have already noted, this convergence of otherwise rather different critiques is revealing. But it has perhaps not been sufficiently remarked that in the trifunctional system of origins as reconstituted by Georges Dumézil, the bourgeoisie corresponds to nothing whatsoever. Of course, it appears attached to the third function, the economic function, that of production and consumption. But it is

---

[79] Berl, *Mort de la pensée bourgeoise*, 197.

[80] For a deep examination of the anti-bourgeois character of certain ideological concepts of postmodernity, *cf.* Panagiotis Kondylis, *Der Niedergang der bürgerlichen Denk- und Lebensform. Die liberale Moderne und die massendemokratische Postmoderne* [*The Decline of the Bourgeois Way of Thinking and Living: Liberal Modernity and Mass Democratic Postmodernism*] (Weinheim: VCH-Acta humaniora, 1991).

merely a commercial excrescence that, constituting itself outside the tripartite system, has gradually grown to displace this
system entirely and invade the entirety of the social domain:
the history of the past eight or ten centuries shows how the
bourgeoisie, which was nothing at the beginning, has ended by
becoming everything. So we can define it as the class that separated the people from the aristocracy, that cut the ties that rendered them complementary, and that, too often, set them
against one another. So it is the "median" class in the proper
sense of the term, the intermediary class. Édouard Berth said so
in the following terms:

> There are only two nobilities, that of the sword and that
> of work; the bourgeois, the man of the shop, of business,
> of the bank, exchange premiums, the stock exchange, the
> merchant, the intermediary, as well as his counterpart,
> the intellectual, also an intermediary, both foreign to the
> world of the army as well as that of work, are irremedia-
> bly condemned to a platitude of thought and heart.[81]

Perhaps in order to escape this platitude it will be necessary to
restore both the aristocracy and the people.

---

[81] Édouard Berth, *Les nouveaux aspects du socialism* [*The New Aspects
of Socialism*](Paris: Marcel Rivière), 1908, 57.

CRITIQUE OF HAYEK

"Laissez faire la misère, laissez faire la mort."

— Antoine Buvet[1]

The Club de l'Horloge held its fifth annual university in Nice October 20–22, 1989, on the theme: "Liberalism in the service of the people" (*sic*). The general tenor was that of a "national-liberal" conservatism. Thus, Henry de Lesquen, president of the Club, declared that "There would be no authentic liberal society as long as the conception of man resulting from the Western humanist and Christian tradition has not prevailed."[2] The thesis he developed on this occasion consisted mainly in opposing two great liberal traditions, one with its origin in Locke's ideas, and the other derived from Hume and Burke. There was thus supposedly a "bad liberalism" based on empiricism and the blank slate and resulting in the libertarian or anarcho-capitalist current, and a "good liberalism" concerned with preserving traditions and thus perfectly compatible with a "national" point of view.

This way of looking at things was legitimized with constant reference to a thinker now dead, Friedrich A. (von) Hayek. If the reception accorded this reasoning was somewhat reserved,[3] the

---

[1] "Let poverty happen, let death happen." — Trans.

[2] *La Presse française*, November 4, 1989.

[3] Thus, in response to Henry de Lesquen, Jacques Garello, leader of the "new economists," recalled that "Liberals are liberals, and are not on the Right" (*La Nouvelle Lettre*, September 2, 1989). Previously he had written: "One cannot protect privileges, industries, one cannot exclude the foreigner in the name of the nation. In this respect, liberals are not nationalists" (*La Nouvelle Lettre*, May 11, 1987). For his part, Hayek explicitly rejected the "conservative" label ("Why I Am Not a Conservative," Postscript to *The Constitution of Liberty* [Chicago: University of Chicago Press, 1960]), which should not surprise us since, as Philippe Nemo re-

theme of "national liberalism" (or conservative liberalism) has nonetheless recurred often in the history of ideas.[4] A study of Hayek's work is a good way of assessing it.[5]

---

calls, "Liberalism is no less an enemy of conservatism than is socialism" (*La société de droit selon F. A. Hayek* [*The Society of Laws According to F. A. Hayek*] [Paris: PUF, 1988], 369). For a point of view opposed to that of the Club de l'Horloge but coming from the same political family, *cf.* Jean-Claude Bardet, "Le libéralisme est un ennemie" ["Liberalism Is an Enemy"] in *Le Choc du mois*, November 1989, 18-20 (article commented upon negatively by Jean-Marie Le Pen in *Le Figaro-Magazine*, February 17, 1990). We note that the distinction between the two liberalisms in certain respects recalls the quarrel in the United States which for the past several decades has opposed the "paleoconservatives" such as Russell Kirk to the "neoconservatives" such as Norman Podhoretz, as well as to libertarians (Murray N. Rothbard, David Friedman, etc.).

[4] It is primarily in Germany, the Netherlands, and the Anglo-Saxon countries that we have most frequently seen explicitly "national liberal" movements or parties arise during the last century. On the French case, *cf.* Edmond Marc Lipiansky, *L'âme française ou le national-libéralisme. Analyse d'une représentation sociale* [*The French Soul or National Liberalism*] (Paris: Anthropos, 1979).

[5] Born in Vienna in 1899, professor at the London School of Economics from 1931, Friedrich A. (von) Hayek moved toward liberalism under the influence of Ludwig von Mises, from whom he would later separate. During the 1930s his positions suffered considerably from the success of Keynes's ideas. In 1944, publication of his polemic *The Road to Serfdom* contributed to his fame and led, in April 1947, to the creation of the Mont Pelerin Society. It also earned him an invitation to the United States. A Professor of Moral Philosophy at the University of Chicago, 1950-56, Hayek drew from his courses the material for the most celebrated of his works, including the three volumes of *Law, Legislation, and Liberty* (London: Routledge & Kegan Paul and Chicago: University of Chicago Press, 1973-1979). Returning to Austria in 1956, he continued to teach at the University of Salzburg, retiring in 1969 and moving to Freiburg-im-Breisgau, Germany. In 1974 he shared the Nobel Prize for Economics with Gunnar Myrdal. In the 1970s and 1980s his work was rediscovered by American libertarians, as well as in France by the group known as the "new economists." He died March 23, 1992. His works also include the following volumes: *Monetary Theory and Trade Cycle* (1929), *Prices and Production* (1931), *Monetary Nationalism and International Stability* (1933),

I.

Within the domain of liberal doctrines, the originality of Hayek's reasoning is certain. Keeping his distance from "continental" liberalism (except Tocqueville and Benjamin Constant),

---

Collectivist Economic Planning (in collaboration with Ludwig von Mises, 1935), *The Political Idea of the Rule of Law* (1937), *Profits, Interest, and Investment* (1939), *The Pure Theory of Capital* (1940), *The Counter-Revolution of Science* (1944), *Individualism and Economic Order* (1948), *The Constitution of Liberty* (1960), *Studies in Philosophy, Politics, and Economics* (1967), *New Studies in Philosophy, Politics, Economics, and the History of Ideas* (1978), *Denationalization of Money* (1974–1976), *1980's Unemployment and the Unions* (1980), *Money, Capital, and Fluctuations* (1985). His last book, *The Fatal Conceit: The Errors of Socialism* (Chicago: University of Chicago Press, 1989), edited by W. W. Bartley III, is the first work in *Collected Works of Friedrich A. Hayek* in twenty-two volumes now appearing from the University of Chicago Press. The most complete bibliography of Hayek up to July 1983 is in John Gray's book *Hayek on Liberty* (London: Basil Blackwell, 1984), 143–209. Of the abundant secondary literature on Hayek, *cf.* especially Fritz Machlup, ed., *Essays on Hayek* (New York: New York University Press, 1976); Eamonn Butler, *Hayek: His Contribution to the Political and Economic Thought of Our Time* (London: Temple Smith, 1983); Chiaki Nishimaya and Kurt R. Leube, eds., *The Essence of Hayek* (Stanford: Hoover Institution, 1984); *Hayek's "Serfdom" Revisited* (London: Institute of Economic Affairs, 1984); Kurt R. Leube and Albert H. Slabinger, eds., *The Political Economy of Freedom: Essays in Honor of F. A. Hayek* (Munich/Vienna: Philosophia, 1984); Philippe Nemo, *La société de droit selon F. A. Hayek*; Gilles Dostaler and Diane Ethier, eds., *Friedrich Hayek: philosophie, économie et politique* [*Friedrich Hayek: Philosophy, Economics, and Politics*] (Paris: Economica, 1989); Guido Vetusti, ed., *Il realismo politico di Ludwig von Mises e Friedrich A. Hayek* [*The Political Realism of Ludwig von Mises and Friedrich Hayek*] (Milan: Giuffrè, 1989); Jérôme Ferry, *Friedrich A. Hayek: les éléments d'un libéralisme radical* [*Friedrich A. Hayek: Elements of a Radical Liberalism*] (Nancy: Presses universitaires de Nancy, 1990); Bruno Pays, *Libérer la monnaie. Les contributions monétaires de Mises, Rueff et Hayek* [*Free the Currency: The Monetary Contributions of Mises, Rueff, and Hayek*] (Paris: PUF, 1991); Barry J. McCromick, *Hayek and the Keynesian Avalanche* (New York: Harvester Wheatsheaf, 1992); Renato Cristi, *Le libéralisme conservateur. Trois essais sur Schmitt, Hayek et Hegel* [*Conservative Liberalism: Three Essays on Schmitt, Hayek, and Hegel*] (Paris: Kimé, 1993).

Hayek aimed to return to the sources of Anglo-Scottish individualism and liberalism (Hume, Smith, Mandeville, Ferguson) while doing without the concepts of reason, pure equilibrium, natural order, and the social contract. In order to do this, he first sketches a broad fresco. Humanity, in his recounting, has adopted two opposed social and moral systems in the course of its history. The first system, the "tribal order," reflects "primitive" conditions of life. It refers to a closed society whose members all know one another and determine their behavior with a view to concrete aims they perceive and determine in a relatively homogeneous manner. In this face-to-face society arranged with a view to collective aims, human relations, largely determined by "instinct," are essentially based on solidarity, reciprocity, and altruism within the group.

This "tribal order" gradually came undone as bonds between persons were extended in more impersonal social structures, eventually giving way to modern society, which Hayek first calls the "great society" then the "extended order," and which corresponds rather closely to Popper's "open society." This modern society (of which liberalism, capitalism, free trade, individualism, etc., are the most widespread dominant ideologies) is fundamentally a society that does not know closure. So social relations can no longer be regulated on the face-to-face model. In this society, says Hayek, "instinctive" behavior, having become useless, is replaced by abstract contractual behavior (except, possibly, within very small groups such as the family). Order is established there spontaneously, in the abstract, not as the product of a will or design, but as the effect of multiple interrelations arising from the activity of human agents. The "great society" is therefore defined as a social system that spontaneously manages the absence of any common aim.

While Ludwig von Mises still had a tendency to see in liberal institutions the product of a conscious choice based on abstract rationality, Hayek held that in the "great society" these institutions were slowly selected by habit. In other words, it was not by logical deduction or even rational analysis that men have gradually mastered their environment and given themselves new institutions, but by way of rules—Hayek defines man as a "rule-following animal" — formed under the influence of experience and consecrated by time. Reason is thus not the cause, but only the product, of culture. Usage cannot be decreed; it is inherent in the way things are, and this is why we cannot identify the origin of institutions that have endured through time. So culture results from the "transmission of learned rules of just conduct that were never invented and whose function is not understood by individual agents."

Modern society thus forms for Hayek a "spontaneous order" that no human will can reproduce or surpass, and which was formed according to a model inspired by the Darwinian scheme. Modern society is not fundamentally a matter of either nature or design but of a cultural evolution where selection operates automatically. In this view, social rules play the role attributed to mutations in neo-Darwinian theory: some are kept because they reveal themselves as more effective and confer an advantage on those who adopt them (these are the "rules of just conduct"), while others are abandoned. Philippe Nemo writes: "Rules are not invented *a priori* but selected *a posteriori* thanks to a process of trial, error, and stabilization."[6] A rule will be kept or rejected according to whether experience reveals it to be *useful* or not to the whole system constituted by the rules that already exist. Hayek writes:

> It is the gradual selection of increasingly impersonal and abstract rules of conduct, liberating the free will of the individual while insuring an ever-stricter domestication of the instincts and drives inherited from the preceding phases of social development, that have allowed the emergence of the Great Society by making possible the spontaneous coordination of the activities of increasingly extended human groups.

And again: "If liberty has become a form of political morality, this is a consequence of a natural process of selection which causes society gradually to select the system of values that best

---

[6] Nemo, *La société de droit selon F. A. Hayek*, 75.

answers to the constraints of survival then applicable to the greatest number." So culture is above all "memory of the beneficial rules of behavior selected by the group."[7]

Thus, the emergence of modernity appears as the "natural" result of the evolution of a civilization that gradually consecrated individual liberty as the general and abstract principle of collective discipline, i.e., as liberation from traditional society and a passage "to a system of abstract disciplines where each person's actions toward the others are guided by obedience no longer to known ends but to general and impersonal rules not deliberately established by man, and whose role is to allow the construction of orders more complex than we can understand." This social Darwinist vision is of course related to the idea of progress. It implies, as we shall see farther on, an optimistic and utilitarian reading of human history: the "great society" is *better* than the "tribal order," and the proof it is better is that it won out.

Having laid down diachronically, i.e., historically, the distinction between his two great models of society, Hayek then redeploys them synchronically, opposing *taxis* to *kosmos*. The first term, *taxis*, defines the order instituted voluntarily, characteristic of any political project associating men for the sake of a common goal, any form of planning, state intervention, administered economy, etc. Obviously, in Hayek's eyes, this is a resurgence of the "tribal order." The word *kosmos*, on the other hand, refers to the spontaneous, self-generated order naturally resulting from usage and practice, and which characterizes the "great society." This spontaneous order does not exist with a view to any goal. Members of society participate in it while pursuing only their own objectives, with the interaction of their particular strategies bringing about mutual adjustments. The *kosmos* forms independently of human intentions and projects. According to the famous formula of Adam Ferguson (1723–1816), it was "the result of human action, but not the execution of any human design."[8]

This definition of modern society as fundamentally and necessarily opaque leads Hayek to reject the classic definition of

---

[7] Nemo, *La société de droit selon F. A. Hayek*, 86.

[8] Adam Ferguson, *Essay on the History of Civil Society*, 1767.

competition as a phenomenon requiring for its proper functioning as complete a knowledge as possible on the part of economic
and social actors. Hayek rejects the idea of the transparency of
the market: pertinent information can never be completely available to agents. On the contrary, he says, what best justifies the
market economy is precisely that information is always incomplete and imperfect, for under such conditions the best policy
will always be to let everyone do as best he can with what he
knows. So competition will be the effect of *laissez-faire*, whereas
in the classic model it is rather *laissez-faire* that results from the
hypothesis of pure and perfect competition.

While the characteristic trait of the "great society" is the necessary excess of pertinent information in comparison with available, appropriable information, what he calls the "synoptic" illusion consists in believing in the possibility of perfect information. Hayek's reasoning is as follows: knowledge of social
processes is necessarily limited, since it is in a permanent state of
collective formation. No individual and no group can have access to all of it. So no one can claim to have access to, or be able
to take into account, the totality of parameters. Now, the success
of social action demands a complete knowledge of the facts pertinent to such action. Since such knowledge is impossible, no
one can claim to act on society in conformity with its interests,
nor even undertake an action perfectly adequate with respect to
the end in view.

From an epistemological observation, Hayek draws a sociological consequence: a certain amount of ignorance cannot be
overcome; the incompleteness of information involves the impossibility of foreseeing the real consequences of our actions,
something that leads us to doubt the practical reliability of our
knowledge. Since man cannot be omniscient, the best course for
him is to rely upon tradition, i.e., habit consecrated by experience. As Philippe Nemo writes: "True rationalism consists in
recognizing the value of normative knowledge handed down by
tradition, in spite of its opacity and irreducibility to logic."[9]

The market is obviously the capstone to this entire system. In

---

[9] Nemo, *La société de droit selon F. A. Hayek*, 85.

a society exclusively composed of individuals, exchanges carried out within the framework of the market in fact represent the only conceivable form of integration. For Smith as for Mandeville, the market constitutes an abstract form of social regulation, directed by an "invisible hand" and expressing objective laws supposed to regulate interpersonal relations in the absence of any human authority. The market is thus meant to be intrinsically anti-hierarchical: it is a mode of decision-making in which no one voluntarily decides for anyone but himself. The social order is thus confounded with the economic order as the unintended result of actions undertaken by agents to realize their own best interest.

Hayek adopts the Smithian theory of the "invisible hand," i.e., the analysis of totally impersonal mechanisms supposedly at work in a free market. But he makes some important adjustments. In Adam Smith this theory remains macro-economic: individual acts, although manifested in an apparently disordered way, end by concurring miraculously in the collective interest, i.e., the well-being of all. This is why Smith still allows for public intervention when individual ends do not realize the general good.

Hayek refuses to allow this exception. Classical liberalism also holds that the competitive market allows for the optimal satisfaction of given ends. Hayek responds that the ends are never given, since they are unknowable, and that as a result one cannot credit the market with any capacity to express the hierarchy of ends or demands. Such a pretention is even tautological, since "The relative intensity of the demand for goods and services, the intensity to which the market will adjust production, is itself determined by the apportionment of income, which in its turn is determined by the mechanism of the market." Having neither goal nor priority, the market is not ordered toward any end: it leaves ends undetermined and only furnishes agreement on means (it is "means-connected").

On the other hand, in classical theory, the optimal allocation of scarce resources at the level of society as a whole is theoretically assured by the adjustment of competitive markets forming a general equilibrium. Following Ludwig von Mises, and anticipating the critique developed afterwards by G. L. S. Shackle and Ludwig Lachmann, Hayek rejects this static vision inspired by Walras and tries to substitute an optimal institutional system for a socially optimal system of production, thus replacing general static equilibrium with a partial dynamic equilibrium.

Finally, contrary to the classical economists, Hayek states that it is not the freedom of agents that allows exchange, but exchange that allows their freedom. We shall see farther along what we should think of this affirmation, which has a central place in Hayek's system. Its consequences, in any case, are fundamental. From the classical point of view, the market in the strict sense of the term refers to the economic sphere alone, with the role of the state being to complete the market by guaranteeing its proper functioning and even sometimes substituting itself for the market.

From the neoliberal point of view, which is that of universalized economics, the market becomes an explanatory model, a template applicable to all human activities: there is a marriage market, a crime market, etc. The political domain is itself redefined as a market in which entrepreneurs (politicians) seek to get themselves elected by responding to the demand of voters who are themselves aiming at satisfying their best interests.

Hayek indirectly legitimates this vision of things by positing the market no longer merely as an economic machine allowing the providential adjustment of plans elaborated in private by individuals, but as an ordered formation, an *order* established spontaneously, i.e., prior to or independently of any individual action which, by means of the price system, allows an optimal flow of information. Under these conditions, the market covers the entire social realm. It is no longer just the model for human activity but that activity itself.

Far from limiting itself to the field of economic activity properly so-called (Hayek tends to reserve the word "economy" for the description of elementary units such as companies and households), it becomes a general regulatory system for society pompously styled "catallaxy" (a neologism borrowed from von Mises). It is no longer merely an economic mechanism for the

optimal allocation of resources in a universe traditionally described as governed by scarcity, a mechanism directed to some
positive finality (the happiness of individuals, enrichment, well-
being), but a sociological as well as "political" order, the formal
instrumental support for individuals' opportunity freely to pursue their particular objectives—in short, a structure, i.e., a process without any subject, spontaneously arranging the coexistence of most private ends, and which imposes itself on everyone
insofar as, by nature, it forbids individuals or groups to seek to
reform it.

The principle affirmed here is obviously that of an individual
activity strictly associated with the model of commercial exchange. Freedom remains defined simply as the absence of constraint, of coercion. It expresses "the situation in which each
agent can use what he knows with a view to what he wants to
do," a situation only guaranteed by the order of the market. So it
is not the means of attaining an objective that a social action
could render concrete, but the impersonal gift that historical evolution has accorded men with the emergence of the abstract order of exchange. Outside the market, no freedom!

Pierre Rosanvallon correctly says that "Liberalism somehow
makes the *depersonalization of the world* the condition for progress
and freedom."[10] Hayek's reasoning obviously shares this aim of
replacing the power of men with as impersonal a form of social
regulation as possible. John Locke already stated that those who
hold authority should only set down general, universal rules.
For Hayek, social solidarity—since it does not flow from adherence to any collective finality, but from the mutual adjustment of
every agent's anticipations—is both logical and functional. A
social state is coherent when its rules of behavior are not contradictory and are in conformity with its evolution. Just as for
Popper we cannot decide on what is true but only eliminate
falsity (the criterion of falsifiability), according to Hayek we

---

[10] Pierre Rosanvallon, *Le libéralisme économique. Histoire de l'idée de
marché* [*Economic Liberalism: History of the Idea of the Market*] (Paris:
Seuil, 1989), vii (1st ed.: *Le capitalisme utopique* [*Utopian Capitalism*]
[Paris: Seuil, 1979).

cannot define just rules but only determine negatively those that are not unjust. The least unjust rules are those that do not prevent the functioning of the market, that conform most closely with an impersonal, abstract order, and that deviate as little as possible from established usage. The good society, then, is one where the legislator's law (*thesis*) follows as closely as possible the custom (*nomos*) that allowed the emergence of the market order. It follows that a constitution must not include substantial rules of justice, but only neutral, abstract rules that determine the limits of legislative or executive action.

The objective of the law, in other words, is no longer to organize individual actions with a view to the common good or any determinate project, but to codify rules whose only function is to protect individuals' freedom of action, i.e., to indicate "to each what he can count upon, what material objects or services he can use for his projects, and what field of action is open to him." Hayek adds that the law can only protect the formation of individual anticipations if it is itself in conformity with the order of things already instituted and, conversely, only the anticipations that form in accordance with this established order can be considered legitimate. So the rules are purely formal norms with no substantial content, a necessary condition of their universal validity. In fact, Hayek emphasizes, "It is only if they are applied universally without regard for their particular effects that they will serve to maintain the abstract order." Of course, individuals will all be posited as equal with respect to the formal rules, but since these refer to a very concrete reality that is none other than liberal capitalism, their equality will itself have nothing substantial about it: formal equality will march in step with real social inequality.

A society organized on the basis of commercial exchange will thus be able to elicit the adhesion of everyone without ever proposing common goals. It institutes an order of pure means, leaving everyone responsible for his own ends. What unites men in catallaxy, defined as "the order brought about by the mutual adjustment of many individual economies in a market,"[11] is not

---

[11] Hayek, *Law, Legislation, and Liberty*, vol. 2 (Chicago: University

in fact any community of ends but a community of means expressed in the abstract legal order. Like Hume and Montesquieu, Hayek believes in the pacifying power of trade. By avoiding the dangers of face-to-face relations proper to the "tribal order" and the debate over collective ends, the market neutralizes rivalries, pacifies the passions, and tends to the extinction of conflicts. When all members of the "great society" share the same adhesion to a system of means substituted for a debate over ends, conflicts will disappear or find their solution automatically.

This model of society poses a problem of interpretation from the start. At first glance, e.g., one might be tempted to consider the idea of *spontaneous* order as an avatar of *natural* order as conceived by the counter-revolutionaries most hostile to voluntarism. But this would be a mistake, for Hayek does not present spontaneous order as referring to an original and permanent state constitutive in some way of the entire human social order, but on the contrary as an order attained over the course of humanity's history and reaching its apogee in the modern era. It is an order, one might say, that results from a "natural" evolution, but which is not therefore a "natural order."

The way Hayek affirms the autonomy of the social realm, moreover, gives his reasoning an appearance of holism, insofar as he posits the market as an encompassing totality that functions as such and that implies trading relations between agents that obviously could not be found in the isolated individual. Finally, the idea of spontaneous order seems to refer to the systemic concept of self-organization, especially since Hayek himself several times sought to connect his theses with P. A. Weiss's systemics, cybernetic models (Heinz von Forster), complexity concepts (John von Neumann) and "autopoiesis" (Francisco Varela, Humberto Maturana), the thermodynamics of open systems (Ilya Prigogine), etc.[12]

---

of Chicago Press, 1976), 108–109.

[12] On Hayek and self-organisation, *cf.* Jean-Pierre Dupuy, "L'autonomie et la complexité du social" ["Autonomy and Social Complexity"] in *Science et pratique de la complexité* (Paris: Documentation française, 1986), 293–306. *Cf.* also Milan Zeleny, ed., *Autopoiesis,*

In fact, Hayek is reformulating in a learned manner ideas advanced well before him by Bernard Mandeville, Adam Smith, and Adam Ferguson, all three founders of a new modern theory of "civil society." The originality of these authors within the body of liberal thought is to mark themselves off at once from the naïve utilitarianism of a Jeremy Bentham and from the philosophy of natural law. Their reasoning consists in studying no longer the question of the *origin* of society (which had led John Locke to advance the hypothesis of the social contract) but of its *regulation,* i.e., its way of functioning. In a 1990 thesis,[13] M. Gautier has very correctly shown that this evolution corresponds to the transition from a vision of the world as a theodicy to a vision of the world as a sociodicy. The essential point is the abandonment of the fiction of the contract and recognition of the necessity of the social bond as a component of human nature: since society constitutes the natural framework of human existence, there is no longer any occasion to search out the secret of its "origin" in a contractual agreement between individuals previously living in isolation. The mechanism of the *market* as the basis of social life is then substituted for the artifice of the contract, which allows one to escape the quandaries characteristic of the contract theories inherited from Hobbes or Locke. This is precisely the basis of the Smithian theory of the "invisible hand." It involves considering habits, customs, and even traditions that accompanied the emergence of the market. Carried to its logical conclusion, as was done by Ferguson, commercial exchange becomes the specific modality of the social relation whose basis is custom.

Claude Gautier is thus justified in speaking of "impure

Dissipative Structures, and Spontaneous Social Orders (Boulder: Westview Press, 1980); and Francisco Varela, *Principles of Biological Autonomy* (New York: Elsevier North Holland, 1979). Let us remember that the concept of uncertainty associated with that of complexity goes back to Heisenberg's formulation of the indeterminacy principles in 1927.

[13] Claude Gautier, *La genèse de la societé civile libérale. Mandeville-Smith-Ferguson* [*The Genesis of Liberal Civil Society: Mandeville-Smith-Ferguson*], Paris: Université de Paris, I, January 1990.

individualism" to describe this new liberal procedure that aims at basing "the relation of co-emergence of the one and the whole on a specific anthropology," i.e., in posing the problem of reconciling individual interests and the social whole from a perspective in which the social contract no longer plays a key role. The consequences are significant. If the market model by itself explains the functioning of society, it follows that the economy represents the best way of realizing politics. Hence an increasingly accusatory attitude toward the public power, for if man is naturally social, it is no longer necessary to "force" him to live in society: "The state no longer constitutes the social bond; it merely guarantees its permanence." What is more, public power must always be neutralized so as never to invade civil society. So politics finds itself radically delegitimized in its calling to carry out a specific end. By rejecting the theory of the social contract and affirming the idea of a spontaneous order beyond the categories of nature and artifice, Hayek places himself directly in this tradition. This is what explains the apparent holism of his system, in which the market assimilated to the social "whole" constitutes the supreme form of regulation at the supra-individual level.

But this appearance must not mislead us. We can only really speak of holism when the whole possesses its own logic and finality, i.e., characteristics that differ in nature from those of its constitutive parts. Now, this is precisely the idea Hayek rejects insofar as it constitutes according to him the specific mark of the "tribal order." In the "great society," the individual may well never be posited in pure isolation, since it is admitted that he has always lived in society and that from the moral point of view he is only fully human in relation to his fellows. Still, the social relation must be seen from the exclusive perspective of the multiplicity of parties. Just as the market is only conceived as a procedure for aggregating individual preferences, society is only organized and understood on the basis of the existence and action of individuals: it is only the play of particular interests that constitutes society. So the social is deduced from the individual, not the other way around: the individual—essential actor and primordial value—constitutes an unsurpassable explanatory absolute. The result is that understanding of the whole derives from that of the parts, and that there can be no collective entity such as a people, culture, or nation that possesses an identity distinct from the sum of individual identities included within it. Finally, it is admitted that individual behavior is oriented only according to the ends they themselves propose. Members of society are so many social atoms "free to use their own knowledge for their own objectives," and the search for their best interest is obviously supposed to guide their choices. Of course, Hayek is not so naïve as to believe all men behave rationally, but he does state that such behavior is most advantageous, so that in a society where it is comparatively more profitable to act rationally, rational behavior will gradually spread by selection or imitation. So the individual is indeed called upon to behave like an economic agent on the market in his social life. We remain within the paradigm of methodological individualism and the *Homo oeconomicus*.

In the end, Hayek does not posit the individual as an autonomous being so much as an independent being, since as Jean-Pierre Dupuy emphasizes, "Autonomy is compatible with submission to a supra-individual sphere valid for all, with a normative law limiting individual selves according to the rules of a self-founded normativity," whereas "Independent selves are incapable of positing an order as a voluntary and conscious project."[14] Beyond all consideration of the formation of structures ordered on the basis of chance variations (system theory, the thermodynamics of dissipative structures), this distinction makes clear the limits upon any reconciliation one might be tempted to undertake between Hayek's ideas and the systemic concept of self-organization: the latter implies an antireductionist vision where the whole is inevitably more than the sum of its parts.

---

[14] Pierre Dupuy, "L'individu libéral, cet inconnu: d'Adam Smith à Friedrich Hayek" ["The Liberal Individual, this Unknown: From Adam Smith to Friedrich Hayek"], *Individu et justice sociale. Autour de John Rawls* [*Individual and Social Justice: With Reference to John Rawls*] (Paris: Seuil, 1989), 80.

II.

Having defined the formative principles of the "great socie-ty" — specifically, the order of the market — Hayek can pass on to the study of the ideology he opposes, which he calls *constructiv-ism*. This ideology, he says, rests on a "synoptic illusion" that consists in believing social arrangements can result from the in-tentions and voluntary actions of men, in other words that it is possible to build or reform society in view of a given project. Constructivism states that "Human institutions only serve hu-man deigns if they have been deliberately elaborated on the ba-sis of such designs." Now, as we have seen, Hayek states that it is not possible to connect institutions with any deliberate act of will, for the latter demands complete information that we never have. So constructivism amounts to systematically overestimat-ing the role social engineers, reformers, and politicians can play in the public domain.

At first, Hayek located the source of constructivism in scien-tism, i.e., the servile imitation by the human sciences of the con-cepts, methods, and objectives proper to the physical sciences. Later he sought the origin of this "illusion" in Descartes. Carte-sian mechanism, which he calls the "French disease," suggests that logico-mathematical intelligibility must be sought in the so-cial sciences as well as elsewhere; and that because of this, insti-tutions can be constructed and reconstructed at will like so many artifacts mentally conceived to serve a particular end. Hayek states that this is a "presumptuousness of reason" for, according to him, reason cannot determine just finalities bound to the common good, but only the formal conditions of agents' activi-ty.[15]

---

[15] Hayek draws a distinction here between "constructivist" ration-alism and "evolutionist" rationalism, which corresponds fairly closely to the opposition between historicist rationalism and critical rational-ism in Popper. This critique of rationalism has usually been judged excessive by libertarian authors, and more generally by American liberals, all rather inclined to appeal to rationalism. *Cf.* on this subject the special issue of *Critical Review* devoted to Hayek on his 90th birthday, *F. A. Hayek's Liberalism,* Spring 1989, especially the articles

In Hayek's view, the archetype of constructivism is socialism, which corresponds to a sort of resurgence of the "tribal order" within the "great society" itself. According to Hayek, the success of socialism comes from its appeal to now anachronistic "atavistic instincts" of solidarity and altruism! However, from Hayek's point of view, the term "socialism" is to be taken in the broadest possible sense. It gradually comes to designate any form of "social engineering," any kind of political-economic project. Moreover, Hayek attacks the heirs of Descartes just as much as the partisans of a holistic or organicist conception of society, from the counter-revolutionaries all the way to the romantics. Socialism in the strict sense, Marxism, fascism, social democracy — all, according to him, partake of "constructivism," which begins with even the most modest forms of state intervention or social reform. To assign any finality to production, to impose an imperative of solidarity, to redistribute income for the benefit of the least favored, to adopt environmental legislation or social protection, to propose a progressive income tax, to institute the least form of economic protection, the mildest currency controls — all this is part of a "constructivism" that can only reveal itself a catastrophe since the order of the market by its very definition forbids any attempt to act intentionally upon social facts. So Hayek constantly repeats that there can never be agreement on ends, and that above all we must never seek to find one, for any effort in this direction will end in catastrophe. Any interventionism, any planning, any political project is pregnant with latent totalitarianism! This leads Hayek to advocate extremely radical positions, e.g., when he recommends privatizing the issuance of money,[16] justifies the formation of monopolies,[17] rejects any

---

by Laurent Dobuzinskis ("The Complexities of Spontaneous Order," 241–66) and David Miller ("The Fatalistic Conceit," 310–23).

[16] The final premonetarist representative of monetary theories of the business cycle, Hayek thinks that by introducing competition into the supply of money we can abolish inflation! In his essay *Denationalization of Money: The Argument Refined* (London: Institute of Economic Affairs, 1978; 1st ed. 1974–1976), he puts forward the idea that money can be issued at will by private companies, since consumers will be called upon to try out the various forms of money until they have

form of macro-economic analysis, and even goes so far as to claim, in his final book (*The Fatal Conceit*) that any socialist system is destined to make its population die of starvation![18]

The classical liberal school kept the idea of social justice, at least as a transitory regulation. Hayek rejects it totally and subjects it to one of the most violent critiques ever seen.[19] Social justice, he proclaims, is a "mirage," an "inept incantation," an "anthropomorphic illusion," an "ontological absurdity," in short, an expression that quite simply makes no sense, except of course within a "tribal order," i.e., within a social domain instituted by particular persons with a view to well-defined objectives. To

---

identified the "best" (and we may hope they do not go bankrupt in the meantime). This suggestion has been taken up by the Club de l'Horloge (*Lettre d'information du Club*, second trimester 1993, 7). For a critique of this point of view: Christian Tutin, "Monnaie et libéralisme. Le cas de Hayek" ["Money and Liberalism: The Case of Hayek"] in Arnaud Berthoud and Roger Frydman, eds., *Le libéralisme économique. Interprétations at analyses* [*Economic Liberalism: Interpretations and Analyses*] (Paris: L'Harmattan, 1989), 153–78. In contrast to the Chicago School, Hayek rejects the quantitativist theory of money, saying that money can never be sufficiently measured or controlled.

[17] While classical liberals were generally favorable to anticartel legislation, certain neoliberals, especially the libertarians, today challenge the idea that there exists a strict relation between levels of concentration and monopolistic effects. *Cf.* Henri Lepage, *Demain le libéralisme* [*Tomorrow, Liberalism*] (Paris: Livre de Poche-Pluriel, 1980), 241–63.

[18] In the same spirit, an extremist disciple of Hayek goes so far as to write quite seriously that "All the unpleasant traits of Nazism, including the extermination of minorities, are found in any political society which takes seriously the ambition of realizing social justice" (François Guillaumat, *Liberalia*, Spring 1989, 19)! Recalling that Hayek announced in 1935 the imminent collapse of the Soviet system, Mark Blaug ("Hayek Revisited," *Critical Review*, Winter 1993–1994, 51–60) draws attention to Hayek's inability to draw from his theories the slightest political or economic prediction that could be empirically verified. Other authors have remarked that Hayek never gives a precise definition of "totalitarianism," a term which in his writings apparently covers everything that is opposed to liberalism.

[19] *Cf.* especially vol. 2 of *Law, Legislation, and Liberty*.

demonstrate this "obvious" proposition, Hayek redefines catallaxy as a social game. Being impersonal, the rules of the game are equally valid for everyone. So all the players, in this sense, are equals. But this obviously does not imply that they can all win, since in every game there are winners and losers. On the other hand, given that only human behavior resulting from deliberate will can be described as "just" or "unjust," using these terms to describe anything other than the result of a voluntary human act is a logical error. So the social order can only be described as just or unjust insofar as it results from the voluntary action of men. Now, Hayek has been at pains to show that it does not. Since the social game does not have an author, no one is responsible for its results, and it is both childish and ridiculous to consider it productive of "injustice." In reality, it is no more unjust to be unemployed than not to have won the lottery, for only the behavior of the "players" can be declared just or unjust, not the results they get. Since the social realm does not result from any intention or project, no one can be responsible for the least favored not drawing the big prize. It would therefore be improper for the "losers" to complain. Rather than giving way to "atavistic instincts," which lead them to believe naïvely that any phenomenon has an identifiable cause, and to seek the party responsible for the "injustice" they are suffering, the best thing for them would be either to blame themselves or to admit that their "bad luck" is just how things go.

Thus, Hayek writes: "The way advantages and burdens are apportioned by the mechanism of the market would in many cases be regarded as very unjust *if* this apportionment were the result of a deliberate decision by this or that person. But this is not the case." Once this premise has been granted, the conclusion becomes automatic. Demanding social justice is unrealistic and illusory. Wanting to realize it is an absurdity that would result in destroying the rule of law. Philippe Nemo coolly writes that social justice is "deeply immoral."[20] So the traditional

---

[20] Nemo, *La société de droit selon F. A. Hayek*, 188. Robert Nozick thinks any voluntary exchange is just, whatever the conditions. This is also true when a worker accepts a pittance so as not to die of star-

concept of distributive justice, whether following the principle of arithmetic equality or proportional (geometric) equality, is rejected from the start. Any idea of instituted solidarity directed toward the concept of the common good is similarly condemned as an "archaic tribal demand." As Hayek emphasizes, "The great society has nothing to do with, and cannot in fact be reconciled with, solidarity in the true sense of the pursuit of known common ends." Hayek even rejects equality of opportunity, for this would amount to cancelling out the differences between the "players" before the game begins, which would vitiate the results. Of course, labor unions should also disappear, for they are "incompatible with the foundations of a society of free men." As for those who complain of alienation from the commercial order, they are "non-domesticated or uncivilized" persons.[21] Behold "liberalism in the service of the people"!

The theory according to which the market is never unjust because of its impersonal and abstract nature obviously has the great advantage of forbidding us from assessing its reality through its concrete effects. Since the general interest amounts at best to the maintenance of public order and providing a certain number of public services, and justice to the definition of formal and universal rules meant to govern the behavior of agents, the market is never subject to substantial evaluation, i.e., in view of its results. The same goes for justice, which can have no substantial content since there is no normativity proper to ends, no "content" of life in society. Moreover, since one cannot define social justice positively, any debate concerning its essence becomes pointless. The system is thus perfectly airtight. We owe obedience to the market order because it was not willed by anybody and imposed itself on its own. Man must follow the established order without trying to understand it and especially without rebelling against it. Secondarily, the "losers" must give

---

vation: no one forced him to do so! In a book that made a big splash in the United States, *Anarchy, State, and Utopia* (New York: Basic Books, 1971) Nozick defends the thesis of the "minimal state" based on an analysis that owes a great deal to game theory.

[21] *Law, Legislation, and Liberty*, vol. 2, 147.

themselves a new philosophical morality according to which "It is simply normal to accept the course of events when they are unfavorable to you." This is a naked apology of success, whatever its causes or the means it uses, as well as the radical negation of equity in the traditional sense of the term. It is also the perfect way of providing the "winners" with a good conscience and forbidding the "losers" to revolt. Hayek's point of view thus issues in a "real theoretical justification of indifference to human unhappiness."[22] In the end, the market replaces the Leviathan.

Moreover, the "great society" reveals itself as extremely *unpolitical*.[23] Since public order is posited as unintentional, no great political project can any longer be based on will or reason, since there can be no social mastery of historical processes. In the end, the reign of the market tends to deprive the public power of any object. Contrary to Carl Schmitt, who puts law in a state of dependence on authority and the capacity for political decision-making, Hayek affirms that authority cannot and must not be obeyed except insofar as it applies the law. (He remains extremely discreet on the nature of legal obligation.) But at the same time, against Kelsen's legal positivism, which identifies law with the decision of the legislator and makes it the essential source of justice and law, Hayek also declares that law has always existed, and that it exists prior to the authority of the legislator and the state. His panegyric upon the common law aims to show that law is prior to all legislation, which forms the basis of the theory of legal normativism. The bases of the rule of law are thus established anew, their only rationale being to preserve the

---

[22] Yvon Quiniou, "Hayek, les limites d'un défi," in *Actuel Marx* [*Current Marx*], first trimester 1989, 83. Philippe Nemo, *La société de droit selon F. A. Hayek*, transposes this indifference as "a non-psychological attachment to an abstract other." Hayek writes: "In its purest form, this ethos [of the open society] regards it as the prime duty to pursue a self-chosen end as effectively as possible without paying attention to the role it plays in the complex network of human activities" (*Law, Legislation, and Liberty*, vol. 2, 145).

[23] We are here using the term *"impolitique"* proposed by Julien Freund, *Politique et impolitique* [*Political and Unpolitical*] (Paris: Sirey, 1987).

"spontaneous order" of society and manage the resources available to it. Under these conditions, politics is reduced at best to preserving the formal legal rules and administration of a civil society already ordered by the market; it does not have to produce that society, assign it a purpose, diffuse values through it, or create cohesion within it. With the same vigor, Hayek rejects the concept of sovereignty, whether of the prince or of the people, in which he sees merely a "constructivist superstition." He writes: "In a society of free men, the highest authority must in normal times have no power of positive commands whatsoever."[24] Since his essential goal is to put public power in a state of dependence on "nomocracy," he even goes so far as to deny that "political necessities" can exist. Philippe Nemo adds: "In the end, the very idea of political power is incompatible with the concept of a society of free men."[25] Since there is no politics without power (*potestas*) or authority (*auctoritas*), we are indeed being invited to eliminate politics entirely.

Accordingly, democracy is given a purely legal and formal definition. Hayek affirms without disguise that the liberalism he advocates is only conditionally compatible with democracy. Of course, he adheres to constitutionalism, the theory of representative and limited government. But we do not find in his writings any theory of the state. He knows only "government," which he defines as an "administrator of common resources," i.e., as "a purely utilitarian device." He adds that democracy is only acceptable in the form of a method of government that does not question liberal principles. In fact, the Hayekian postulate ends in the negation of democracy understood as a regime endowed with substantial content (identity of views between governors and governed) and resting on popular sovereignty. Like the market, democracy (or what remains of it) becomes an affair of impersonal rules and formal procedures without content.[26]

---

[24] *Law, Legislation, and Liberty*, vol. 3, 130.

[25] Nemo, *La société de droit selon F. A. Hayek*, 361.

[26] For a critical examination of the idea that existing rules of conduct in democracy are identical with those of the market, *cf.* Gus DiZerega, "A Spontaneous Order Model of Democracy: Applying Hay-

Moreover, Hayek is equally critical of decision by majority vote, in which he sees an arbitrary principle antagonistic to individual freedom. Decision by majority vote, declares Philippe Nemo, is satisfactory "as a method of decision, but not as an authoritative source to determine the content of decisions."[27] From this conception flows a rejection of the concept of the people as a political category, the negation of the idea of national sovereignty ("There does not exist any will of the social body that could be sovereign") and the rejection of any form of direct democracy.[28]

Paradoxically, this "unpolitical" ideal aligns Hayek's ideas with Marxist "constructivism." For Marx, the withering away of the state in the classless society results from politics no longer having any reason to exist. This is because Marx, who never rids himself of a certain individualism, only considers man a social animal insofar as he participates individually in the construction of society. As the liberal author Bertrand Nezeys writes: "From a Marxist point of view, socialism must represent the triumph of an individualistic society, or simply of individualism; private society merely represents an alienated form of it."[29] Pierre Rosanvallon remarks on this subject that "Anticapitalism has become synonymous with anti-liberalism, while socialism had no other real goal than fulfilling the program of the liberal utopia."

---

ekian Insights to Democratic Theory," a presentation to the Society for the Study of Public Choice, San Francisco, March 1988.

[27] Nemo, *La société de droit selon F. A. Hayek*, 121.

[28] We note that the Club de l'Horloge, which appeals to Hayek's ideas, also declares itself in favor of extending direct democracy, particularly by the establishment of the popular referendum. Such demands are indefensible from a Hayekian point of view, which denies popular sovereignty and the substantial value of voting.

[29] Bertrand Nezeys, *L'autopsie du tiers-mondialisme* [*The Autopsy of Third Worldism*] (Paris: Economica, 1988), 130. For his part, Louis Dumont thinks that in *The German Ideology* Marx's individualism reaches its "apotheosis." *Cf.* also John Elster, "Marxisme et individualisme méthodologique" ["Marxism and Methodological Individualism"] in Pierre Birnbaum and Jean Leca, eds., *Sur l'individualisme* [*On Individualism*] (Paris: Presses de la Fondation nationale des sciences politiques, 1986).

In fact, he adds,

> Utopian socialism rejects capitalism *in toto* but remains
> blind to the deeper sense of the economistic ideology with-
> in which it is shaped. In the same way, liberalism de-
> nounces collectivism, but only understands it as a kind of
> radical despotism; it does not analyze it in its relation to
> individualism, insofar as it is itself a vehicle for the illusion
> of a depoliticized society in which democracy is reduced
> to consensus.[30]

It remains to be seen how far this ideal is not itself fundamentally totalitarian, at least if one admits with Hannah Arendt that
totalitarianism resides in the desire to nullify politics even more
than in the will to make it penetrate everywhere.

III.

We have seen that Hayek's critique of constructivism is closely bound up with his representation of the social whole as an
aggregate concerning which individuals can only have incomplete information. So the question is whether the conclusions
Hayek draws from this representation are well-founded.

That human information is always incomplete is obviously
indisputable. Contrary to what Hayek seems to believe, this is
just as true for the "tribal order," even if the number of parameters to be taken into consideration is smaller there. We can also
admit that in human societies, many social facts come about by
themselves without our being able to trace them back to intentions or deliberate projects, under the effect of slow processes,
interactions, or retroactions without precisely identifiable authors, processes of which cybernetics and systemics give a convincing idea, thereby agreeing with certain intuitions of organicist thought. Moreover, this is the case with the capitalist system
that Marx was able to characterize accurately as an "automatic
subject." Nor will anyone deny the value of traditions validated

---

[30] Rosanvallon, *Le libéralisme économique*, 226–28.

by historical experience. Finally, no one will have difficulty acknowledging that there frequently exists a gap between a project
and its realization, a gap Jules Monnerot called "heterotelia,"
and which manifests itself in unforeseen consequences or fallout,
often described as "perverse effects." But the logical impossibility of undertaking any social or political action or trying to shape
the social order in view of a given purpose in no way follows
from all of this, nor does it follow that any voluntary act aimed
at improvement will only make things worse.

At first, Hayek pretends to believe that any constructivism is
a form of rationalism, which betrays his "technical" conception
of voluntary acts. Now, human practice rarely results from a rational examination of pro and contra. This is true in the "tribal
order" where Hayek elsewhere says that "instincts" are king.
But it is still true in the "great society," especially in the realm of
politics, where the determination of a collective finality inevitably rests on value judgments whose premises are rarely rationally based. Hayek then argues as if human decision required
knowledge of all existing parameters, these alone being able precisely to evaluate consequences and results. This statement proceeds from a complete misunderstanding of what decision is,
particularly that (far from engendering a purely linear process
that would reflect a sort of omniscience) it constantly calls for
corrections, since after their initial decision men can always multiply subsidiary decisions aimed at reorienting the chain of cause
and effect in view of information received and results obtained.
On this subject, Gérard Roland writes:

> Contrary to what Hayek claims, an action's success does
> not necessarily depend on a complete knowledge of the
> pertinent facts. It is perfectly possible to believe that no
> scientific, technical, economic, political, social, or other ac-
> tion undertaken in the entire history of humanity up to
> this very day has been based on such complete know-
> ledge. This is perhaps why no action is completely exempt
> from error with respect to its original intention, but this rel-
> ative absence of knowledge has never constituted an abso-
> lute obstacle to the success of an individual or collective

human action. . . . The process of knowledge is never and has never been totally preliminary to action. On the contrary, it is closely and dialectically involved in action. The successes and failures of actions undertaken nourish knowledge for future actions, which will meet with success or failure thanks to new knowledge, and so on in a process that is not necessarily linear and unforeseeable but is always marked by goals men have fixed for their actions.[31]

In fact, the critique of constructivism obviously clashes with common sense, viz., that "Analyzing suffering, a crisis, or an evil is always analyzing it as a problem, as a soluble problem whose solution is technical."[32] To claim that a man cannot, and above all should not, correct a situation for which no person is originally responsible is, in this regard, a pure paralogism. In fact, it is irresponsible not to act on effects, even if no person is responsible for causing them. So the question is not whether a situation can rightly be called "just" or "unjust" according to abstract criteria, but whether it is just to accept what is not acceptable for ethical, political, or other reasons. Should we not seek to improve the security of ships or airplanes on the pretext that "no one is responsible" for the nature of the sea or air? By shifting the criterion of justice from human subjectivity to the objective situation, by making a pretext of the lack of any identifiable author of a situation in order to conclude the impossibility of modifying it, Hayek certainly throws a light on his personal preferences, but in no way does he demonstrate that man is by definition powerless in relation to a social fact unwilled by anyone.

In the end, Hayek seems to argue from man's lack of omniscience in order to mark him with radical powerlessness. Now, a

---

[31] Gérard Roland, *Economie politique du système soviétique* [*Political Economy of the Soviet System*] (Paris: L'Harmattan, 1989), 19–20.

[32] Arnaud Berthoud, "Liberté et libéralisme économique chez Walras, Hayek et Keynes" ["Liberty and Economic Liberalism in Walras, Hayek, and Keynes"], in Berthoud and Frydman, *Le libéralisme économique*, 49.

man's power to modify a state of things depends much more on the means of which he disposes than upon the extent of his "information." But in Hayek everything transpires as if there were no alternative between a utopian will to reconstruct the entire social order from scratch by making a clean slate of the past, and complete submission to the established order (or disorder). In this all-or-nothing logic, metaphysical in its aim at the absolute, any political project, any will to reform or transform, can only appear as an unbearable disruptionism. Such a procedure obviously goes with the classic liberal condemnation of the autonomy of politics for the simple reason that, since politics is above all a matter of project and decision, *there is in the end no non-constructivist politics.* But this is also a reasoning that can turn against its author. If in fact, as Hayek says, we can never anticipate the real results of our actions, so that the most logical attitude is to do nothing to try to change the society in which we live, it is hard to see why we should try to make the liberal order triumph, which will impose itself much more surely in virtue of its intrinsic excellence and the advantage it confers upon societies in which it prevails. Nor do we see why we must follow Hayek in his monetary or constitutional proposals,[33] which represent in relation to the present situation a more or less radical innovation.

The entire Hayekian critique thus leads us back to an *incapacitating* system destined in practice to comfort the worst sort of conservatism. To say that the market is neither just nor unjust amounts in fact to saying that the market along with its effects must be removed from human judgment, that it is the new divinity, the new and unique God before whom one must bow. So man must not seek out on his own values that might be incarnated in society, but only recognize in society as it is the system

---

[33] Hayek advocates a separation of legislative powers involving the institution of an upper chamber that functions somewhat like a Constitutional Council. It would be reserved for persons over the age of 45 who have given proof of their "honesty," "wisdom," and "judgment" and who would be elected for a term of fifteen years. *Cf.* especially F. A. Hayek, "Whither Democracy?," in Nishiyama and Leube, eds., *The Essence of Hayek*, 352–62.

of values that allows him to be a member. He must concern him-self with his personal and private ends without ever questioning the social order or preoccupying himself with the evolution of human history, which can only proceed in the best fashion apart from him. Here we see the kind of "autonomy" Hayek assigns the individual: he is only emancipated from political power exercised in the name of the whole of society in order to be rendered powerless for projects that might associate him with his fellows. Hayek says this forcefully: "Man is not master of his destiny and never will be." Man can indeed do as he likes, but he cannot will what he does. The object of a society that only functions well insofar as he never tries to take control of it, his freedom at the collective level is thus defined in terms of powerlessness and submission. Freedom according to Hayek can only be exercised within a framework that denies it. So it is no exaggeration to say that man is thereby dispossessed of his humanity, for if there is one fundamental characteristic proper to being human, it is being endowed with a historical capacity to conceive and carry out collective projects. In unburdening humanity of this capacity, in making the monotheism of the market the new empire of necessity, Hayek stealthily leads us back to the "pretribal" stage of pure animality.[34]

So it is obvious one cannot appeal to the Hayekian analysis to justify a return to tradition. Hayek only praises tradition from an instrumental point of view, to legitimate the market order, in fact. In his eyes, traditions only have value insofar as they constituted "prerational regulations" that favored the emergence of an impersonal and abstract order of which the market constitutes the most perfect result. When he speaks of them favorably, it is to evoke the slow development of societies toward modernity, the sedimentation of ideas which (at least in the West) allowed

---

[34] *Cf.* on this subject Gilles Leclerq, "Hier le libéralisme" ["Liberalism Yesterday"], *Procès*, 1986, 83–100, who also sees in liberalism "an essentially, if subtly, totalitarian doctrine." From a similar viewpoint, but marked especially by Christian social teaching: Michael Schooyans, *La Dérive totalitaire du libéralisme* [*The Totalitarian Drift of Liberalism*] (Paris: Editions Universitaires, 1991).

the "great society" to triumph. Any tradition running in any other direction can only be rejected. Now, there is a principled contradiction between traditions which, by definition, are always proper to singular cultures and the universality of the formal rules Hayek recommends adopting. And since it is commonly admitted that Western modernity has everywhere functioned as a steamroller of traditions, it is easy to see that Hayekian "traditionalism" only refers to the tradition . . . of the extinction of traditions.

In this respect, Hayek remains faithful to the reasoning of certain of his predecessors, especially David Hume, to whom he frequently refers. In the eighteenth century, in his political essays, Hume already criticized the ideas of Locke and those like him who gave too important a place to reason. For him, reason is unable by itself to oppose the passions, which can only be channeled by "non-arbitrary artifices" not resulting from any pre-established design. Among these non-arbitrary artifices figure the habits, customs, and institutions consecrated by usage. Justice itself is a "grown institution," custom revealing itself the best substitute for reason for guiding human practices. The emphasis placed on traditions can thus hold back the passions while doing without the fiction of the social contract. However, for Hume, institutions do not result from any "selection" occurring over the course of history: if they are not arbitrary, it is because they correspond to general principles of the understanding.[35]

The true nature of Hayekian "traditionalism" appears clearly in his critique of the "tribal order," of which the different forms of constructivism constitute so many anachronistic recrudescences. The "tribal order" is in fact nothing but *traditional* society as opposed to *modern* society, or *community* as opposed to *society*.

---

[35] On Hume as a precursor of liberalism, *cf.* Didier Deleule, *Hume et la naissance du libéralisme* [*Hume and the Birth of Liberalism*] (Paris: Aubier Montaigne, 1979). For a contrary point of view: Dianel Diatkine, "Hume et le libéralisme économique" ["Hume and Economic Liberalism"] in Berthoud and Frydman, *Le libéralisme économique*, 3–19.

And it is precisely all the traits characteristic of traditional and communitarian, organic and holist societies which we find condemned by Hayek as so many traits antagonistic to the "great society." The tradition Hayek defends is, on the contrary, a "tradition" that has no collective finality, nor common good, nor social value, nor shared symbolic imagination. In short, it is a "tradition" valued only insofar as it is born of the disaggregation of archaic societies and finishes off this disaggregation: the paradox of an anti-traditionalist form of thought that advances beneath the mask of a "defense of traditions"!

Yvan Blot writes: "Liberalism of the traditionalist type is national, for the nation itself issues from tradition and not from any arbitrary construct of the mind."[36] This lapidary formulation, unfortunately, states a double falsehood. Firstly, the modern idea of the nation is indeed an arbitrary construction of the mind, since it is above all a creation of the philosophy of the Enlightenment and the French Revolution—the Kingdom of France, which proceeded it historically, was itself built up in a fundamentally voluntarist and "constructivist" manner by the Capetian dynasty. Secondly, it is notorious that liberalism, Hayekian or otherwise, cannot assign the nation any privileged place, for the domain in which its conception of society unfolds is not a territory delimited by political boundaries but a market.

Whereas for the mercantilists, the ("national") *territory* and (economic) *space* were still confused, Adam Smith in his *Wealth of Nations* carries out a decisive dissociation between the two concepts. For Smith, the borders of the market are constantly being constructed and modified without ever coinciding with the political borders of nation or kingdom: it is the extent of the market, not that of the territory, which is the real key to wealth. Smith even seems in this respect the "first consistent internationalist" (Pierre Rosanvallon).

The same postulate will be adopted by the entire liberal tradition: the nation can have a relative value as regards the self-identification of citizens, but it cannot establish itself as a criterion of economic activity, nor serve as a pretext for controlling or

[36] *Présent*, October 6, 1989.

limiting exchanges. The old ideal that aimed to make legal, political, and economic spaces coincide on a given territory and under a given authority is thus broken. From the point of view of
economic activity, borders must be considered as if they did not
exist: *laissez faire, laissez passer.*

A correlate is that the merchant is no longer under the control
of any non-economic form of belonging. As Adam Smith writes:

> A merchant . . . is not necessarily the citizen of any particu-
> lar country. It is in a great measure indifferent to him from
> what place he carries on his trade; and a very trifling dis-
> gust will make him remove his capital, and, together with
> it, all the industry which it supports, from one country to
> another.[37]

The entire equivocation of "national-liberalism" is there.

IV.

But we must return to the Hayekian conception of the market. By instrumentalizing traditions, Hayek is seeking a basis for
the legitimacy of the market in order to resolve the question of
the basis of obligation within the social pact. This preoccupation
is constant in liberal thought. It is always a matter of finding a
natural basis for the social order: "sympathy" for Smith, "custom" for Hume, etc. This way of proceeding poses the problem
of the "state of nature," a hypothesis to which Locke's thought is
still subject. He has recourse to the fiction of a primitive scene:
the social contract. As we have seen above, in the doctrinal current that flows from Smith, this fiction becomes useless: the "invisible hand" whose intervention produces the necessary adjustments to the market also allows us to explain the permanence of the social order. However, contrary to other liberal authors, Hayek does not instantly draw the conclusion that the
market is "natural." On the contrary, he admits that it emerges
at a particular time in human history, and he posits only this

---

[37] Smith, *Wealth of Nations*, Book III, chapter 4.

emergence as *natural*: without its having originally been a natural phenomenon, the market is supposed to appear "naturally" under the effect of a gradual process of selection that operates on its own. Hayekian naturalism is thus bound up with the idea of an ineluctable form of progress based on objective laws uncovered by cultural evolution.

All Hayek's skill is seen in this idea, which, by combining evolutionary theory and the doctrine of the "invisible hand," allows us to conclude the "naturalness" of the market without its being given as original, i.e., going without any idea of natural order or "self-evident truth." At the same time, Hayek accepts the liberal postulate according to which there exist objective laws such that the free interaction of individual strategies results not merely in an order but in the best order there can be. In doing so, he does not escape the classic logical impasse into which liberal thought runs when it tries to explain how a viable social order can constitute itself on the exclusive basis of individual sovereignty. The difficulty is having to "presuppose the presence of the whole in each part. In fact, if the social were not already there in some fashion, contained in the parts, it is hard to see how these could agree."[38] The postulate called for is that of a continuity between parts and whole. Now, this postulate is untenable, if only for the reasons stated by Bertrand Russell in his theory of logical types ("the class cannot be a member of itself any more than one of its members can be the class"). In other words, there is necessarily a discontinuity between the whole and its parts, and this discontinuity defeats liberal pretentions.

The Hayekian vision of "primitive" man living in the "tribal order," although very different from those of a Hobbes or Locke,

---

[38] Roger Frydman, "Individu et totalité dans la pensée libérale. Le cas de F. A. Hayek" ["Individual and Totality in Liberal Thought: The Case of F. A. Hayek"], in Berthoud and Frydman, *Le libéralisme économique*, 98. This logical impasse weighs especially heavily upon any theory founded on the hypothesis of the social contract: for isolated individuals to decide contractually to enter society, they must have at least an approximative knowledge of the result before making that decision, in which case the state of nature can no longer be radically opposed to the social state.

or indeed from Rousseau, is without much anthropological pertinence. To represent traditional societies as privileging voluntaristic ("constructivist") behavior is particularly bold, since these societies are ruled by traditions oriented toward the repetition of what has been inherited. It would be easy to show that the "great society" is more receptive to innovative projects and deliberate designs. In other words, traditional and "tribal" societies display a spontaneous order, and modern societies display instituted order. Alain Caillé correctly observes that making justice depend on conformity with the traditional order of practice would "paradoxically lead to showing that the only conceivable just society is the closed society and not the liberal great society."[39] By definition, the society where *themis* strays least far from *nomos* is indeed traditional society, closed on itself (but open to the cosmos): from a strictly Hayekian point of view, it is more "just" (or rather, less "unjust") insofar as it tends to perpetuate itself in identical form by basing itself on custom.

The idea according to which institutions that have lastingly imposed themselves all the way to our own days always result "from the action of men, but not from their designs" is no less questionable. English law, often cited by Hayek as a typical example of an institution derived from custom, was in reality born in a relatively authoritarian and brutal manner "following royal and parliamentary interventions, and is the result of the creative work of jurists belonging to the centralized administration of justice."[40] More generally, the entire English liberal order is the result of the conflict between Parliament and the Crown in the seventeenth century and in no way from any spontaneous evolution.

As for the market, if it is certainly not the most natural form of exchange, neither can its birth be ascribed to any slow evolution of customs and institutions from which "constructivism"

---

[39] Alain Caillé, *Splendeur et misère des sciences sociales. Esquisses d'une mythologie* [*Splendor and Misery of the Social Sciences: Sketches of a Mythology*] (Geneva: Droz, 1986), 340.

[40] Blandine Barret-Kriegel, *L'Etat et les esclaves* [*The State and the Slaves*] (Paris: Calmann-Lévy, 1980, 115.

was absent. The reverse is true: the market constitutes a typical example of an *instituted* order. As we have seen, the logic of the market, a phenomenon both singular and recent, only developed at the end of the Middle Ages when emerging states, concerned with monetizing their economies so as to increase their fiscal resources, began to unify local and long-distance commerce within "national" markets they could more easily control. In Western Europe, and especially in France, the market, far from appearing as a reaction against the state, was born at its initiative, and it was only during a second period that it emancipated itself from "national" constraints as the autonomy of the economic realm became greater. A strictly voluntary creation, the market at its beginnings was one of the means used by the nation-state to liquidate the feudal order. It aimed at facilitating taxation in the modern sense (intercommunal exchanges, not being commercial, were formerly inaccessible to taxation), which involved the gradual suppression of autonomous organic communities and, consequently, centralization. In this way both the nation-state and the market call forth an atomized society in which individuals are gradually removed from all intermediate forms of socialization.

In the end, the dichotomy drawn by Hayek between spontaneous order and instituted order appears unacceptable. Quite simply, it has never existed. To say that society evolves spontaneously is just as reductionist as to say that it is transformed only under the effect of the voluntary action of men. And the assertion that the logic of the spontaneous order cannot interfere with that of the instituted order without resulting in catastrophic consequences is also entirely arbitrary: all of history is made up of such a combination. The image of the social order formed by purely "unconscious" practice independently of any collective aim or finality is nothing but armchair theorizing. No society has ever been like this. The self-organization of societies has been both more complex and less spontaneous than Hayek claims. If rules and traditions do indeed influence the life of men, we cannot forget (unless we fall into a purely linear and mechanical vision of human life) that men also react in their turn upon rules and traditions. In the end, Hayek does not see that societies are never instituted in spontaneous practice alone and based on individual interests alone, but firstly in the symbolic order based on values whose representation always involves a departure from such practice.

The question also arises of how we passed from the stage of "tribal" and traditional order to that of the "great society." Hayek does not lay much stress on this point; nevertheless, it is essential for his demonstration. How was a society of a given type, let us say communitarian and holist, able to give birth "naturally" to an essentially individualistic society, i.e., a society of the opposite type? Of course, we can answer this question by following Louis Dumont, i.e., by describing the emergence of modernity as the result of a slow process of secularizing Christian ideology. But Hayek does not attach the slightest importance to ideological factors, and, what is more, it would be inconvenient for his thesis if the "great society" should arise from a break of a "constructivist" type. (What could be more constructivist, in fact, that the will to create a new religion?) Whence his recourse to the evolutionary schema, i.e., a social Darwinism of which the idea of progress serves as vehicle.

Of course, Hayek does not fall into any crude form of biologism. His social Darwinism, developed at length in *The Constitution of Liberty*, consists rather in positing human history as the reflection of a cultural evolution functioning on the model of biological evolution as it is conceived in the Darwinian or neo-Darwinian model. Not only, as in all liberalism, is economic competition supposed to favor progress just as the "struggle for life" allows selection to operate in the animal kingdom, but traditions, institutions, and social facts are explained in the same way. At the same time, the surreptitious inference from fact to norm is constant: liberal society and the market economy impose themselves as *values* all the better in that they have been "naturally selected" over the course of evolution. Value is thus a function of success: the winners deserve to win; the losers deserve to lose. This conception is expressed especially in Hayek's last book where capitalism is intrinsically valorized, no longer so much because of its economic effectiveness as because it represents the *nec plus ultra* of human evolution.[41] This identification of value with success is obviously characteristic of any evolutionist vision of history. If evolution "selects" what is best adapted to the conditions of the moment, clearly all history that has occurred can only be regarded approvingly and optimistically. Selection consecrates the best, the proof they are the best being that they have been selected. The replacement of the "tribal order" by the "great society," the emergence of modernity, the success of individualism at the expense of holism are simply in the order of things. The state of evolution, in other words, reflects exactly what *ought* to be. Human history can then rightfully be read as a progress, reinterpreted by Hayek as the forward march of "liberty."[42] As Henri Lepage writes: "In a universe without progress,

---

[41] The way Hayek defines social evolution by the emergence of increasingly complex societies is strongly reminiscent of Herbert Spencer, who already identified evolution with progress. Certain libertarians on the other hand have criticized the Hayekian idea of a "natural selection" of institutions. *Cf.* Timothy Virkkala, "Reason and Evolution," *Liberty*, September 1989, 57–61, and David Ramsay Steele, "Hayek's Theory of Cultural Group Selection," *Journal of Libertarian Studies*, VIII, 2, 171–95.

> The idea of cultural evolution, or natural group selection, remains extremely obscure. What is the unity implied in cultural evolution and how does it function? Like Marxism, the Hayekian theory of cultural evolution neglects historical contingency (the fact, e.g., that certain religions disappear not because the represent a lesser Darwinian advantage than their rivals, but because state power persecutes them). . . . This is why his attempt to justify the political ideas of classical liberalism with an evolutionary or synthetic philosophy is finally a failure, just as happened with Herbert Spencer before him. (E. R. Kuehnelt-Leddihn, "The Road from Serfdom," *National Review*, April 27, 1992, 36–37)

[42] "Over time, and with occasional steps backward, history choses the winners. This thesis is perhaps familiar to us: Francis Fukuyama's bestseller on the end of history owes at least as much to Hayek as to Hegel" ("In praise of Hayek," *The Economist*, March 28, 1992, 77).

liberty would lose its reason for being."

This parallel between cultural and biological evolution raises numerous methodological problems, starting with the question of precisely to what the liberal order is best "adapted." In this respect, Hayek's quasi-mechanical application of the theory of natural selection to social values and institutions does not escape the critique that stigmatizes it as tautological. As Roger Frydman remarks:

> The evolutionary-utilitarian perspective that inscribes cultural developments in a finalized sequence is either banal or unverifiable. Banal because human institutions are necessarily adequate to their ends or to the survival of each society that produces them. Unverifiable because, if it is legitimate to posit that institutions are adapted (even if not necessarily as a whole, and always relative to particular objectives), nothing lets us escape this vicious circle to say it was the best or most adapted that were finally selected.[43]

Jean-Pierre Dupuy adds that if Hayek "had followed to their conclusions the logical and systemic theories of self-organization of which he was a partisan from the beginning, he would have understood that they cannot accommodate themselves to the vicious circles of neo-Darwinism concerning the selection of the best adapted."[44]

Moreover, this evolutionary model runs up against Western singularity—which, as in any ethnocentric vision, is here posited as the very incarnation of normality when it really represents the exception. Hayek never explains why the liberal order and the market were not selected as the forms most adequate to social life outside the realm of Western civilization. Nor does he explain why in other parts of the world the social order "spontaneously" evolved in other directions . . . or did not evolve at all.[45] More generally, Hayek seems not to have seen that all

---

[43] Frydman, "Individu et totalité dans la pensée libérale."

[44] Dupuy, "L'individu libéral, cet inconnu," 119.

[45] On this question, *cf.* John Gray, *Hayek on Liberty.*

forms of spontaneous order, including that of the West, have not necessarily been compatible with liberal principles. A social system can evolve "spontaneously" toward a traditionalist or "reactionary" order as easily as toward a liberal order. And it was by arguing for the "naturalness" of traditions that the counterrevolutionary school led by Bonald and Joseph de Maistre developed its critique of liberalism and pled for theocracy and absolute monarchy! Hayek reasons as if opinion were spontaneously liberal, something contradicted by historical experience, and as if it were formed autonomously, which has yet to be proven. It is true he could scarcely do otherwise: if the advent of the liberal order cannot be explained by "natural selection" alone, his whole system collapses immediately.

The fact, however, is that the market order has not been "selected" everywhere. So how can we state that the selection from which this order is supposed to result is "natural?" And above all, how do we demonstrate that this order is the best there is? Here, Hayek's difficulty is passing from the statement of a supposed fact to the enunciation of a norm. Just because institutions are not the product of voluntary human designs (a supposed fact), he concludes that men absolutely must not seek to transform them voluntarily (a norm). But then he falls into a classic contradiction: "is" is not "ought." In fact, Hayek knows perfectly well that his preference for a given system of values, the liberal, cannot be logically justified. This is why he dissimulates his choice behind considerations of an evolutionary character that confer upon his reasoning an appearance of objectivity.

Besides, there is a certain contradiction between the fact of affirming that all moral rules are valid insofar as they result from a "selection" guaranteeing their well-adaptedness to social life, and the necessity Hayek finds himself in of showing that liberal society is objectively the best. The question arises whether the liberal order is best by virtue of its intrinsic qualities or if it is the best because it has been "consecrated" by evolution. Now, these are entirely different things. If we respond that the liberal order is best because it has been "naturally selected" over the course of history, then we must explain why it has not been selected everywhere, and also why orders opposed to it have sometimes existed. If on the other hand we answer that it is the best because of its intrinsic virtues (the position of the classical liberal school), then the market is no longer a norm, but merely a model, i.e., one system among others, and it is no longer possible to demonstrate its excellence based on a fact external to those virtues, viz., evolution.

In fact, Hayek can only escape this dilemma by falling back into the utilitarianism from which he claimed to have freed himself, i.e., by affirming that the market constitutes no longer a way to coordinate all human activities without planning, but simply the generic model most favorable to human development. He does not miss the chance to have recourse to this argument, e.g., when he explains that the "great society" imposed itself "because the most effective institutions have prevailed in a competitive process." But such reasoning has two disadvantages. Firstly, it amounts to basing the demonstration on a totally arbitrary judgment, viz., that all human aspirations must be ordered according to a principle of effectiveness allowing the maximum of material enrichment, which is merely another way of saying that there is no value higher than such enrichment (whereas Hayek claims elsewhere that the economy's principal goal is not to create wealth). But then, secondly, we no longer see what is the advantage of the market defined as an epistemological tool allowing us to arrive at a general order. If the market's superiority only lies in its capacity to produce wealth, and if the highest priority is seeking wealth, there is no longer any reason why the disinherited should be satisfied with their lot and find the unequal distribution of possessions "normal." So Alain Caillé is right to ask: "Doesn't making the efficiency of the market the criterion and aim of justice amount to introducing into the definition of the market considerations we pretended to ignore?"[46] By falling back on a utilitarian appreciation of the market, Hayek himself invalidates everything he says about the "non-injustice" of the "great society."

The Hayekian critique of utilitarianism thus appears at least ambiguous. Connected in his writings to the denunciation of

---

[46] Caillé, *Splendeur et misère des sciences sociales*, 315.

"constructivism," as are the critiques of rationalism and positivism, it is at best aimed at the narrow utilitarianism of Jeremy Bentham, who defines general happiness as the sum of the greatest possible number of individual happinesses. According to Hayek, this definition leaves too great a place to the idea of the common good. In fact, it legitimates the idea of sacrifice, which it inscribes in a strict relation of numerical quantity. Pareto posited in principle that if some could gain by a social transformation without others thereby suffering, that transformation was recommended. Bentham's utilitarianism breaks with this principle by going farther. If the essential point is the satisfaction of the majority, we can allow that a transformation which increases the gains of the greater number while increasing the losses of a small number is also justified. This idea that the sacrifice of a few is legitimate when it is the condition for everyone else's advantage, which is also one of the bases of the victim mechanism in the theory of the scapegoat,[47] is rejected by Hayek simply because he does not accept the concept of "collective utility" even when defined as a mere sum of individual utilities. His position on this point is no different from that of Robert Nozick or even John Rawls, who writes:

> Each person possesses an inviolability founded on justice that even the welfare of society as a whole cannot override. For this reason justice denies that the loss of freedom for some is made right by a greater good shared by others. It does not allow that the sacrifices imposed on a few are outweighed by the larger sum of advantages enjoyed by many.[48]

However, we may wonder whether this rejection is sincere. When Hayek urges the losers of the "game" of catallaxy to accept their

---

[47] In the fourth Gospel one of the chief priest, Caiaphas, declares: "It is expedient for us that one man should die for the people, and that the whole nation perish not" (John 11:50).

[48] John Rawls, *A Theory of Justice* (Cambridge, Mass.: Belknap Press, 1971), 3.

lot as the least unjust thing there is, does he not impose self-sacrifice upon them for the sake of the proper functioning of the general order of the market? There is an equivocation here which takes us back to the "impure individualism" we have already discussed. Let us remember that it is above all individualism that Hayek opposes to utilitarianism, but also that he himself falls back into this same utilitarianism in spite of himself each time he boasts of the effectiveness of the "invisible hand," each time he legitimizes the market by its intrinsic virtues or directly identifies value with success.[49]

V.

Alain Caillé defines the two contradictions coextensive with critical liberal rationalism in the following terms:

The first relates to the fact that critical reason is not self-sufficient. To be critical, reason must find something other than itself to criticize, and this something must not be purely negative. The second contradiction follows from the first. Critical reason can only believe itself capable of exhausting the entire domain of reality if it supposes that reality amounts to the negative rationality which would constitute its whole identity. So critical liberal reason supports itself upon an identitarian representation of the social relation that contradicts the idea of liberty.[50]

For his part, Max Weber has shown there always exists a contradiction between formal and substantial rationality, and that they can always conflict. Thus the problem of the substantial

---

[49] Significant in this respect is the definition Hayek gives of the issue of distribution resulting from the market: "To each according to the utility of his contribution as perceived by the others." Some liberal authors do not hesitate to classify Hayek among the theoreticians of utilitarianism. *Cf.* for example Leland B. Yeager, "Utility, Rights, and Contract: Some Reflections on Hayek's Work," in Leube and Slabinger, eds., *The Political Economy of Freedom*, 61–80.

[50] Caillé, *Splendeur et misère des sciences sociales*, 340–41.

content of liberty cannot be regulated by merely honing the procedures supposed to guarantee it. The hypothesis of the spontaneous adjustment of economic and social agents' multiple competing projects under a regime of total freedom of exchange, an adjustment posited as optimal (not in the ideal sense, but in the sense of the possible, i.e., with reference to the real cognitive conditions of the life of the members of the society), as if there were no irreducible antagonism of interests, crises destructive of the market, etc., reveals itself as profoundly utopian. The idea that we could fuse the values of liberty and the spontaneous order resulting from practice rests in fact on the idea of a society with no public space.

Hayek, as we have seen, does not limit himself to saying, as the classical liberals do, that the market maximizes everyone's well-being. He affirms that it constitutes a "game" that increases the odds of all players considered individually attaining their particular ends. This affirmation runs into an obvious objection: how can we say that the market maximizes individuals' chances of realizing their ends if we have laid down the principle that these ends are unknowable? Moreover, as Alain Caillé writes:

> If such is the case . . . it would be easy to argue that the market economy has multiplied the individuals' ends more than their means of realizing them; that is has, according to the psychological mechanism analyzed by Tocqueville, increased dissatisfaction. This is one way of reminding us that individual's ends do not fall from the sky, but proceed from the social and cultural system within which they are placed. So we do not see what would prevent us from thinking that the members of a primitive society, e.g., have far greater chances of realizing their individual ends than those of the great society. Hayek would undoubtedly respond that the primitive men were not "free" to choose their own objectives. This would have to be proven, as it would equally have to be proven that modern individuals freely determine themselves as such.[51]

---

[51] Caillé, *Splendeur et misère des sciences sociales*, 320–21.

The representation of catallaxy as a game offering "impersonal" chances, and in which it is normal for there to be winners and losers, is in reality indefensible. The existence of abstract rules is not enough to guarantee that all will have the same chances of winning or losing. Hayek forgets precisely that the chances of winning are not the same for everybody and that the losers often turn out to be the same people every time. At that point, the results of the game cannot be considered a matter of chance. They are not, and for them to become so, at least over the long run, the game would have to be "corrected" by voluntary interventions by the public power, something Hayek vigorously rejects. What, then, are we to think of a game where, as if by accident, the winners win ever more while the losers lose ever more? To accuse spontaneous order of "injustice," claims Hayek, amounts to falling into anthropomorphism or "animism," or even the logic of the scapegoat, since it amounts to seeking a responsible party, a guilty party, where none exists. But, as Jean-Pierre Dupuy has noted, the argument is easily reversed, for if there has been one decisive gain from social evolution, it is surely that we no longer consider it just to condemn an innocent party. From this perspective, it is rather the negation of the very notion of social injustice that "moves us backwards." Guarding against the logic of the scapegoat, Hayek himself falls straight into it: the scapegoats, in his system, are simply the victims of social injustice forbidden even to complain. To state that social justice does not mean anything amounts to transforming those who suffer injustice into scapegoats of a theory meant to legitimate injustice. The sophistry consists in saying that the social order is neither just nor unjust even as we conclude that it must be accepted as it is, i.e., . . . as if it were just.

All the ambiguity here comes from Hayek sometimes presenting the market as intrinsically creative of liberty (this is his fundamental thesis), and sometimes presenting liberty as a means to the general effectiveness of the market. But then what is the real goal being sought: individual liberty or economic effectiveness? Hayek no doubt would say that these two aims are the same. But it would still have to be determined how they stand in relation to one another. In fact, the definition of liberty given by Hayek shows that in the end, it is the latter whose function is to guarantee the market, which thus becomes an end in itself. For Hayek, liberty is neither an attribute of human nature nor a complement of his reason, but a historical conquest, a value that originated from the "great society." It is, moreover, a purely individual, negative, and homogenous liberty. Hayek goes so far as to say that liberty is strangled whenever one pleads for (plural) liberties.[52] So the market only creates the conditions for liberty because liberty has been put in the service of the market. The ethics of liberty is thus reduced to the ethics of well-being, which amounts to falling back into utilitarianism. Hayek offers us a merely instrumental vison of liberty: its value is precisely equal to how well it allows the functioning of the commercial order.

To identify the market with the social order as a whole, finally, amounts to the most reductionist form of economism. As Roger Frydman writes:

> The market is inevitably an economy. It forms a system that presupposes coherence between a social arrangement and the objectives it can satisfy. For the market to work, it must itself be based on a social relation that can be expressed in quantifiable terms, and it must propose commercial ends for itself, or at least transform such ends into products that enterprises can monetize and profit from. So we do not escape the need to justify commercial society in terms of its economic performance, and to select rules of just conduct with a view to these same objectives.[53]

In the end, the only "defensible sort of legislation is that which suits products of human activity *qua* merchandise implemented in a competitive process."[54] This is also Alain Caillé's conclusion:

---

[52] *"Liberties appear only when liberty is lacking"* (*The Constitution of Liberty*, 12).

[53] Frydman, "Individu et totalité dans la pensée libérale," 120.

[54] Frydman, "Individu et totalité dans la pensée libérale," 120.

The sleight-of-hand trick of liberal ideology (of which
Hayek furnishes us the most perfect illustration) resides in
the identification of the rule of law with the commercial
state, in its reduction to the role of an emanation of the
market. From that point on, the plea for individuals to be
allowed to choose their own ends gets flipped around into
a demand placed upon them to have no ends that are not
commercial.[55]

Liberal doctrine is that which claims anything can be bought
and sold on a market described as self-regulating. It corresponds
to the economic ideology that Pierre Rosanvallon says "expresses first of all the fact that relations between men are understood
as relations between commercial values." It thereby inscribes
itself in the negation of the difference traditionally posited (at
least since Aristotle) between economics and politics, or rather it
only refers to this difference in order to reverse the order of subordination between the two. It then results in what Henri
Lepage rightly calls "generalized economics," i.e., the reduction
of all social facts to a (liberal) economic model by way of methodological individualism, legitimating itself with the conviction
that

> If, as economic theory affirms, economic agents behave
> relatively rationally and usually pursue what they most
> prefer when it comes to producing, investing, consuming,
> there is no reason to think it would be different in their
> other social activities: e.g., when electing a representative,
> choosing a course of training, a trade, taking a spouse,
> having children, arranging for their education . . . . The
> paradigm of *Homo oeconomicus* is thus used not only to ex-
> plain production and consumption behavior, but also to
> explore the entire field of social relations based on the in-
> teraction of individual decisions and actions.[56]

---

[55] Caillé, *Splendeur et misère des sciences sociales*, 347.
[56] Lepage, *Demain le libéralisme*, 25–26.

Hayek's project differs from classical liberalism in its will to find a new foundation for the doctrine at the highest level without needing to have recourse to the fiction of the social contract and while trying to escape the criticisms commonly addressed to rationalism, utilitarianism, the postulate of general equilibrium, or pure and perfect competition based on a transparency of information. To carry this out, Hayek was led to move the issues upstream, making the market into a global concept, insurmountable because of its totalizing character. The result is a new utopia resting on as many paralogisms as contradictions. In reality, it is clear that "Without peace having being bought by the welfare state, the market order would have long since been swept away" (Alain Caillé). A society that functioned according to Hayek's principles would explode in a short time. Its institution, moreover, would amount to the purest "constructivism," and no doubt would even demand a state of a dictatorial type. As Albert O. Hirschman writes, "This supposedly idyllic privatized citizenry that pays attention only to its economic interests and indirectly serves the public interest without every taking a direct part in it—all of this could only be realized under political conditions amounting to a nightmare."[57] That people can claim today to be renewing "national thinking" by basing themselves on this sort of theory says a great deal about the collapse of such thinking.

---

[57] Albert O. Hirschman, *Vers une économie politique élargie* [*Towards an Expanded Political Economy*] (Paris: Minuit, 1986), 27.

REPRESENTATIVE & PARTICIPATIVE DEMOCRACY

Representative democracy, essentially liberal and bourgeois, in which representatives are authorized by election to transform the popular will into governmental acts, today constitutes the most widespread political regime in Western countries. One consequence is that we have developed the habit of considering democracy and representation as somehow synonymous. But the history of ideas shows that they are not synonymous at all.

The great theorists of representation are Hobbes and Locke. For both, the people contractually delegates its sovereignty to rulers. In Hobbes, this delegation is total, and it does not result in a democracy. On the contrary, it invests a monarch with absolute power (the "Leviathan"). In Locke, the delegation is conditional. A people only agrees to give up its sovereignty in exchange for guarantees concerning fundamental rights and individual liberties. Popular sovereignty between elections remains suspended for as long as the governors respect the terms of the contract.

For his part, Rousseau considers the demands of democracy antagonistic to any sort of representative regime. For him, the people do not enter into any contract with the sovereign; their relations are exclusively a matter of law. The prince is merely the executive of the people, who remain the only holders of legislative power. He is not even invested with the power that belongs to the general will; it is rather the people who govern through him. Rousseau's reasoning is very simple: if the people is represented, its representatives hold the power, and in that case it is no longer sovereign. The sovereign people is a "collective being" that cannot be represented except by itself. So to renounce its sovereignty would be like renouncing its liberty, i.e., destroying itself. As soon as the people has elected its representatives, "It is a slave; it is nothing" (*On the Social Contract*, III, 15). Liberty, as an inalienable right, implies the plenitude of an exercise without which there can be no true political citizenship. Under such conditions, popular sovereignty can only be inalienable. So any representation amounts to an abdication.

If we admit that democracy is a regime founded on the sovereignty of the people, we must acknowledge that Rousseau is correct.

Democracy is the form of government corresponding to the principle of the identity of the ruled and the rulers, i.e., of the popular will and the law. This identity itself refers to the substantial equality of citizens, i.e., to their all being equally members of the same political society. To say that the people is sovereign not by essence but by vocation, to say that by this title it possesses the constitutive power, means that it is from the people that public power and the laws proceed, and that the people constitute the source of political legitimacy. So the rulers can only be executive agents who must conform to the ends determined by popular will. The role of representatives is thus maximally reduced, with the representative mandate losing all legitimacy as soon as it is directed to ends or projects not corresponding to the popular will.

Now, this is the very reverse of what happens today. In liberal democracies, the primacy is given to representation, and more precisely representation-incarnation. The representative, far from being merely charged with expressing the will of his electors, himself incarnates this will merely on the basis of having been elected. This amounts to saying that he finds in his election the justification that allows him to act not according to the will of those who elected him, but according to his own—in other words, that he considers himself authorized by the vote to do whatever he thinks is good.

This system is the basis of criticisms that, in the past, never ceased being directed against parliamentarism, and that echo today through debates on the "democratic deficit" and the "crisis of representation."

In the representative system, once the voter has delegated his political will to the one who represents him, power's center of gravity inevitably resides in the representatives and the parties into which they are grouped, and no longer in the people. So parliamentary sovereignty is substituted for popular sovereignty.

The political class soon forms a professional oligarchy that defends its own interests amid a general climate of confusion and irresponsibility. Nowadays, those possessing the power to decide hold it far more often by nomination or cooptation than by election. Thus an oligarchy of "experts," officials, and technicians emerges alongside the political class.

A government of laws, whose virtues are regularly celebrated by liberal theoreticians—despite all the ambiguities attached to the expression—does not appear able to correct this situation. Resting upon an ensemble of procedures and formal legal rules, it is in effect indifferent to the specific ends of politics. Values are excluded from its preoccupations, thus leaving the field free to the clash of interests. The laws have authority here from the mere fact that they are legal, i.e., in conformity with the constitution and the procedures foreseen for their adoption. So legitimacy gets reduced to legality. This positivist-legalist conception of legitimacy invites us to respect institutions for their own sakes, as if they constituted an end in themselves, without the popular will being able to modify them or control their functioning.

Now, in democracy, the legitimacy of power depends not only on conformity with the law, nor even on conformity with the constitution, but above all on the conformity of governmental practice with the ends assigned to it by the popular will. Justice and the validity of the laws cannot, then, reside entirely in state activity or in legislation produced by the party in power. By the same token, the legitimacy of law cannot be guaranteed by the mere existence of judicial review: it is also necessary, for law to be legitimate, that it answer to citizens' expectations of it and include purposes oriented toward the service of the common good. Finally, we can only speak of the legitimacy of the constitution when the authority of the constituting power is recognized as always able to modify form or content. This amounts to saying that the constituting power cannot be totally delegated or alienated, that it continues to exist and remains superior to the constitution and constitutional rules even when they flow from it.

It is obvious that we can never totally escape representation, for the idea of a governing majority in modern societies runs into insurmountable difficulties. Representation, which is never more than a makeshift, does not exhaust the democratic principle. It can to a great extent be corrected by the implementation of participative democracy. Such a reorientation today even appears a vital necessity because of the overall development of society.

The crisis of institutional structures and the disappearance of foundational "grand narratives," the growing disaffection of the electorate for political parties of the classic type, the renewal of associative life, the emergence of new social or political movements (ecological, regional, identitarian, populist, sovereigntist) whose common characteristic is no longer defending negotiable interests but existential values, let us glimpse the possibility of recreating an active citizenry from the grass roots.

The crisis of the nation-state, due especially to the globalization of economic life and the development of phenomena of planetary significance, suggests two methods by which it may be overcome: from above, with various attempts at the international level aiming to recreate a coherence and effectiveness of decision-making that would allow us at least in part to guide the process of globalization; and from below, with a renewal of the importance of smaller political units and local forms of autonomy. Both tendencies, which do not simply oppose but complement one another, involve remedying the democratic deficit currently perceived.

But the political landscape is undergoing other transformations. On the Right, we observe a break in the old "hegemonic bloc" because capitalism can no longer rely on its alliance with the middle classes due to the completion of its late modernization, the evolution of production costs, and the transnationalization of capital accelerated by the economic crisis. At the same time, while the middle classes are disoriented and often threatened, the popular classes are increasingly disappointed by the governmental practices of a Left or a Right that, after having practically renounced all principles, tend increasingly to identify with the interests of the upper level of the middle bourgeoisie. In other words, the middle classes no longer feel represented by the parties of the Right, while the popular milieus feel abandoned and betrayed by the parties of the Left.

To this we may add that the effacement of older points of reference, the collapse of models, the disintegration of the great ideologies of modernity, the omnipotence of a commercial system that (sometimes) provides the means of existence but never reasons for living, have all led to the reemergence of the crucial question of the meaning of man's presence in the world, the meaning of individual and collective existence, and this at a time when the economy is producing ever more goods and services with ever fewer men, which has the effect of multiplying forms of exclusion in a context already heavily marked by unemployment, precarious employment, fear for the future, insecurity, reactive aggressiveness, and tensions of all kinds.

All these factors call for a thoroughgoing reshaping of democratic practices that can only move in the direction of a truly participative democracy. In a society becoming increasingly "unreadable," the principal advantage of direct democracy will be to eliminate or correct distortions due to representation, to assure better conformity of the law with the general will, and to form the basis of a legitimacy without which institutional legality is merely a travesty.

It is not at the level of the great collective institutions (parties, unions, churches, the army, schools, etc.), all of which are today more or less in crisis and therefore cannot play their traditional role of social integration and intermediation, that it is possible to recreate such an active citizenry. Nor can the control of power be the exclusive apanage of political parties whose activity too often amounts to nothing more than patronage and electoral machinery. Participative democracy today can only be a grass roots democracy.

This grass roots democracy is not aimed at generalizing discussion at all levels but rather at determining (with the participation of the greatest possible number) new decision-making procedures in conformity with its own requirements as well as with those that flow from the citizens' aspirations. Nor can it be reduced to a mere opposition of "civil society" to the public sphere, something that would amount to extending even further the grip of private life and abandoning political initiative to obsolete forms of political power. On the contrary, the point would be to allow individuals to test themselves as citizens and not as members of the private sphere, while favoring as much as possible the flowering and multiplying of new *loci* of public initiative and responsibility.

The procedure of popular referendum (whether resulting from the decision of rulers or from popular initiative, whether voluntary or obligatory) is merely one form of direct democracy among others—and one whose scope has perhaps been overestimated. Let us emphasize once again that the political principle of democracy is not so much that the majority decides as that the people are sovereign. Voting is merely one technique for consultation and revealing opinion. This means that democracy is a political principle that must not be confused with the means it employs any more that it should be reduced to a purely arithmetical or quantitative idea. Citizenship is not exhausted by voting. It consists rather in uncovering all the methods allowing consent to be manifested or refused, of expressing approbation or rejection. So we should systematically explore all possible forms of active participation in public life, which are also forms of responsibility and autonomy, since public life affects all of our daily lives.

But participative democracy does not have a merely political scope. It also has a social scope. By favoring relations of reciprocity, by allowing the recreation of a social bond, it can aid in the reconstitution of organic forms of solidarity which today have weakened, recreating social fabrics that have disintegrated in the face of rising individualism and the headlong rush to the system of competition and self-interest. Insofar as it is productive of elementary sociality, participative democracy will go hand in hand with the rebirth of living communities, preference for shorter supply chains, local autonomy, the recreation of solidarity between neighbors, among neighborhoods, in workplaces, etc.

This participative conception of democracy is radically opposed to the liberal legitimation of political apathy, which indirectly encourages abstention and results in the reign of managers, experts, and technicians. In the end, democracy rests less on the form of government properly speaking than on the people's participation in public life, so that the maximum of democracy amounts to the maximum of participation. To participate is to take part; it is to feel oneself part of a whole, and to assume the active role that results from that belonging. As René Capitant has said: "Participation is the individual act of the citizen acting as a member of the popular collectivity." We see here how the concepts of belonging, citizenship, and democracy are connected. Participation authorizes citizenship, which results from belonging. Belonging justifies citizenship, which allows participation.

The French republican slogan "liberty, egality, fraternity" is well-known. If liberal democracies have exploited the word "liberty," if ancient popular democracies seized upon "equality," organic or participative democracy based on active citizenship and the sovereignty of the people might be the best way of responding to the imperative of fraternity.

LIBERALISM & DEMOCRACY

Liberal democracy is in decline today, as witnessed not only by several recent essays published mainly in the English-speaking world,[1] but also by the rise of a new phenomenon to which the significant name "illiberal democracy" has been given. Like the rise of populism — a form of "leprosy" according to Emmanuel Macron — the appearance of "illiberal democracy" is a new phenomenon indicating the exhaustion of the representative parliamentary system in favor of a form of democracy both more sovereigntist and more respectful of the popular will.

The expression "illiberal democracy" is obviously ambiguous, and no one will contest that it might result in some cases in purely authoritarian regimes, just as it might be the sign of a powerful renewal of democracy. But exactly what should we understand by such renewal?

The term "illiberalism" appeared in the 1990s, but it only became popular after the appearance of a celebrated article by Fareed Zakaria published toward the end of 1997 in the journal *Foreign Affairs*,[2] which has since been followed by a book that has provoked much debate.[3]

Fareed Zakaria defines illiberal democracy as a doctrine that separates the classical exercise of democracy from the principles of the rule of law. It is a form of democracy where popular sovereignty and election continue to play an essential role, but

---

[1] *Cf.* Thomas Frank, *One Market under God: Extreme Capitalism, Market Populism and the End of Economic Democracy* (London: Secker & Warburg, 2001); Mabel Berezin, *Illiberal Politics in Neoliberal Times: Culture, Security and Populism in the New Europe* (Cambridge: Cambridge University Press, 2009); Edward Luce, *The Retreat of Western Liberalism* (New York: Atlantic Monthly Press, 2017); and Patrick J. Deneen, *Why Liberalism Failed* (New Haven: Yale University Press, 2018).

[2] "The Rise of Illiberal Democracy," *Foreign Affairs*, November-December 1997.

[3] Fareed Zakaria, *The Future of Freedom: Illiberal Democracy at Home and Abroad* (New York, W. W. Norton & Co., 2003).

where there is no hesitancy about infringing certain liberal principles (constitutional norms, individual liberties, separation of powers, etc.) when circumstances demand. This results in a rejection of individualism and "rights language," a rejection of Kantian visions of "perpetual peace," and so a rejection of a significant part of the heritage of the Enlightenment. "We thus find ourselves closer to Rousseau's general will than to Montesquieu's separation of powers," notes Jacques Rupnik.[4] American neoconservative Daniel Pipes speaks of "civilizationists" to describe the association of populists with "illiberals."[5]

In his article, Zakaria states that illiberal democracy is today getting stronger "from Peru to the Palestinian authority, from Sierra Leone to Slovakia, from Pakistan to the Philippines," which is perhaps a slight exaggeration. What is certain, however, is that in Europe, in the countries of the Visegrád Group, viz., Hungary, Poland, Czechia, and Slovakia, but also in Croatia, Slovenia, Romania, Austria, and now Italy, governments oriented toward "illiberalism" have been established over the past few years in a context marked by the discrediting of the old institutional parties and the muddling of the Left-Right distinction. "We may speak of illiberal democracy from the Baltic to the Adriatic," observes Jacques Rupnik.

The political scientist Sylvain Kahn, author of a recent *History of European Construction since 1945*,[6] does not hesitate to speak of an "Orbánization" of Europe. It is in fact Viktor Orbán, Hungarian Prime Minister since May 2010, constantly reelected with an absolute majority ever since, who first openly claimed this label in a 2014 speech at his Fidesz Party's Summer University: "The Hungarian nation is not a simple sum of individuals," he

---

[4] *Le Monde*, May 8–9, 2016.

[5] Pierre Rosanvallon, who defines it as a "political culture which rejects the liberal vision as a matter of principle," compares "illiberalism" with Bonapartism, which in his eyes constitutes the French political tradition par excellence ("Fondements et problèmes de 'l'illiberalism' français" ["Foundations and Problems of French 'Illiberalism'"], remarks to the Académie des sciences morales et politiques, 2001).

[6] Sylvain Kahn, *Histoire de la construction de l'Europe depuis 1945* [*History of the Construction of Europe Since 1945*] (Paris: PUF, 2018).

declared, "but a community that needs to be organized, strengthened, and developed, and in this sense, the new state that we are building is an illiberal state, a non-liberal state." He added that we must "understand systems that are not Western, not liberal, . . . and yet make nations successful."

Orbán, who proposes to the Hungarian people and the European nations a solidarity against what threatens their common values, observes that liberal democracy was "not capable of obliging governments to serve national interests, . . . protect public wealth and protect the country from debt." He adds that democracy is not necessarily liberal: "One can be democratic even without being liberal."[7] In September 2017, Orbán declared before the Hungarian parliament that the adaptation by the countries of Central Europe of "Western liberalism would mean spiritual suicide for the Central Europeans."

A month later, on October 23, a Hungarian national holiday, Orbán once again attacked the "global force that would make European nations a standardized cluster" and denounced "the financial empire that has imposed new migratory waves, millions of migrants, and new invasions of populations to make Europe a mixed-race land."

For taking these positions, Orbán of course has attracted the thunder of the European Commission in Brussels, George Soros, and all liberal forces in the world. His response: "We are not going to be a colony! We never accepted the Vienna diktat of 1848; then we opposed Moscow in 1956 and 1990. Today we shall not let anyone dictate our behavior to us."

The causes of "illiberalism's" rise are obvious, and match in many ways those which explain the success of populist parties. Both involve the observation that liberal democracies have been transformed nearly everywhere into financial oligarchies cut off from the people: ineffectiveness, impotence, corruption, parties transformed into mere electoral machines, the reign of experts,

---

[7] *Cf.* Viktor Orbán, "Hungary and the Crisis of Europe," *Hungarian Review*, January 2017, 3–17. *Cf.* also Teréz Barna, "Viktor Orbán et la renaissance de la Hongrie" ["Viktor Orbán and the Rebirth of Hungary"], *Égards*, June–August 2017, 7–24.

short-term views, etc. To this observation is added a more serious one: in liberal democracies, nations and peoples no longer
have any means of defending their interests. What is the point of
popular sovereignty if governments no longer have the necessary independence broadly to determine their own orientation in
matters of economics, finance, the military, and foreign policy?
Can we continue to impose legal principles that instead of favoring the cohesion of peoples, end by dissolving them?

We recall the disillusioned remarks made on March 3, 2018,
by Nicolas Sarkozy at a forum in Abu Dhabi, according to which
"modern democracies destroy leadership. How can we see 10,
15, or 20 years ahead and at the same time have an electoral
rhythm of four years like the United States? The great leaders of
the world come from countries that are not great democracies."

The expression "illiberal democracy" is apt: it is a democratic
theory hostile to liberalism. So it represents a historic break with
the era where, in Western countries, the expression "liberal democracy" was regarded as a pleonasm. To understand this, emphasizes Fareed Zakaria, we must stop identifying liberalism
and democracy: "Constitutional liberalism is theoretically different and historically distinct from democracy." This is also what
political scientist Philippe C. Schmitter, former professor at Stanford and the University of Chicago reminds us: "Liberalism, either as a conception of political liberty, or as a doctrine about
economic policy, may have coincided with the rise of democracy. But it has never been immutably or unambiguously linked to
its practice."

So what is it that separates and even opposes liberalism and
democracy? How are liberal principles distinct from democratic
principles? And why can liberalism be considered, finally, an
antipolitics?

Democracy involves the sovereign power of the *demos* or, if
you prefer, popular sovereignty as a constitutive power. Democracy is the form of government corresponding to the principle of
an identity of views between the rulers and the ruled, the primary identity being that of a people concretely existing by itself as a
political unit. All citizens belonging to that political unit are
formally equal.

The principle of democracy is not the natural equality of men but the political equality of all citizens. As Hannah Arendt writes: "We are not born equal; we become equal as members of a group by virtue of our decision mutually to guarantee ourselves equal rights." "Competence" to participate in public life is based solely on being a citizen: suffrage obeys the rule "one citizen, one vote" and not "one man, one vote." In a democracy, a people does not express propositions that are "truer" than others by means of suffrage. It makes known its preferences and whether it supports or disavows its leaders. As Antoine Chollet correctly writes: "In a democracy, the people are neither wrong nor right; rather, they *decide*." This is the very basis of democratic legitimacy. This is why the question of who is a citizen and who is not is the fundamental question for all democratic practice. This is also why the territorial boundaries of a political unit are essential. At the same time, the democratic definition of liberty is not the absence of constraint, as in liberal doctrine or Hobbes ("the absence of external impediment," we read in *Leviathan*, chapter 14), but is identical with each person's ability to participate in the collective definition of social constraints. Liberties, always concrete, apply to specific domains and particular situations.

Liberalism is entirely different. Whereas politics is neither a "sphere" nor a domain separate from others, but an elementary dimension of any human society or community, liberalism is a doctrine that on the political level divides society into a certain number of "spheres" and claims that the "economic sphere" must be made autonomous from political power, whether for reasons of efficiency (the market only functions optimally if nothing interferes with its "natural" functioning), or for "anthropological" reasons (freedom of commerce, says Benjamin Constant, frees the individual from social power, for it is by definition economic exchange that best permits individuals freely to maximize their interests). Economics, originally perceived as the realm of necessity, thus becomes the realm of liberty *par excellence*.

Redefined in a liberal sense, democracy is no longer the regime that consecrates the sovereignty of the people, but that which "guarantees the rights of man." The rights of man take priority over the sovereignty of the people to the point that the latter is no longer respected except insofar as it does not contradict the former: the exercise of democracy is thus subjected to conditions, starting with that of respecting the "inalienable rights" every individual possesses by reason of his mere existence. Confounded with a "rule of law" that has now become the unsurpassable horizon of our age, democracy transforms itself into a movement towards ever greater equality of condition. Such equality, supposed to result from the free confrontation of rights, is henceforward conceived as synonymous with sameness. The rule of law dissolves politics under the corrosive effect of the multiplication of rights. As Marcel Gauchet says: "By being constantly invoked, the rights of man end by paralyzing democracy."

The rule of law, which we should recall, is firstly a rule of private law, implies the primacy of law over political power and rests on the imperative of obedience to the law. While relying on the metaphysics of the rights of man which alone is supposed to guarantee human dignity, it consecrates the power of general laws as general norms imposed on everyone, starting with the rulers. Legitimacy is thus reduced to mere legality, with positive law ruling in a purely impersonal and procedural manner. Carl Schmitt has shown that this system eliminates the very concept of legitimacy and proves incapable of functioning in emergency situations where norms are no longer valid. As Jacques Sapir has correctly noted: "Schmitt considers that liberal parliamentarism creates conditions for supplanting legitimacy with legality." This replacement of politics with law ends by emptying politics of its substance. "The political machine is only an artificial device whose purpose is realizing the best possible discussion of the content of law," writes Fabrice Flipo.[8] Schmitt sums it up in a single sentence: "The rule of law is never more than the rule of

---

[8] Fabrice Flipo, *Réenchanter le monde. Pouvoir et vérité. Essai d'anthropologie politique de l'émancipation* [*Re-Enchant the World: Power and Truth. Essay on the Political Anthropology of Emancipation*] (Vulaines-sur-Seine: Éditions du Croquant, 2017), 41.

those who establish and apply legal norms."[9]

The rule of law necessarily goes hand in hand with liberal individualism and its conception of a purely "negative" liberty that concerns only the individual, but never the collectivity. This is what explains liberalism's fundamental hostility to the concept of sovereignty—except, of course, the sovereignty of the individual. For it, any form of sovereignty going beyond the individual is a threat to his liberty. So it condemns political sovereignty and popular sovereignty on the grounds that legitimacy only belongs to the individual will.[10] "As soon as there is sovereignty, there is despotism," as Pierre Paul Royer-Collard (1763–1845) already said. With the individual posited as the absolute sovereign, the state enjoys no intrinsic legitimacy.

Not recognizing the validity of any democratic decision that might infringe on liberal principles or the ideology of the rights of man, liberalism has never admitted that the people's will should always be respected. Distrusting the people, it also distrusts universal suffrage, whose adoption it tried to hinder, especially in France where liberals have been more clearly marked than elsewhere by a rationalist tradition that tends to disqualify opinion. In the past, it tried to reserve the advantage of voting to the rich or "most competent," which explains why it long favored property qualifications (in the United States we find this idea expressed by Alexander Hamilton, considered the "father of American capitalism," at the time of the Constitutional Convention of 1787).

Liberalism has also adhered to the principle of representation: all liberal democracies have also been representative parliamentary democracies, which means that parliamentary sovereignty has been substituted for popular sovereignty. For liberalism, power is not fundamentally the power to direct, but to *represent*, society. However, a people scarcely needs to be represented, for

---

[9] Carl Schmitt, *La notion de politique – Théorie du partisan* [*The Concept of the Political – Theory of the Partisan*] (Paris: Flammarion Champs, 1992), 111–12.

[10] *Cf.* Bernard Manin, *Les principes du gouvernement représentatif* [*The Principles of Representative Government*, 1996] (Paris : Flammarion, 2008).

it is only truly sovereign when it makes itself present.

In every representative government there is an obvious anti-democratic bent, as Rousseau well knew: "The instant a people gives itself representatives, it is no longer free; it no longer exists" (*On the Social Contract*, III, 15). Political participation in such a regime is in fact limited to mere electoral consultations, which means that the *demos* is no longer a group of actors but only of voters. It is implicitly affirmed here that the people cannot speak directly, that it should not directly give its own opinion on the problems of the hour or decisions that affect its future, that there are even subjects that should be removed from its assessment, with decisions and choices made only by the representatives it has elected, i.e., by elites which in most cases continually betray those from whom they have received power. In the first rank of these are the experts, who regularly confuse means with ends. Emmanuel Joseph Sieyès in 1789 already defined the representative regime as that which allowed the people's will to be "interpreted" better than the people could do themselves. When an election is held, we say "the people have spoken," which simply means that they have nothing further to do but to shut up.

Democracy being first of all a "-cracy" (*kratos*), liberalism can only try to limit it, for it distrusts the people's power as it does all power. To the equality of citizens, it opposes the freedom of individuals. The essential point is then to limit power (whence the insistence on the separation of the legislative, executive, and judicial powers and the necessity for checks and balances), and thereby to limit authority—without seeing that in a democracy the basis of authority is primarily systemic.[11]

In order to set up checks and balances, liberalism limits popular sovereignty in various ways. In France, the increasingly extensive powers accorded to the Constitutional Council, tasked with verifying the consistency of political decision with the arrangements of the Constitution, tend in this direction. The method consists in integrating into the normative parts of the Constitution things that have nothing to do with it—or even considering ideals

---

[11] Cf. David Estlund, *L'autorité de la démocratie* [*Authority and Democracy*, 2008] (Paris: Hermann, 2011).

(liberty, equality, fraternity) as legal principles with normative value, which they are not. The decision of July 16, 1971, to integrate into the constitution the preamble to the constitution of 1946 thus obliges Parlement to adopt only laws "conformable" to this purely declaratory text. The same goes for the Declaration of the Rights of Man of 1789, also incorporated into the "constitutional bloc." To this we may add limitations resulting from the European treaties, the power of judges, the decisions of the European Court of Human Rights, etc. These are all ways of exerting the primacy of human rights and pure legality over popular sovereignty. Liberal democracy is democracy with no *demos*, no people.

Carl Schmitt, who famously defined the relation specific to all political activity—its "criterion"—not by enmity as is too often said, but by the possibility of a dialectical distinction and antagonism between friend and enemy, affirms the unpolitical character of liberalism. One reason is liberalism does not admit that conflict is an irreducible part of human nature: it believes it can make conflict disappear either by favoring the development of "peaceful commerce" ("We have arrived at the age of commerce, an age that must necessarily replace that of war,"[12] said Benjamin Constant) and endless discussion—the latter being understood on the model of commercial negotiation[13]—or conjures up an apocalyptic scenario in which war supposedly opposes an absolute Evil to a Good assimilated to "humanity." As Schmitt observes: "Liberalism has attempted to transform the enemy from the viewpoint of economics into a competitor and from the intellectual viewpoint into a debating adversary."[14] In reality, "any political unit is necessarily either the center of decision, which commands the grouping into friend and enemy, and then it is sovereign in this sense (and not in any absolute sense), or it

---

[12] Benjamin Constant, *De l'esprit de conquête et de l'usurpation* [*The Spirit of Conquest and Usurpation*] (1814).

[13] Already in the nineteenth century, Donoso Cortés observed that "it is of the essence of bourgeois liberalism not to decide . . . but, instead of deciding, to attempt to start a discussion." Carl Schmitt developed this idea at length.

[14] Schmitt, *The Concept of the Political*, 28.

simply does not exist."[15]

The ideology of the rights of man does not want to recognize anything but humanity and the individual, even though everything political—peoples, cultures, states, territories—is situated between these two concepts. Thus politics involves the existence of borders, without which the distinction between citizen and non-citizen (or foreigner) loses all meaning. Humanity is not a political concept: one cannot be a "citizen of the world," for the political world is not a *universum* but a *pluriversum*. Politics implies a plurality of opposing forces. Humanity cannot be a political unit because it cannot have an enemy on this planet—unless metaphorically. This is why liberalism can only wage war against those it represents as "enemies of humanity," thereby making war more terrible than ever. Schmitt cites the saying attributed to Proudhon: "Whoever invokes humanity wants to cheat." He deduces from this, as Michael J. Sandel writes, that "universal principles are inapt to fix a common political identity."[16] Again, Schmitt writes: "A completely pacified globe would be a world without the distinction of friend and enemy and hence a world without politics."[17]

We can now better understand in what sense liberalism is fundamentally unpolitical. It is so already in its general conception of man: man is not for it a political and social being whose motto might be *inter homines esse*,[18] but an economic being (*Homo oeconomicus*), separate from his fellows, seeking to maximize his best interest ever more effectively. It is so in its adherence to free trade, which implies the sidelining of any form of political authority (its utopian character results precisely from the impossibility of economic exchange totally escaping the power relations that prevent it from functioning "freely"[19]). It is so in its conception of government practice: the very Saint-Simonian way it

---

[15] *Cf.* Schmitt, *The Concept of the Political*, 38.

[16] Michael J. Sandel, *Democracy's Discontent: America in Search of a Public Philosophy* (Cambridge, Mass.: Harvard University Press, 1996).

[17] Schmitt, *The Concept of the Political*, 35.

[18] "To be among men"—Trans.

[19] Cf. Simon-Pierre Savard-Tremblay, *Despotisme sans frontières* [*Despotism without Frontiers*] (Montreal: VLB, 2018).

seeks to reduce the government of men to the administration of things attests to its hope of "neutralizing" political questions by reducing them to technical questions, with technology itself considered eminently "neutral"—which it obviously is not—without seeing that even if technology were merely an instrument, the question would immediately arise of who would make use of it and for whose benefit. By reducing government to governance, i.e., the implementation of technical competence aimed at merely administrative management, liberalism falls under the heading of what Jean-Claude Milner rightly calls the "politics of things."[20]

Finally, liberalism is unpolitical in its idea that governments do not have to take any position with regard to the "good life," which also results in the withering away of politics, at least if we believe with Aristotle that "the end of politics consists in nothing less than allowing people to develop their properly human capacities and virtues," politics not being "economics by other means."[21] So liberalism cannot demand that members of society give their lives to confront a threat to their common existence, since from its point of view "no program, no ideal, no norm, no expediency confers a right to dispose of the physical life of other human beings."[22] No sacrifice is possible where interest and egoism are consecrated, where the individual is both *terminus a quo* and *terminus ad quem*.[23]

---

[20] Jean-Claude Milner, *La politique des choses* [*The Politics of Things*] (Lagrasse: Verdiar, 2011. Jean-Claude Michéa also emphasizes that "the principal obsession of liberals has always been to discover automatic piloting systems for society which would definitively render the 'ideological' government of men needless" (*La double pensée. Retour sur la question libérale* [*The Double Thought: Return of the Liberal Question*] [Paris: Flammarion-Champs, 2008], 204).

[21] Michael J. Sandel, *Justice: What's the Right Thing to Do?* (New York: Farrar, Straus & Giroux, 2009), 200. Here we see just how inconsistent those liberals or libertarians are who do not hesitate to appeal to Aristotle, for whom ethics issues in a politics, whereas for them it issues in its negation.

[22] Schmitt, *The Concept of the Political*, 48.

[23] "Starting point" and "final goal"—Trans.

In Schmitt's eyes, liberalism thus signifies "total depoliticization." The domination of liberalism, he explains, inevitably involves depoliticization by the polarity of morality (the rights of man) and economics (the market). Liberals can "do politics," of course—liberal democracy knows how to be authoritarian when it likes!—but not in accordance with their principles: "The negation of the political, which is inherent in every consistent individualism, leads necessarily to a political practice of distrust toward all conceivable political forces and forms of state and government, but never produces on its own a positive theory of state, government, and politics."[24] Conclusion: "There exists no liberal politics, only a liberal critique of politics."[25]

But Carl Schmitt also emphasizes—and this is the most important point—that any depoliticized society ends up "serving a foreign, politically active people."[26] This allows us to return to our original subject.

Another essential cause of the emergence of illiberal democracies comes from our having entered, as Spengler put it, the *Jahre der Entscheidung*, the "years of decision." As long as the economic situation was relatively stable, we could get along with legal rules and formal constitutions. But as soon as circumstances become uncertain, when threats grow until it is no longer a question of how to live but of how to survive, in short, as soon as we pass into an emergency situation, the hour of decision has struck, for by definition habitual norms cannot anticipate anything unforeseen. As Carl Schmitt writes, it is the state of exception that reveals the identity of the sovereign: he is sovereign "who decides on the exceptional case."[27] Now, decisionism is the natural adversary of a liberalism that considers mere constitutional arrangements enough to organize powers.

It is certainly not an accident that illiberal democracies are

---

[24] Schmitt, *The Concept of the Political*, 70.

[25] Schmitt, *The Concept of the Political*, 70.

[26] Carl Schmitt, *Constitutional Theory* (1928) (Durham: Duke University Press, 2007), 248.

[27] Carl Schmitt, *Political Theology* (1922) (Cambridge, Mass.: MIT Press, 1985), 5.

starting to multiply at the very moment the European Union is crashing headlong into the migratory crisis. At a time of mass immigration, we are rediscovering that any human community "inevitably finds itself confronted with the problem of its day-to-day anthropological cohesion" (Jean-Claude Michéa), i.e., with controlling the conditions of its own social reproduction. The economic and financial crisis, economic globalization, followed by the migrant crisis, have given birth to a feeling of urgency, especially in countries whose historical imagination remains haunted by the memory of the Ottoman invasions and which do not want to see imposed on them a "multicultural" model that they consider a total failure. The rise of illiberal democracies attests to the generalization of this feeling, related to the development of an existential threat to freedom, identity, or their citizens' way of life.

Schmitt was not wrong to say that a democracy is all the more democratic insofar as it is less liberal. Liberal theory wants a good constitutional order to be enough to allow the members of society to live the way they prefer without having to submit to interference by the public powers. The friend/enemy dialectic can supposedly be overcome in this way. But this theory falls to pieces the moment an enemy appears that poses an existential threat to us. Politics then resumes its rights. A political society that renounces power and sovereignty already has nothing political about it. It can only renounce its primary mission, guaranteeing the conditions of its self-preservation. Liberal democracies are quite simply not up to facing the urgency of current challenges or the breadth of current threats. So the hour of illiberal democracies is striking.

The Third Age of Capitalism

In a book that made a certain splash, Luc Boltanski and Ève Chiapello looked at how capitalism continues to mobilize millions of individuals for a cause lacking any finality other than itself: the accumulation of capital.[1] Seeking to identify the "beliefs that contribute to justifying the capitalist order and support it by legitimating modes of action and dispositions consistent with it," they observe that in each age capitalism includes a basic figure, an element of individual excitation, and a discourse justifying it in terms of the common good. This leads them to distinguish between three different periods.

The first capitalism, which dominated the entire nineteenth century, was incarnated in the figure of the "bourgeois" so well described by Werner Sombart, and by the entrepreneur or "captain of industry," who displayed above all a taste for risk and innovation. This patrimonial and familial capitalism was largely in solidarity with the bourgeois classes that exercised power. The vital element was represented by the will to discovery and enterprise. The legitimating discourse was simply the cult of progress.

The second form of capitalism developed in the 1930s: that of the giant corporations and the Fordist compromise, where the proletariat gradually renounced social criticism in exchange for a guarantee of joining the middle class. Rising salaries favored consumption, which mitigated conflict. The emblematic figure of this second capitalism was the CEO or company president, as well as upper management. The impulse to action resided in the company's will to develop itself as much as possible. The legitimating discourse emphasized increases in purchasing power as well as the rewards of "merit" and competence. This period, which corresponded to the era of welfare state redistribution, Keynesianism, and the constant expansion of the middle class, ended (along with France's Thirty Glorious Years) with the 1973 oil crisis.

---

[1] Luc Boltanski and Ève Chiapello, *Le nouvel esprit du capitalisme*, [*The New Spirit of Capitalism*] (Paris: Gallimard, 1999).

Since then, we have entered the "third age" of capitalism, a stage that corresponds to the passing from a still embedded capitalism to the unbridled capitalism of the present world — the "turbo-capitalism" of which Edward N. Luttwak speaks.[2] Its essential figure is that of the project coach or networker who limits himself to coordinating the activities of temporary teams. His key values are autonomy, creativity, mobility, initiative, conviviality, and development. The new capitalism bypasses the principle of hierarchy with a new form of personnel management. There are ever-fewer "bosses" and ever-more "responsible parties" working in teams. The manager attentive to human resources, adaptable, flexible, "communicative," replaces the rigid manager and planner. The employee is mobile, with very little loyalty to the company employing him. Because of increasing competition, the company functions less "internally." It externalizes its services, which are supplied by subcontracting and precariousness. The Taylorist or Fordist company gradually gives way to the *network company*, a phenomenon that appears in tandem with the emergence of a postmodern, essentially "connected" world. The element of excitation is represented by the development of new technologies. The legitimating discourse is that of a "new economy" that will lead humanity into a new era of durable growth.

The chief characteristic of this new capitalism lies in the extraordinary rise in the power of the financial markets. The surge in stock prices began in the mid-1980s on Wall Street before spreading to Europe. The result has been an obsession with creating value for stockholders and an exorbitant demand for capital profitability. A 15% return on capital is now expected, at a time when GDP growth is not more than a few percentage points. Whereas formerly the profitability of a company's assets was measured exclusively by returns on its equities, today, in order to compensate for a lack of information concerning future profitability, companies are appraised with the help of presumptive ratios based on market shares obtained.

---

[2] Edward N. Luttwak, *Turbo-Capitalism: Winners and Losers in the Global Economy* (London: Weidenfeld & Nicolson, 1998).

The stock market, which fluctuates in a random manner, ceases to reflect the situation of companies or economies: listed share value no longer bears any relation to real value. The sudden rise of Western stock markets breaks the relation of equality between the growth rate of the real economy and the yield on investments. Economic value is becoming ever less related to objectively measurable value and ever more closely related to a virtual wealth deemed to match individuals' unlimited desire. The entrepreneurial dynamic that aimed at creating something lasting is supplanted by an immaterial financial dynamic without any objective basis. This distortion between the real economy and the financial economy, between stock market value and value added, and between the consumer and the stockholder, supports the illusion that the accumulation of shares is equivalent to the production of goods. There is a headlong rush fueled by credit, with stock shares increasingly resembling fiat money in the making. The speculative "bubble," which continues to expand, can burst at any moment, resulting in a new stock market crash. This is what happened in 2008 with the subprime lending crisis and is threatening to happen again today.

This supremacy of the stock market led logically to the domination of "institutional investors," the famous *"zinzins,"*[3] collectors of savings, who today manage some 10 trillion dollars (including 2.85 trillion Euros worth of managed stock shares in France) and are currently imposing the Anglo-Saxon version of capitalism on the entire world.

Among these *zinzins* who dominate the world of stocks, the best known are pension fund managers, insurance companies, and mutual funds. Pension funds are collective savings accounts created by professionals or companies in order to pay retirees' pensions in the form of rent. Their activity consists in investing the funds in the financial markets looking for the biggest profits. In today's dollars, their shares have grown from 17 billion in 1950 to 5 trillion in 1997. In 2009 they reached 20 trillion; in 2015 more than 36 trillion!

---

[3] *Cf.* Erik Israelewicz, *Le capitalisme zinzin* [*Crazy Capitalism*] (Paris: Grasset, 1999).

This fashion for pension funds, whose miraculous virtues are constantly celebrated, actually involves an enormous risk for those who, by means of them, are willing to gamble on the stock market with their retirement pensions. It amounts to transferring to salaried workers, whom it puts at the mercy of a stock market crash, the financial risks formerly borne by companies and states.[4] Moreover, pension funds are one of the major factors behind world financial instability, with their massive capital input bringing about an artificial overvaluation that feeds into speculative bubbles, while their positive impact on the real economy is practically zero. Their potentially destabilizing role, especially in emerging markets, has also been highlighted by the most recent financial crises.

With their threats or their actual decision, institutional investors have changed the face of capitalism. Their considerable weight, their means of exerting pressure, have caused the emergence of new management norms while permanently limiting governmental room for maneuver. Everywhere they have imposed their own style, objectives, demands. Through risk-capital, stock options, and employee stock portfolios they have given priority to corporate governance by stimulating the desire for an immediate return on investment. Through mergers, reciprocal shareholding, and stock-exchange takeovers they have given birth to a new class of entrepreneurs who derive their power from the pure power of markets. By demanding practically usurious profitability rates on invested capital they have forced entrepreneurs to submit to their conditions.

---

[4] *Cf.* Michel Husson, "Jouer sa retraite en bourse?" ["Gambling Your Retirement on the Stock Market?"], *Le Monde diplomatique*, February 1999, 1, 4–5. The discussion regarding pension funds is indissociable from the debate on the role of capitalization (as opposed to distribution) in the retirement system. At the same time, it turns on the dependency ratio as measured by the proportion of retirees to active workers. *Cf.* on this subject René Passet, "Le grande mystification des fonds de pension" ["The Great Mystification of Pension Funds"], *Le Monde diplomatique*, March 1997; François Chesnais, "Demain, les retraites à la merci des marchés" ["Tomorrow, Pensions at the Mercy of the Markets"], *Le Monde diplomatique*, April 1997.

The penetration of French stock market capitalization by foreign investors, the big Anglo-Saxon pension funds chief among them, has been revealing in this respect. France holds the record in this domain. Big international investors' share in French companies is today over 40% (46.7% of market capitalization of the CAC 40 [a French stock market index] in 2014 as opposed to just 41.9% three years earlier). By 1998, net investments in French stock by non-residents had risen to 70 billion francs, as opposed to only six billion for residents. In 2013 the total amounted to 499 billion Euros! Moreover, since a decision made in 1993 by Nicolas Sarkozy, then Minister for the Budget, French dividends received by non-residents are tax exempt. So there is a difference in the constraints to which resident and nonresident investments are subject, and thus in their yield. The logical consequence, given the means of which the *zinzins* dispose, is the gradual buying out of most stock in French companies by foreign investors. In 2000, the collapse of Alcatel following the decision of an American fund to sell off half its Alcatel stock illustrates the dangers of such dependence, which only continues to grow.[5]

Laurent Joffrin remarks:

In this way the liberal model expands without fanfare merely by financial pressure. Forced to assure extravagant levels of "value creation" (commonly known as profit) to these pitiless shareholders, French companies make the necessary sacrifices at their employees' expense: stagnant French salaries go to fill the pockets of retirees on the other side of the Atlantic.

The "Rheinish capitalism" recently described by Michel Albert[6] is thus constantly losing ground to financial capitalism,

---

[5] The constantly repeated argument according to which French companies' own pension funds will allow them to avoid takeover by foreign investors, thus stabilizing their own investments while favoring the growth of the Paris stock market, runs into the fact that stock markets do not bring any fresh money to companies (among other objections).

[6] Michel Albert, *Capitalisme contre capitalisme* [*Capitalism Against*

which is shaking its very foundations. This "Rheinish" capitalism based on the banking system and industrial conglomerates likes to consider itself concerned to preserve a minimum of social cohesion. But the economic difficulties of recent decades have reinforced the idea that the Anglo-Saxon model is destined to impose itself everywhere—all the more in that it is favored by the extraterritoriality of American law. In any case, the convergence of economic models is one of the main postulates of the "new economy," wherein the same interpretive model is applied to nation-states as to companies when evaluating their competitiveness.

In reality, since the American example constitutes the basic reference point for the "new economy," this supposed convergence of economic systems—a convergence that abstracts from the cultural, social, or institution particularities of each country and interprets every problem that derives from any local situation as a delay—results simply from all countries being classed according to how widely they deviate from the United States, "a young country that has eradicated all prior forms of socialization and is therefore the merchant's country *par excellence*," as Robert Boyer notes, adding: "We compare every other society with this one, the emblematic figure of capitalism, only to discover them 'archaic' or 'emergent.' In other words, most American analysts apply to other economies the conceptual tools they use to analyze American society, supposing them both necessary and sufficient."[7] We thus lose sight of the American system's exceptionality in comparison with the diversity of existing situations.

The first demand of institutional investors, of course, is deregulation. At the heart of the liberal credo lies a belief in the existence of a natural (self-regulating) process of adjustment that supposedly allows the market to reach an optimal state if it is not hindered in any way—which does not prevent partisans of the market from discretely converting to interventionism any

---

Capitalism] (Paris: Seuil, 1991).

[7] Robert Boyer, "L'internationalisation approfondit les spécificités de chaque économie" ["Internationalization deepens the specificities of each economy"], *Le Monde*, February 29, 2000, 19.

time they find it advantageous.[8] Deregulation consists in suppressing anything that might disturb the adjustments proper to the "market mechanism" and, secondarily, in attributing any negative effects one might observe to human ill-will ("salary rigidity," public debt, cultural "obstacles," etc.) rather than to the market itself.

An essential component of this liberal conception of the economy, namely deregulation, has continually spread since the 1980s, starting from the British and American experiments. An important turning point came in 1986, when Ronald Reagan and Margaret Thatcher convinced their G7 partners to accept the principle of financial deregulation. The countries accepted it because such deregulation allowed them to finance their public debt through "securitization," meaning that government debt could be transformed into equities that could be bought and sold on the stock market. A vast movement of financial "disintermediation" then began, allowing big companies to finance themselves directly on the financial markets, which involved lessening the role of banks. It has been the traditional role of banks to act as a screen between companies and savers by allowing a sort of "mutualization" of risks, and by absorbing a part of the conjunctural shocks that create a mismatch between savings and investment. The disappearance of this screen meant that from then on the individual saver had to endure all the risk of his investments in financial markets, which increased his vulnerability. At the same time, new financial instruments were created such as the futures and foreign exchange markets.

This liberalization of the financial markets was both one of the essential driving motors and one of the most visible consequences of globalization. Like deregulation and privatization, it is part of a single tendency: the shift from bank liquidity to a purely financial form of liquidity, i.e., financial instruments continue to gain liquidity to the point that they can be used as monetary instruments.[9]

---

[8] We recall especially the way corporations called for governments to help them during the Asian financial crisis.

[9] *Cf.* André Orlean, *Le pouvoir de la finance* [*The Power of Finance*]

On the pretext of deregulation and greater efficiency, the new capitalism is thus demanding total legal freedom of maneuver by arguing that any restriction upon such freedom will reduce efficiency. In this way they are freeing themselves of any rule apart from immediate profit. The result: whereas great stock market raids used to be extremely rare in Europe, mergers and acquisitions are now multiplying at an unprecedented rate.[10] Of course, between 1885 and 1913 there had already been a movement toward corporate concentration, but it was not of these dimensions. Moreover, a century ago mergers were aggressive and served to conquer new parts of the market, whereas two-thirds of today's mergers are mainly defensive. Another characteristic of these operations is that they are carried out "on paper" for the most part, i.e., by public exchange offers profitable to the shareholders of the targeted companies, but they contribute further to the speculative "bubble." Such mergers involve colossal sums. To give just one example: in January 2000, the purchase of Time Warner, the number one communications company in the world, by AOL created a group worth 300 billion dollars. On a world scale, such mergers and acquisitions represented more than 5 trillion dollars in 2015, as compared to 3.16 trillion in 1999.

The principle of competition, supposed to favor diversity and quality, thus results in the creation of immense cartels or monopolies with more power than many states. In 2016, the ten most valuable companies in the world were all American, and

---

(Paris: Odile Jacob, 1999).

[10] As a reminder we may cite the mergers or buybacks from just one year, 2017, between PSA and Opel/Vauxhall, Alstrom and Siemens, Danone and WhiteWave, Unibail-Rodamco and Westfield, Essilor and Ray Ban, Body Shop (L'Oréal) and Natura Cosméticos, Vivendi and Bolloré, Suez and GE Water, Thales and Gemalto, Safran and Zodiac, Ingenico and Bambora, etc. Such concentrations also affect the banking sector as we have seen in France with the merger of Paribas-Société Générale and the buyout of CCF by the British HSBC. This development has involved the sudden disappearance of a certain number of large French concerns including, most famously, Pechiney, Elf, Seita, Aérospaciale, Rhône-Poulenc, etc.

the top three were technology giants: Apple (with 600 billion dollars of stock market capitalization), Google, and Microsoft. In most sectors, especially that of culture and communication, this development involved the homogenization of supply (each company tries to do better, but to do *the same thing* better) and "reverse selection," i.e., situations in which solutions decided upon turned out to be disadvantageous for those involved.[11]

The *zinzins'* true role is clearly to restructure world capitalism. As Dominique Plihon explains, "By buying and selling their participation, pension funds increase capital circulation and accelerate the emergence of a new configuration wherein investors assume control of productive capital, and also create a class of *rentiers* among white-collar workers themselves."[12]

We have gone from trading raw materials to trading industrial products to trading financial products. This development is today justified by belief in a new type of durable growth tied to the rise of "new technologies" — media, the Internet, mobile telephones, etc. Just as the development of the original form of capitalism was favored by the steam engine and railroads, the new capitalism owes most of its good fortune to the explosion in communications technologies: the computer, the first tool created by man to replace the human brain, is characterized by the instantaneous transportation of immaterial data and allows the endless proliferation of networks.

Put on the market by the Pentagon at the end of the 1980s, the Internet has proven a formidable tool. The number of users is shortly to pass four billion (already 52 million in France), electronic commerce (online trading, advertising, live stock market reports) is reaching 80 billion Euros per year in France. At the beginning of March 2000, news of the IPO of a new online subsidiary of France Télécom allowed that telephone company to earn 295 billion francs in a single day, something unprecedented on the Paris stock market. France Télécom thus reached a market

---

[11] One speaks of "reverse selection" where there exists a large difference between immediate and long-term preferences.

[12] Dominique Plihon, "Au nom des entreprises?" ["On Behalf of Businesses?"], *Le Monde diplomatique*, February 1999, 4.

capitalization of 1.47 trillion francs, the equivalent of France's entire state budget at that time. Ignacio Ramonet notes that "an investor who had simply put 1000 dollars into each of the five big Internet companies (AOL, Yahoo!, Amazon, AtHome, eBay) on the day of their IPO would by April 9, 1999, have made a profit of a million dollars!"[13]

Market capitalization of Internet stocks has elicited a kind of madness, as attested by the multiplication of start-ups. Here again the model is that of a virtual economy and headlong rush. "Companies that have never made a profit and are not close to doing so have been evaluated in figures that represent several centuries of doing business."[14] Disappointments were not slow in coming. By the end of March 2000, 700 billion dollars (twice the debt of some African countries) went up in smoke within twenty-four hours on the New York stock exchange. A few days later, the collapse of Nasdaq (the market on which tech stocks are listed) resulted in a new loss of 800 billion dollars.

Because they allow any activity, anywhere on the planet it occurs, to become international immediately, the new technologies are of symbolic significance. One of the characteristics of the new capitalism is in fact the abolition of distance and time. Money circulates instantaneously from one end of the planet to the other, and this mobility, which contrasts with the heaviness of governmental bureaucracies whose impotence it highlights and whose obsolescence it accelerates, is found on all levels: between purchasers and subcontractors, multinational firms and countries, financial markets and companies. Mobility ("displacement differential") tends to be set up as an absolute norm, with the imperative of profitability commanding the movement of men and the delocalization of enterprises. "A twenty-first-century technology has been placed in the service of a nineteenth-century ideology," writes Jack Dion.[15] Capitalism is more nomadic than ever.

---

[13] Ignacio Ramonet, "Nouvelle économie" ["New Economy"], *Le Monde diplomatique*, April 2000, 1.

[14] Yves Le Hénaff, "Le temps des tulipes" ["Tulip Time] *Politis*, April 13, 2000, 13.

[15] Jack Dion, "Les archaïsmes de la nouvelle économie" ["The Ar-

The first capitalism was certainly a "wild" capitalism, but it also included an element of security tied to the reign of bourgeois morality and its key values (family, patrimony, savings, employer charity). This element of security was reinforced in the second capitalism with the Fordist compromise and the emergence of the welfare state: the activity of employers was carried out within a framework of regulatory arrangements, fiscal legislation, hard-won labor legislation, social structures, cultural traditions, etc. These two forms of capitalism were also founded on hierarchic relations of domination within which a certain degree of challenge was still possible. Bernard Perret observes:

> Hierarchic organization paradoxically leaves more room for democratic elaboration and the consolidation of noncommercial regulations. In a word: it is precisely because the domination of money appears there explicitly as a relation of domination between persons that the Fordist company was able to provide the main setting for social democracy's struggles.[16]

All this was blown to pieces with the third age of capitalism. Rediscovering its original appetite, but with greatly multiplied means at its disposal, it tends to make any system of security disappear, the basic idea being that in an economy where competition is taking precedence over organizations and institutions, social concerns absolutely must not disturb the free play of the market. Because of deregulation, salaried workers are seeing the advantages and rights acquired by decades of trade union struggle disappear one after the other, under Left-wing as well as Right-wing governments. At the same time, the new structure of work (ever more goods produced and services provided by ever fewer men) causes growth to become "rich in unemployment" (in the words of Alain Lebaude), while flexibility results

chaisms of the New Economy"] in *Marianne*, April 10, 2000, 11.

[16] Bernard Perret, "Contester le capitalisme ou résister à la société de marché?" ["Contest Capitalism or Resist Market Society?"], *Esprit*, January 2000, 129.

mainly in the devaluation of the concept of status, as precariousness and exclusion increase.

Unemployment, formerly related to the business cycle, becomes structural and permanent. On the one hand, we see a tendency for agricultural and industrial employment to decline, to
which are added budget constraints that weigh on the creation
of public employment and the inherent limits on the development of tertiary commercial sector jobs. On the other hand, the
search for employees is increasingly becoming delocalized and
international. Such workers find themselves victims of systematic social, fiscal, and environmental dumping. Finally, and most
importantly, large industrial enterprises not only no longer create jobs, but are trying to increase their productivity by doing
away with them.

The increasing influence pension funds exert on corporate
management practices also plays a role, of course.

> The only imperative that counts for them is increasing the
> profitability of their stocks and maximizing their value.
> The priority is no longer, as it was in the Fordist era, to as-
> sure the growth of industry, but to realize productivity
> gains: if necessary, by shutting down production centers
> considered insufficiently profitable or, more precisely, that
> fail to live up to the exalted standards of profitability de-
> manded by investors. Under this new regime, the size of a
> company and the number of its employees become adjust-
> able variables.[17]

Until recently, a company tended to hire when it was profitable. This is even how profit was justified: the better companies
do, the less unemployment there will be. Today, the reverse is
true. When Michelin simultaneously announced the abolition of
7500 jobs and a 22% increase in its earnings, the news was greet-
ed with immediate favor by the markets. Similarly, when Lionel
Jospin's government approved the closure of the Renault factory
in Vilvorde in June 1997, American investment firms, which held

---

[17] Plihon, "Au nom des entreprises?," 4.

5% of the company's capital, applauded loudly. Unemployment is thus contributing to profits, at least in the short term (for no account is being taken of consequences on purchasing power or consumption). In such a context, the growth in jobs can be explained essentially by that of part-time work and short-term or precarious jobs, especially in the service sector.

Since liberal economists are convinced the market society is the best that can be imagined, the aim is to privilege structural reforms that increase incentives to work and at the same time reduce the income of non-activity, i.e., that distributed by the welfare system. On the one hand, we create structural unemployment, on the other we do ever less for the unemployed, while the numbers of the richest and the poorest increase in tandem.

The social exclusion that results from this is fundamentally different from the lot of workers whose labor-power capitalism previously limited itself to exploiting. The emergence of the networked world has been accompanied by new forms of alienation based on differences in ability, especially cognitive, but also of mobility and capacity for adaptation. Given the personal profile demanded in expanding sectors of the economy (abstract intelligence and technical competence), the underqualified become increasingly unemployable and thus useless. They are no longer exploited but excluded. As Boltanski and Chiapello write:

> In the topography of the network, the very concept of the common good is problematic because, since belonging or not belonging to the network remains largely undetermined, it is unclear between whom any "good" might be placed in "common," or by the same token between whom the scales of justice might be established.[18]

In the world of networks, social justice quite simply makes no sense. Those who slip through the cracks are definitively excluded. Bernard Perret speaks justifiably of an elective and volatile society "based on the avoidance of disturbing factors and thereby

---

[18] Boltanski and Chiapello, *Le nouvel esprit du capitalisme*, 159.

always generating exclusion."

To disguise this tendency, champions of the "new economy" emphasize the now-decisive importance of creating shareholder value. As Jacques Julliard remarks,

> For a long time, company management identified completely with capital. Thus, in the classic French system, the figure of the CEO, who was both Chairman of the Board of Directors and President of the company, perfectly assured this identity of the shareholders with management. Today the tendency of capital to become autonomous, encouraged by the increasing importance of pension funds, turns the CEO into a demanding inspector and guarantor of corporate profitability.[19]

Shareholders in fact are becoming ever more important within this system. Henceforth they—and no longer the CEOs or managers—demand mergers and firings in order to increase their dividends. This has been seen in France, where it was finally shareholders who decided the battle between the Banque Nationale de Paris and Paribas, while the finance minister was reduced to the role of spectator. Shareholders are thus presented as the miracle recipe by the champions of "popular capitalism" as well as by liberals, who go so far as to explain with a straight face that this allows the realization of the old socialist dream of the appropriation of companies by their workers.[20]

Shareholding employees thus find themselves in an almost

[19] Jacques Julliar, *Le Nouvel Observateur*, October 14, 1999.

[20] *Cf.* Guy Sorman, *La nouvelle solution libérale* [*The New Liberal Solution*] (Paris: Fayard, 1998). In another book, *Marx à la corbeille. Quand les actionnaires font la révolution* [*Marx in the Trash: When Shareholders Make the Revolution*] (Paris: Stock, 1999), another ultraliberal, Philippe Manière, also celebrates the increasing power of shareholders, to the point of preaching "capitalist democracy," i.e., the emergence of citizenship through the purchase of shares: political changes will no longer be decided by voters but by shareholders! Since in France less than one household in eight holds any corporate stock, such a project would amount to restoring the old system of property qualifications.

schizophrenic double bind. As salaried workers, they have an interest in freeing themselves from the "harsh discipline of capitalism," in particular from the extremely risky character of any activity aimed at turning a quick profit, whereas they reinforce that discipline by acquiring shares themselves. Moreover, their interests as employees are directly the opposite of their interests as shareholders, since as shareholders their profits depend closely on the success of social policies hostile to them as employees. As Dominique Plihon observes: "These employee-investors lose in a double sense. As employees they endure the consequences of the 'flexibility' demanded by the unbridled search for maximum immediate profit; as investors they assume the main risks associated with the instability of financial markets."[21] With most capital remaining concentrated in a very limited number of hands, employee stockholding without any redefinition of their real power within companies represents in the end only a surplus for patrimonial capitalism.[22]

The substitution of this patrimonial capitalism (in which the dividends paid to shareholders plays a major role) for the old capitalism based on salaried workers obviously accentuates inequalities, for the distribution of capital holdings is always more uneven than that of salaries. The stock-option system that rapidly growing companies use to reward their managers also allows some of them to acquire enormous fortunes. Capital always remains better remunerated than labor. That stock shares earn more than real growth simply means that annual payments not coming from profits on shares (salaries, essentially) are declining.

In this way the whole face of the global company is gradually changing. Formerly the gains of the winners benefited the losers at the bottom of the social pyramid to some extent. This is no longer the case. The growth in unemployment marks the end of

---

[21] Plihon, "Au nom des entreprises?," 4.

[22] This term is primarily associated with French economist Thomas Piketty and features prominently in his book *Capital in the Twenty-First Century* (Cambridge, Mass.: Harvard University Press, 2013).—Trans.

the age when those who entered the middle class (and their descendants) were sure not to fall back into the proletariat. While liberals serenely repeat that free trade is "a system in which all win" (Alain Madelin), the "hourglass" model of society is what actually gets established, with the rich getting richer, the poor ever more destitute and excluded, and the middle class shrinking.

While the world as a whole is still getting wealthier, and ever more enormous quantities of money are circulating, income and capital inequality are continually increasing both between countries and within each country. In American companies the difference between the average salary and the highest went from a factor of 20 to a factor of 419 within the space of 30 years! The fortunes of the three richest men in the world, Jeff Bezos ($112 billion), Bill Gates, ($100 billion), and Warren Buffett ($84 billion) are today greater than the gross national product of the 48 poorest countries in the world put together, countries where more than 700 million people live. Everywhere the gap is widening between the well-connected and those with no connections—between the financial elites and the mass of precariously employed, the more modest white-collar workers, the long-term unemployed, inactive and underqualified young people—between the urban centers that benefit from globalization and the "peripheral" countryside where those who live in a state of permanent social, cultural, and political insecurity are relegated. This new form of social breakdown on a planetary scale is also typical of the third age of capitalism.

At the same time a trendy elite, a deterritorialized, egoistic and volatile "hyperclass" (Jacques Attali), is becoming established whose members are neither entrepreneurs nor capitalists in the old sense, but wealthy individuals with highly portable assets. They possess knowledge and control the great communication networks, i.e., all the instruments by which cultural works are produced and distributed, and do not have the faintest desire to direct public affairs, knowing better than anyone the decreasing power of those who do. It is enough for them to control those persons.

Laurent Joffrin writes:

It is undeniable that a "neo-bourgeoisie" now dominates French society, as it does many other democratic societies. As much as by its wealth or occupation of eminent positions, this new class is characterized by its *mobility*: professional, intellectual, and geographic. Concentrated in the professions that "move" — communications, finance, or cutting-edge technology — they hold symbolic power as much as material power, and thereby have the means of influencing public opinion. It forms part of a world of rapidity, adaptation, and competition. They form a relaxed set of people, international, tolerant, slightly cynical, with a cosmopolitan culture and a varying but generally high purchasing power. . . . Nothing is more fundamentally foreign to them than national borders, statuses, guarantees, rules, prohibitions: in short, the protections that to ordinary mortals seem an indispensable barrier to the hazards of existence. . . . Sheltered from the vicissitudes of a society subject to openness and *anomie*, protected by their private security guards and their stock options, the new class abandons the common people to their unfortunate fate and criticizes their desire to maintain the old protections as "populism."[23]

Faced with liberals who champion the "self-regulating" market, social-democratic leaders still sometimes claim to regulate, provide a framework for, or "moralize" neo-capitalism.[24] But can they still do so? The socialists have long since abandoned the

---

[23] Laurent Joffrin, "Les deux cents golden boys" ["The Two Hundred Golden Boys"], *Le Nouvel Observateur*.

[24] The principal French theoreticians of state regulation (heteroregulation) are Robert Boyer (*Économie politique des capitalismes. Théorie de la régulation et des crises* [*Political Economy of Capitalism: Theory and Regulation of Crises*] [Paris: Découverte, 2015]) and Michel Aglietta (*Régulation et crises du capitalisme* [*Regulation and Crises of Capitalism*] [Paris: Odile Jacob, 1987]). Besides the classic instruments of budgetary, monetary, and fiscal policy, the regulatory measures most frequently discussed are the minimum wage, work regulations, environmental norms, prudential ratios imposed on banks, etc.

idea of the collective appropriation of the means of production.[25] Whether meant as a corrective or for redistribution, social democratic or "Left-liberal" attempts to find an acceptable compromise between the imperatives of social and democratic life on the one hand and the hegemony of the market and the demands of globalization on the other, are having practically no results. Insofar as they assess levels of well-being in monetary wealth alone, far from questioning the dominant social model, they even reinforce the centrality of paid employment, thereby acquiescing in the process of individualization and the monetarization of social life.[26]

The truth is that the welfare state today is having ever greater difficulty intervening in the economic sphere. Liberals, who have long aspired to "public impotence" in this regard, are congratulating themselves.

The old capitalism was adapted to the nation insofar as corporate profits were essentially realized within its framework, thus contributing (at least indirectly) to national power. Today, these gains are sought outside the framework of nation-states, with the consequence that the normative system of neocapitalism is valid in all countries alike. Financial globalization has shifted the reality of economic power from the level of nations to that of the planet, from classic businesses to international corporations, from the public sphere to private interests. Victims of the increasing power and internationalization of markets, states no longer have the means to formulate a long-term economic policy. The mobility of international investments, constantly shifting about in search of greater profits, directly limits their capacity for action, especially in the social and fiscal

[25] Cf. Gérard Desportes et Laurent Mauduit, La gauche imaginaire et le nouveau capitalism [The Imaginary Left and the New Capitalism] (Paris: Grasset, 1999).

[26] Cf. Bernard Perret, "Les impasses du libéralisme social" ["The Impasses of Social Liberalism"], Ésprit, February 1999, who notes that "reduced to its essential terms, the social question considered from a liberal point of view can be expressed as follows: how do we reduce inequalities to a politically acceptable level while letting the market determine the hierarchy of wealth and social power?" (65).

domains: any will to regulate inconsistent with the interests of
capital is immediately sanctioned by corporations moving their
place of business, the expatriation of managers, and capital
flight. In Europe, more than half the decisions that affect the
gross national product are nongovernmental in nature.

Wolfgang H. Reinicke has analyzed this gap between nation-
states, which continue to derive their legitimacy from the
maintenance of borders that no longer stop anything, and from
markets formerly dependent on political power (as were local
social bodies) that now find themselves emancipated from all
territorial constraint.[27] The creation of wealth, and even of money, now occurs above the level of banks and states, while exchanges are organized to escape fiscal constraints as much as
possible.

So it would be a mistake to think the expansion of neocapitalism could be cancelled by a nation-state practicing a sort of renewed Keynesianism. Not only is the state increasingly impotent
today, but contrary to a still-widespread idea, for a long time
now it has ceased to represent the general interest as opposed to
private interests. In many ways, by rallying to the model of
"governance," it has even placed itself in the service of the market. "The success of capitalism is due as much to the state's role
as to that of the market," as economist Amartya Sen, a 1998 Nobel laureate, reminds us. We are surprised to see a certain form
of the Left forget this role played by the bourgeois state in pro-
moting the market, as well as the "class nature" it formerly attributed to the state.

In their book, Boltanski and Chiapello also inquire about why
relatively recent critiques of capitalism have weakened. They
distinguish the "artistic critique" from the "social critique." The
former, characteristic both of romantic anticapitalism and the

---

[27] Wolfgang H. Reinicke, *Global Public Policy: Governing without
Government* (Washington, DC: Brookings Institution Press, 1998). *Cf.*
also Nigel Harris, *The Return of Cosmopolitan Capital: Globalization, the
State and War* (London: I.B. Tauris, 2002). On the way capitalism and
nationalism were associated in the past, *cf.* Liah Greenfeld, *The Spirit
of Capitalism: Nationalism and Economic Growth* (Cambridge, Mass.:
Harvard University Press, 2002).

libertarian challenge of May 1968, put the emphasis on the inauthentic character of capitalism, criticizing the generalization of commercial values brought about by its domination. Especially in the cultural domain, this found expression in a strong demand for autonomy and creativity. The second critique was aimed rather at the egoism of capital and the exploitation of poverty. A classic tool of the Left and extreme Left since the nineteenth century, it limited itself to denouncing injustice and demanding better salaries and increased security.

These two critiques, which complemented one another without being reducible to one another since they concerned different forms of alienation, are today obviously on the decline. The incorporation of the values fashionable in May 1968 (creativity, conviviality, derision, etc.) into the dynamic of neocapitalism, not so much resulting from any deliberate strategy (contrary to what Boltanksi and Chiapello say) as from a symbiosis, has largely disarmed the "artistic critique." As for the "social critique," it suffered not only from the collapse of alternative theories or systems but also from the rise of individualism and deinstitutionalization, which have drained the membership base of both labor unions and political parties.

The mistake of traditional social criticism, such as we still find in a Pierre Bourdieu, lies in retaining an archaic conception of the forms of "domination." This critique fails to take into account the "displacement effects" of capitalism in the form of outsourcing, the replacement of men by machines, the relative dwindling of the old working class, and the rise of the shareholding class. It has failed to identify the forms of alienation characteristic of the world of networks.

The contradictions between capital and labor have not disappeared, but they only play an occasional role regarding the rationality of the system as a whole. The expansion of market power no longer involves merely the exploitation of labor-power, but induces a series of disturbances of fundamental equilibrium, both regarding politics and the diversity of forms of social exchange. The monetarization of social relations in particular transforms and impoverishes the social bond in an unprecedented way, while public institutions are gradually rendered obsolete.

The new state of affairs is that the world of work has largely renounced overthrowing capitalism, limiting itself to trying to arrange or reform it. There is still conflict over the distribution of surplus value, but none over the best way to accumulate it. This is what Jacques Julliard correctly calls "the internalization of capitalist logic by workers." What seems to disappear in this way is a horizon of meaning justifying the project of profoundly changing the existing system. In fact, everyone gives way because no one any longer believes in the possibility of an alternative. Capitalism is experienced as an imperfect system, but one which remains in the last analysis the only one possible. People increasingly feel that it is no longer possible to escape it. Hence Jean-Claude Michéa's observation: "It is easier today to imagine the end of the world than the end of capitalism." Social life is only experienced within a horizon of fatality. The (provisional) triumph of capitalism resides above all in the fact that it appears as something fated.

The result is a slow conquest of the symbolic imagination and of minds by commercial values, inseparable from the colonization of all spheres of social life by the market, with both phenomena supporting and mutually reinforcing one another. This generalized commercialization of human life means that certain domains that previously escaped the logic of the market at least in part are now subject to it. Information, culture, art, sports, personal care, and social relations in general are henceforward part of the market. As Jacques Robin observes, "As soon as some of the activities of a sector are served by the market, the entire sector tends toward privatization. Thus we see all activities related to education, health, sports, the arts, technoscience, human relations rushing toward the market."[28]

The consequences are well-known. Privatizing transportation provokes a rise in prices and the abandonment of rail lines judged to be "unprofitable." The commercialization of genetically modified organisms is accepted before their effects on the natural environment and health are really known. Nutrition

---

[28] Jacques Robin, "La gauche ingrate contre l'OMC" ["The Ungrateful Left Against the WTO"], *Le Monde*, December 8, 1999.

deteriorates, for price competition pushes companies toward sacrificing the quality of their products. The search for performance leads to the suppression, once again on the pretext of insufficient profitability, of a number of businesses, establishments, or social services that previously provided a certain comfort to daily life. Profitability itself is assessed in purely commercial terms, without taking long-term effects, externalities, and financially incalculable side-effects into consideration.

We have reached the point where the American Francis Fukuyama, one-time theoretician of the "end of history," has been able to congratulate himself that "The World Trade Organization is the only international institution with a chance of becoming an organ of world government" (!)[29] René Passet concludes:

> The masks are falling, and we see emerging the image that the business world means to impose on the universe: one carved up systematically with a view to the profitability of financial capital, a planet in the tentacles of a hydra of interests with only rights and no duties, imposing its own law on states and calling them to account, requiring reparations for any failures of profitability due to social protection, the defense of the environment, culture, and everything that makes up the identity of a nation: cash as the supreme value and men in its service.[30]

After the parenthesis of the twentieth century and the failure of the various forms of fascism and communism, capitalism seems to have rediscovered the outlandish ambitions it had when it first appeared. In certain respects, the capitalism of the third age has far greater affinities with the pre-industrial commercial economy of the eighteenth century than with the manufacturing economy of the nineteenth. The declarations of the ultra-liberal David Boaz, Vice President of the Cato Institute in

---

[29] Francis Fukuyama, *Transversales Science/Culture*, March–April 2000, 3.

[30] René Passet, "Au-delà de l'AMI" ["Beyond the AMI"], *Transversales Science/Culture*, March–April 1998, 19.

Washington, are revealing. He says the twentieth century was never more than a statist parenthesis in the history of free trade:

> Liberalism led first to the industrial revolution and, in a natural process of development [*sic*], to the new economy. Rather than anything entirely new, I think globalism is the prolongation of the industrial revolution. . . . In a sense we have now gone back to the path laid down at the very beginning of the eighteenth century, at the birth of liberalism and the industrial revolution.[31]

And he adds: "The liberal ideal has not changed for two centuries. We want a world in which men and women can act in their own interest, . . . for it is by doing so that they will contribute to the rest of society."[32] In plain language, the more individual egoism reigns, the better the world will be!

Capitalism has preserved the inhumanity of its beginnings but is now taking on new forms. Must we conclude that its reign is irreversible? Capitalism, as has often been said, is nourished by its own crises. But it is uncertain whether it can always overcome its own contradictions. Even if it constantly creates new needs, plans for the obsolescence of its products, and always makes new "gadgets" appear, we cannot exclude the hypothesis that abundance itself will end by harming the market insofar as it can only function in a situation of relative scarcity of manufactured goods. Another paradox is that competitive advantage in the capitalist system is nourished by differences between countries, whereas its universalization results in their disappearance. The idea of a capitalist system capable of regenerating itself indefinitely implies a strictly endogenous mechanism of capital accumulation. But accumulation is not exactly endogenous: it requires an expansion that must eventually run into a limit, if only at the planetary level.

For now, the whole world is living on credit. Cumulative world debt (households, businesses, and states) has passed from

---

[31] *Le Monde*, January 25, 2000.
[32] *Le Monde*, January 25, 2000.

33.1 trillion in 1997 to 237 trillion, i.e., triple the gross world product. Between the third and fourth quarter of 2017, this sum grew by 11 trillion, the equivalent of China's gross national product! As Henri Guaino remarks: "In a certain way, the shift from industrial capitalism to financial capitalism proves Marx right: capitalism is sawing off the branch it is sitting on."[33] Serge Latouche rightly speaks of a "system rolling along at full speed with no reverse gear, no brakes, and no driver." We are dancing on a volcano.

[33] Henri Guaino, "Des brèches s'ouvrent dans le front de la pensée unique" ["Breaches Are Opening in the Front of Unique Thought"], *Marianne*, January 24, 2000, 26.

TO CONSERVE WHAT?
THE AMBIGUITIES OF CONSERVATISM

Conservatism is back in fashion. Is the exhaustion of the Right-Left divide responsible? Or the new "conservatives vs. progressives" divide highlighted by Emmanuel Macron during his presidential campaign? Is it an already distant effect of the "protest for all?"[1] In any case, we are now seeing a revival of interest in conservatism, perhaps surprising in a country where, contrary to what happened in Germany and the Anglo-Saxon nations, conservatism was hastily assimilated to "reaction" and has never enjoyed a good press, at least since the end of the nineteenth century when *Le Conservateur*, created in 1818, was publishing Chateaubriand, Bonald, and Lammenais.[2]

As a current of political thought, however, conservatism has never disappeared. Many works published during these last years (Laetitia Strauch-Bonnart, Guillaume Perrault, Mathieu Bock-Côté, Bérénice Levet, Guillaume Bernard, Philipe Bénéton, Frédéric Rouvillois, etc.) even suggest it is now recovering strength, while a certain number of classic authors are also being rediscovered, from Burke and Tocqueville to Raymond Aron, to cite only the best known. This development is not a bad thing, since it allows us to understand better a doctrine too often dismissed with the observation that its name begins badly.[3] But this doctrine also has its shadowy areas. Conservative, yes, but in order to conserve what?

But let us pause for a moment to consider the causes of this

---

[1] "La Manif pour tous" ("The Demonstration for Everyone") is a French organization founded in 2012 to oppose homosexual marriage and adoption. The name is a play on "mariage pour tous" ("marriage for everybody"), the slogan under which homosexual marriage was promoted in France. — Trans.

[2] *Cf.* our article "Pourquoi n'y a-t-il pas de 'conservatisme' en France?" ["Why Is There No 'Conservatism' in France?"], *Krisis*, May 2009, 24–27, the text of which first appeared in German.

[3] In French, "*con*" means "idiot." — Trans.

conservative revival. First of all, obviously, there is the crisis of the ideology of progress: the increasingly widespread idea that "things were better before" is undermining the idea that the future can only be better (the "sunny tomorrows"). The principled depreciation of the past that is the very foundation of "progressivism" is hard to swallow when we are having the greatest difficulty understanding the present and are unable to believe that the past no longer has anything to say to us.

Another fundamental cause lies in the general loss of points of reference, which has accompanied the rise of the ideology of rights, the gradually weakening prestige of the concept of the nation, the public education crisis, the rallying of the Left to the market system, the appearance of a managerial Right that has unburdened itself of any doctrinal identity to become the party of "modernity," the rising power of "deconstructors," professors of repentance, and theoreticians of suspicion. The legal and institutional recognition extended to any form of individual demand, while it has destabilized the anthropological and normative bases of society, has also involved a blurring of landmarks and a crisis of meaning that has aroused, if not a moral panic, at least a new desire for intelligibility in a world that appears increasingly confused and uncertain. As Gaultier Bès writes, man "needs rootedness and fidelity, intelligible and firm norms," if he is not to feel like "windswept straw."[4] Conservatism answers this need.

There are, of course, many forms of conservatism, especially since it is both an ideology and a temperament: Michael Oakeshott is not Bertrand de Jouvenel. Julien Freund is not Alasdair MacIntyre. Leo Strauss is not Jacques Ellul. Russell Kirk is not Wilhelm Röpke. Robert Nisbet is not Panagiotis Kondylis.

Beyond these differences, what are the positive claims of conservatism? There are at least four.

Firstly, a conservative believes there exists a human nature that makes man a political and social being from the start, i.e., a

---

[4] Gaultier Bès, *Nos limites. Pour une écologie intégrale* [*Our Limits: For an Integral Ecology*] (Paris: Centurion, 2014).

being *in relation*. He thinks this political and social being is imperfect, capable of the best as well as the worst; that to construct himself and reach the excellence of his *telos*, to get the
best out of himself, he must have moral reference points and
institutional frameworks at his disposal. It follows that a society, which is not merely an aggregate of individuals, cannot be
built exclusively on a legal contract and commercial exchange.

Secondly, he considers man above all an heir, i.e., he is part
of a history and defines himself partly by forms of belonging
that he has not always chosen himself. This heir is indebted to
what he has inherited. Conservatism is the party of anchorage,
the party of rootedness and fidelity.

The conservative also has a sense of limits that makes him
critical of those who say "everything is possible" or who believe
more is automatically synonymous with better. To be conservative, says Michael Oakeshott, is "to prefer the familiar to the unknown," which can be understood in two senses: to prefer the
near to the distant, or to prefer what has been tried and proven
to what has never been tried. "The starting point of conservatism
is the sense that good things can easily be destroyed but not created" (Roger Scruton). In other words, what is best in the present
comes from the accumulation of past experiences.

Finally, the conservative is more interested in the particular
than in the universal, or rather he knows that one does not
reach the universal except by way of a particular culture. He
loves diversity and understands that what is valid for some is
not necessarily valid for others. This is what makes him radically hostile to universalist abstractions, to equality conceived
as a synonym for sameness, and to the idea of a history of the
species gradually moving toward world unity.

But conservatism is always threatened with deviation into
pure and simple reaction or into liberalism.

François Huguenin in an important book, *Le conservatisme
impossible*,[5] explained that conservatism was unable to implant

---

[5] François Huguenin, *Le conservatisme impossible: Libéralisme et réac-
tion en France depuis 1789* [*The Impossible Conservatism: Liberalism and
Reaction in France Since 1789*] (Paris: Table ronde, 2006).

itself durably in France because, due to the Revolution of 1789, it never succeeded in distinguishing itself clearly from the counter-revolutionary movement, thereby displaying an intransigence that obliterated the space it should have occupied between the reactionaries and the liberals. Tocqueville, after all, has nothing in common with Joseph de Maistre, Louis de Bonald, or Maurras! The opposite happened in Britain, where the Tories quickly accepted the compromises of parliamentary life and the rules of democracy.

Jean-Philippe Vincent has done a good job of showing how much separates conservatism from the reactionary spirit.[6] For his part, Yann Raison du Cleuziou writes: "Even if the reactionary and the conservative share many of the same dispositions and tastes, politics separates them instantly."[7] Reaction (which is often an individual attitude) can be identified mainly by a certain style. Too often it amounts to nostalgia for a reified refuge in the past. With reaction, "common decency" results in the moral order, which is merely a caricature. Reactionaries certainly have the merit of wanting to transmit something. But from the conservative perspective, transmitting is not enough, for identity is not simply heritage. Transmission is only meaningful if we also transmit the capacity to create thanks to what we have received.

Conservatism knows that nostalgia cannot serve as a program, and that to defend the value of the past is something entirely different from imagining that we can go back where we came from. Moreover, conservatism is oriented less to the past than to what is timeless: what conserves its value for all time. "The renewal of conservative thought is not a return to the past. It is a present response to the climate of extreme uncertainty that weighs upon our societies, an attempt to overcome

---

[6] Jean-Philippe Vincent, *Qu'est-ce que le conservatisme? Histoire intellectuelle d'une idée politique* [*What Is Conservatism? Intellectual History of a Political Idea*] (Paris: Belles Lettres, 2016).

[7] Yann Raison du Cleuziou, "Un renversement de l'horizon du politique. Le renouveau conservateur en France" ["A Reversal of the Political Horizon: The Conservative Revival in France"], *Esprit*, October 2017, 140.

doubt about the ability of our institutions to face the catastrophe in which we are already involved."[8]

In its reactionary version, conservatism is also most often associated with religion ("Christian roots"). So it must conciliate a taste for concrete particularities with belief in the moral unity of the human species, reference to the heritage of the past, and the rejection of the "new man" with the fact that originally Christianity took root in Europe by invoking the Pauline "new man"[9] saved from the heritage of the old Roman *mos maiorum*.[10]

The question of the relations between conservatism and liberalism is more complex. As Philippe Bénéton reminds us: "In the nineteenth century, conservatives opposed liberals and were usually even more radical in their critique of capitalism than the socialists."[11] Now, as the same author notes, conservatism today has become a "conservative liberalism" — the specter of which spreads, with no special concern for logical coherence, from the libertarian current to the various formulas of "national liberalism." How is this possible?

What connects conservatism to liberalism is its distrust of the state, horror of "constructivism," critique of egalitarianism, defense of private property, and very Hayekian conception of a tradition formed under the selective pressure of history (perhaps also, it must be said, its contempt for the popular classes). The problems start when we confuse "collectivism" with the primacy of the common good, private property with the absolute right to own, freedom with egoism, the autonomy of the subject with the independence of the individual.

In relation to the state, e.g., there is an ambiguity about conservatism. One the one hand, it takes sides, rightly, in favor of

---

[8] Raison du Cleuziou, "Un renversement de l'horizon du politique," 142.

[9] In an article published in the first issue of *L'Incorrect* (September 2017), Chantal Delsol writes that "the Left seeks the universal truth of a norm valid for all men." This is entirely correct, but isn't that also what the Christian religion seeks?

[10] "Ancestral custom" — Trans.

[11] Philippe Bénéton, *Le conservatisme* [*Conservatism*] (Paris: PUF, 1988).

intermediate bodies (which many conservatives identify with entrepreneurs) and is reluctant to summarize the play of social forces as a face-off between the state and individuals. On the other, and especially in its republican variant, it gladly recognizes that the weakening of the state went hand in hand with the collapse of sovereignty, to which it is attached, and with the unlimited expansion of the logic of the market, which consecrates the omnipotence of capital as an exclusive source of value.

Much turns on the concept of individualism, to which conservatism may adhere out of detestation for "collectivism," but which can also take it far from its conception of man as an heir. Much turns also on the concept of freedom, especially considered in relation to modernity: for a conservative, not all forms of behavior are equal, not all desires are legitimate. Conservatism can only have great difficulty accepting the liberal state's renunciation of any definition of the "good life" and its boast of (an actually non-existent) "neutrality" on the pretext of allowing everyone to live as he pleases.

Looking more closely, we see that liberalism and conservatism are in fact completely incompatible. Conservatism involves repugnance for the idea of progress (the past is worthless) and the ideology of the rights of man (individual wills are sovereign) which, historically, have always been associated with liberalism. It involves considering man first of all as a being *in relation* and not, as in liberal anthropology, a presocial being called upon to construct himself from nothing. It involves a scale of values where egoism is not posited as the most normal form of human behavior. It involves a rejection of economism and the resulting materialism. It involves the idea that society or the community commands the common good, while liberalism puts the individual at the center of the social field. It involves a defense of rootedness and natural communities that also rejects liberal individualism. It involves an emphasis on duties more than rights. It involves conceiving of liberty on the basis of institutions rather than individual demands. It involves a principled distrust of novelties, while economic liberalism demands incessant transformation by the market, the permanent overturning of productive and social relations.

How can one profess a sense of limits while adhering to an economic system whose essence resides in the limitlessness of the market and the endless accumulation of capital, i.e., a system whose planetary development involves the destruction of everything one would like to conserve? It is hard to be against world government and in favor of the global market at the same time!

Conservatism happily admits that people can give their lives for a worthwhile cause. Across history, the only ideas for which people have collectively given their lives are nation, religion, and class. These are three forms of belonging, the domains of the common. But liberalism, which posits the individual as a being that mainly calculates its best interest, does not recognize a common good beyond a general interest defined as the mere addition of particular interests.

Guillaume Bernard was thus correct to distinguish between liberal conservatism, which is a contradiction in terms, and conservatism as such. Frédéric Saint-Clair, author of *La refondation de la droite*,[12] also writes *à propos* of Roger Scruton:

> He articulates a political conservatism and an economic liberalism majestically, but beyond the intellectual success of his enterprise, one must admit that his approach breaks the momentum of conservatism. If it is simply a matter of taking over from global and inegalitarian economic liberalism, there is no need to go to all this trouble. . . . Now, conservatism could reveal itself to be a natural and powerful opponent of economic liberalism, for it is the only form of thought to break with the obsession over growth. . . . Conservatism constitutes an open door to another model of society, economically and ecologically more reasonable.

The proximity of conservatism and liberalism also risks preventing any frontal assault by the former on the oligarchy, the ruling class today won over to the principles of liberal anthro-

---

[12] Frédéric Saint-Clair, *La refondation de la droite* [*Refounding the Right*] (Paris: Salvator, 2017).

pology, while this latter bears essential responsibility for the destabilization and decline of contemporary society, and it is only by opposing it that nations can hope to preserve their identity and regain control of sociability. Moreover, it is no accident that the popular classes today are the most conservative, since they observe that the neoliberal elites are the most contemptuous of national identity and are undoing the social contract from the top.

Above we wrote: "Conservative, yes, but in order to conserve what?" Let us pose the question in a more radical form: In contemporary society, is there anything that really deserves to be conserved? And if there are good reasons for doubt, why not try to reconcile the terms "conservation" and "revolution"? In the 1920s and '30s, the German Conservative Revolution was the work of a constellation of young conservative authors who thought only a revolution could still save what deserved to be conserved. A not necessarily similar but analogous procedure is today characteristic of the ecologists who observe that only a complete break with capitalism, the myth of growth, and the logic of profit can allow the preservation of ecosystems that represent the systemic condition of life on earth.

"There is nothing more antipathetic to the conservative spirit than the revolutionary spirit," said Russell Kirk. In certain cases, however, conservatives must overcome their allergy to "revolution," without which they will lock themselves into a role as collaborators with a system they otherwise freely criticize. Such an attitude can also take the form of a rejection of extremes that risks limiting conservatives to play the role of those "moderates" so valued by the bourgeoisie and of which Abel Bonnard was once able to make such a pitiless critique. This is exactly what Olivier Ray recently observed:

The existing "system" is not what is preserving the legacy of the past, but what is liquidating it on an unprecedented scale and at an ever-faster pace. This forces authentic conservatives to question the entirety of the system, taking on a revolutionary appearance. In spite of themselves, they are forced to preach change.[13]

Other authors have not hesitated to speak of an emancipatory conservatism, i.e., one that, far from preaching a return to the past, would consist rather in a dynamic reappropriation of what we have transmitted (starting with the organic forms of solidarity destroyed by the rise of modernity) with a view to the creation of new forms of autonomy. In other words: taking inspiration from those who began to implement a new beginning before we did.

There is in fact a "Left-wing" conservatism whose great names are George Orwell, Christopher Lasch, Jean-Claude Michéa, Ivan Illich, Günther Anders, and Pier Paolo Pasolini. All of them emphasize, from a democratic perspective, the advantages of an organic society based on solidarity, mutual assistance, and gratuity. Michel Onfray writes: "If we must have labels, let's say that I am a conservative anarchist." George Orwell, described as a "Tory anarchist" by Jean-Claude Michéa, said nothing different.

Maxime Ouellet and Eric Martin, both professors in Quebec, presented themselves for a time as "Left-wing conservatives" before laying claim to "emancipatory antimodernism." Their basic idea is that there necessarily exists a "conservative moment" within any critical theory, a moment that consists in reconstituting the concrete conditions of the possibility of liberty. As Maxime Ouellet writes:

> Only a dialectical return to the past allows us to de-reify social relations. . . . The revolution cannot arrive if we conceive it from the start as a *tabula rasa*. . . . Social emancipation does not mean disengaging or undoing all the ties of belonging imposed on us by tradition, but rather breaking the Weberian iron cage of capitalist categories, viz., labor, commodity, and value. . . . The common is not possible

---

[13] Interview in *Le Figaro*, April 15–16, 2017. Cited by Christophe Geffroy, "Un renouveau du conservatisme ?" ["A Revival of Conservatism?"] *La Nef*, June 2017, 19.

without institutions that direct *a priori* the use and activity
of distributing that which is in common. . . . A politics of
the common is part of a philosophy of autonomy understood as the capacity for self-limitation.[14]

From this point of view, traditions are not necessarily alienating. Reappropriating them in a dialectical manner can help us
liberate ourselves from the new forms of alienation engendered
by modernity: there are bonds that liberate.

The ambiguities of conservatism obviously weigh upon the
domain of politics. Consider, e.g., "buissonist" politics (proposed by Patrick Buisson). In principle, it is seductive: to unite
conservatives and populists is in fact a worthy goal — and may
also be the key to power — but how are we to understand it? At
the level of political parties, it is hard to see what could erase or
overcome the boundary separating the Front National from the
Républicains, however tenuous it may appear to some. Things
certainly might change in the future: a great conservative
populist party might see the light of day, especially if we continue to see the decline of the middle classes. In the presidential
elections of 2017, however, Fillon was not able to win over the
working class, while Marine Le Pen did not succeed in rallying
the conservatives to her side.

If from a strictly sociological point of view it is a matter of
rallying the popular classes and the declining middle classes
around a few simple but fundamental concerns they share:
identity, historical and cultural continuity, the need for reference points, or even a taste for authority . . . then there is nothing to criticize.

But a blind spot remains: the economic and social domain.
Can the interests of the people and the bourgeoisie, those who
are suffering the most from the neoliberal consensus and those
who ultimately profit from it, be reconciled? Or just how far?

---

[14] Maxime Ouellet, *La révolution culturelle du capital. Le capitalisme
cybernétique dans la société globale de l'information* [*The Cultural Revolution of Capital: Cybernetic Capitalism in the Global Information Society*]
(Montreal: Ecosociété, 2016), 303–15.

And when will they cease to be reconcilable? A thorough debate might enable us to see more clearly into these matters. But as everyone knows, doctrinal vagueness (aided by a lack of education) is the norm in Right-wing parties. For now, calling for "ideological clarification" is like talking about astrophysics with toads.

At a time when economic and social liberalism are tending to fuse in the form of a globalized anti-populist bloc, a renewed conservatism quite possibly has a future. But it must cease to be mistakable for liberalism without falling back into the restorationist rut.

INSECURITY FOR EVERYONE
LABOR IN THE TIME OF "SUPERFLUOUS MEN"

"Life, health, love are all precarious, why should labor
escape that law?"

— Laurence Parisot

The greatest mistake one could make concerning labor is
considering it an intemporal object that always has the same
nature in different forms, plays the same role, and responds to
the same motives. To reduce socio-historic diversity to an essence or a formal unity is the best way not to understand what
one claims to be analyzing. Another mistake is to give too extensive a definition of it, as if any form of metabolic relation in
nature or, more simply, any activity were a form of "labor."

The great religions have already influenced how labor is
seen. Judaism does not devalue labor. Islam makes it into a sacred value. On the contrary, in ancient European societies, labor was seen as degrading (it arises from a painful necessity
contrary to freedom). Over the course of its history, the church
has continually oscillated between the exaltation of poverty
and the condemnation of "idleness," anathematizing usury and
legitimizing productive value. It was in the monasteries that
"labor value" was first recognized, as a complement of prayer
and contemplation. In *La religion industrielle*,[1] Pierre Musso describes the monastery as the ancestor of the workshop, then of
the factory, a shorthand with a certain real basis.

But it was only with the first liberal economists, starting
with Adam Smith, that labor was considered the source of
wealth, and even as the only true human activity. It was with
modernity that labor came to occupy a central place in economic logic and became an end in itself, an idea totally foreign to

---

[1] Pierre Musso, *La religion industrielle* [*The Industrial Religion*] (Paris: Fayard, 2017).

traditional societies, in which the economy was "embedded"
(Karl Polanyi) within society and had not yet been made into a
dominant function. In these societies where the economy occupied only a subordinate place, three things could not be traded
on the market: labor, land, and money. One of the great characteristics of capitalism, on the other hand, was seeing in labor
merely a competitive commodity that should be bought for the
lowest possible price in order to increase the share of added
value (surplus value) coming back to the employer, while assuring that people will spend what they have been allowed to
earn on consumption.

It is too often forgotten: capitalism is not merely capital but
also paid employment. It is not only the system of bourgeois
origin that seeks to transform money into ever more money; it
is not only the system based on the fiction of a self-regulating
market; it is not only the system aiming at unlimited profit and
working to eliminate every limit standing in the way of the development of capital and preaching the commercialization of
all forms of human activity — it is also the system founded on
labor power, the basis of capital development, and the transformation of concrete labor into abstract labor, a concomitant of
the transformation of use value into exchange value. Labor in
the modern sense is a capitalist category.

Labor has gradually become confused with paid employment. This was a silent revolution, but an enormous change.
Previously one had a trade; now one looks for a job. A trade
and employment are not the same thing. With a trade, you see
what you are creating and often consume what you make. It is
a form of autonomy. With a job you are employed; it is a form
of dependence, of dispossession; and you consume only what
others have created. Speaking historically, the universalization
of paid employment that began at the end of the nineteenth
century with the rise of industrial society and manufacturing,
ran up against strong resistance now generally forgotten, especially in the rural world that is now disappearing.

In the salary relation, the laborer sells his labor power for a
salary. This labor power is a commodity with a determinate
value. Any commodity has the double character of a use value

and an exchange value. Use value is concrete and singular, exchange value universal and abstract. Each is a product of a different type of labor. The labor that produces exchange value is "abstract labor," i.e., labor made homogeneous because the market has determined it as socially necessary for production. It consists in the reduction of different kinds of labor to their quantity measured in mathematical time, itself abstract. That this abstract labor can become autonomous is due to money, which reduces every quality to a pure quantity. Money measures the value added ("surplus value"), which the employer draws from the exploitation of labor power, which allows him to produce himself *qua* value. The transubstantiation of labor into money, then of money into capital, yields the self-valorization of value. As Jean Vioulac writes, "The fundamental characteristic of capitalist exploitation is not to extort goods from the laborer, but only value, i.e., to force human labor to produce an abstract universal."

The genesis of the salary relation went hand-in-hand with the dissolution of previous forms of sociality and with the appearance of individuals in the modern sense of the term, i.e., men unbound from their traditional relations of belonging and solidarity. The emergence of the market where one can sell and buy in exchange for the salary on one's labor power implies both the destruction of old social forms and the separation of the laborer from the means of production. Marx says, moreover, that the labor contract has the same presuppositions as the social contract. In the end, the entire diversity of human activity is reduced to a single abstract category, just as all values are reduced to commercial value.

The Left has sought to liberate labor, less often to liberate itself from it. It reduces capitalism to a system of exploitation without questioning the principle of paid employment or asking about the desirability of labor itself. It has not perceived that labor is more alienating than alienated. Finally, it has appropriated the idea that labor is a necessity, an unfortunate fatality (Paul: "If someone does not want to labor, let him also not eat." 2 Timothy 3:10), thus accelerating the establishment of a labor society.

Today we do not see the "end of labor" predicted in the 1930s
by John Maynard Keynes, and more recently by Jeremy Rifkin,
but rather its radical transformation within a context of crisis.

The principal contradiction capitalism runs into today is directly tied to the development of productivity — which was
originally measured by the ratio between the number or volume of objects produced and the labor necessary to do so. The
contradiction is as follows: on the one hand, capital permanently seeks productivity gains allowing it to stand up to competition, which involves the suppression of jobs and an overall
diminution of labor time; on the other, it posits labor time as
the only source and only measure of value. The contradiction
arises when the gains in productivity result in the abolition of
jobs, whereas it is precisely the form "job" that allowed labor to
become the motor of capital expansion.

In the past, this contradiction was disguised by increased
production and the extension of the market, compensating for
the diminution in the expense of labor power. The explosion of
international trade, competition between laborers all over the
world, and debt have thus helped postpone the day of reckoning. But today productivity gains have become so large that the
innovation of manufacturing procedures is running faster than
the innovation of products. With the digital revolution, the
production of wealth is increasingly becoming uncoupled from
human labor power, and for the first time we are doing away
with labor faster than it can be reabsorbed by the extension of
the market. In this way, capitalism is running into an "absolute
historic limit."[2]

It is because there is an intrinsic limit to real valorization
that we have entered an economy of speculation and financial
bubbles over the past twenty years. But it would still be a mistake to think "bad" financial capitalism has killed off "good"
industrial capitalism: it was because the latter no longer offered
enough resources, and because capital-money could no longer
be reinvested profitably in the real economy, that people had to

---

[2] Groupe Krisis, *Manifeste contre le travail* [*Manifesto Against Work*]
(Paris: Léo Scheer, 2002).

turn to speculation on the financial markets. The contradiction between the contemporary labor market and the real production of surplus value threatens the capitalist system today not only with declining profit rates, but with a generalized devaluing of value.

Concretely, ever more commodities are produced, while the quantity of labor necessary to produce them constantly diminishes, which involves a rise in unemployment and a lowering of salaries (and thus of demand). So there are ever more objects produced and ever fewer consumers to buy them. The consequences are that the popular classes sink into poverty and people fall out of the middle classes, while we see a fundamentally predatory and growing appropriation of public and private rent. As Christophe Grand writes: "Technological replacement is at the heart of the contemporary class struggle, because the elites who possess capital seek to benefit from productivity in order to enrich themselves without having to share."[3] An ever-increasing fraction of the population is represented by "superfluous men," with all the consequences this will necessarily have.

In the coming years, this phenomenon will strengthen thanks to the progress of robotics and artificial intelligence (AI).

Automation, today increasingly replaced by robotics, has been developing for a long time, especially in order to carry out excessively repetitive tasks. This movement is accelerating, but while doing so its nature is changing as well. It is already the aim of computer science to automate intellectual operations. Artificial intelligence (AI), which will gain decisive importance in the coming years, can in no sense be reduced to the material objects we have always known. It contributes in an abstract way to the commercialization of existence and the traceability of agents thanks to the algorithmic organization of an ever-larger number of sectors. Now, we are moving toward a general

---

[3] Christophe Grand, "L'avènement de la société de prédation, conséquence du remplacement de l'homme par la machine" ["The Advent of the Predatory Society, Consequence of the Replacement of Man by Machine"], www.journaldumauss.net, March 7, 2015, 1.

expansion of robotics, with driverless public transportation (this has already begun for cars and busses), cashierless points-of-sale, surgical positions, labor overseers, even policemen and soldiers—to say nothing of 3D printing, which is already "printing" houses and will soon permit the fabrication of bodily organs.

Already in 2013, two researchers at the University of Oxford, Carl Benedikt Frey and Michael A. Osborne, estimated that 47% of US jobs are threatened with disappearance.[4] In Europe, one third of jobs are also destined to disappear over the next twenty years thanks to the expansion of robotics, computing, and artificial intelligence. Mass industrialization provoked the emergence of the laboring class and the proletariat; roboticization appears to be provoking the emergence of a non-laboring population.[5]

The classical liberal argument is that there is nothing new about this, that technical progress has always destroyed jobs but that it creates others (Schumpeter's "creative destruction"). They cite the revolt of the Lyonnais silk laborers against looms, the English Luddites, or the Silesian weavers of 1844. They also remind us how tertiary sector jobs replaced those of the primary and secondary sectors. But this is to forget that today not all jobs can find substitutes, that ever fewer can, given the importance of knowledge and the unequal distribution of cognitive capacities. In the past, a peasant could become a laborer without any great problem. But a construction laborer will have much more trouble converting himself into a computer scientist. This is why robotics is now destroying more jobs than it is creating.

But it is also to forget that we have left the age when machines made things *as well as* men do, and entered an age when

---

[4] Carl Benedikt Frey and Michael A. Osborne, "The Future of Unemployment," *Technological Forecasting and Social Change*, 114, January 2017, 254–80.

[5] This is the thesis developed by the historian Yuval Noah Harari in a recent book *Homo Deus: A Brief History of Tomorrow* (London: Vintage, 2017), which has already been translated all over the world.

machines make things *much better*. This changes everything, because it means that machines can compete with functions no longer merely manual, which poses the problem of decision: the machine is in a better position to decide, since it can deal with the information at its disposal better than a human.

It is easy to reassure us by saying that there will always be areas where men cannot be replaced by machines. But the list of domains in which non-organic algorithms are supposed to perform less well than men is getting constantly shorter. For now, there remain above all jobs requiring extensive social interactions, like personal care or ordinary medicine. But personal services (of the rich by the poor), today on the rise, are themselves weak producers of value. How will it be when machines can decide for themselves, and not only reprogram and repair themselves, but mutually manufacture one another, i.e., reproduce, using a language man no longer understands?

In today's society, the centrality of labor is obvious. Although it is a purely contractual relation demanding individuals free of any attachment (in liberal teaching everything should be able to be bought, sold, or rented), labor remains a social form of mediation, a means of socialization, a substitute for the social bond, even as it confers a status. Unemployment is felt as "shameful" because it is a form of exclusion, which causes the only way men can still participate in society to disappear. This is why, as Dominique Méda remarks, "There is a strong correlation between unemployment rates and the importance accorded labor."[6] Let us add that labor, having become a collective fetish, can also be a way to escape the moral panic evoked by the spiritual emptiness of the present world, even if this is increasingly difficult today.

Faced with the rise in unemployment now become structural (and no longer simply a matter of the business cycle), the great tendency today — along with the replacement of productive activities by useless jobs, jobs that are ultimately a matter

---

[6] Dominique Méda, *Travail: la révolution nécessaire* [*Work: The Necessary Revolution*] (La Tour-d'Aigues: L'Aube, 2010).

of social control, designed to nip any tendencies to revolt in the bud — is to try to reduce unemployment by increasing insecurity. This is the application of a liberal principle: "A bad job is better than no job at all." Hence the idea of "flexi-security," which must be understood as: flexibility right away, and we'll see about security later on. The term is in fact an oxymoron, like "permanent development." Thus, one creates pointless jobs, "bullshit jobs" (in David Graeber's words), and laborers with no resources, i.e., people with employment but who do not have anything to live on. Unemployment goes down, but poverty spreads, while at the top of the skyscraper, wealth derived from money creation, financial speculation, and social predation accumulates.

A job associated with a very low salary or of short duration, one that does not offer any guarantee of attaining or maintaining an acceptable standard of living, is known as a precarious job. Precariousness is opposed to durability, stability, security. It manifests itself at the level of labor contracts as well as labor conditions and schedules (with part-time labor becoming more common). It can also be the result of restructuring due to the search for lower labor costs (lay-offs, social plans, relocations). The increased precariousness of labor tends to eliminate the sorts of protection formerly gained through social struggle. A result of the absolute primacy of profitability, combining present instability with future unpredictability, it engenders universal competition and the struggle of all against all.

Temporary labor, subcontracting, internships, or fixed-term contracts are by definition more precarious than open-ended contracts. In France, for now, open-ended contracts remain in the majority, but the percentage of fixed-term contracts continues to grow, and full-time and open-ended employment are no longer the "normal" form of labor. In March 2000, more than one paid job in ten was already fixed-term. Already between 1990 and 2000 there was recorded a 60% rise in fixed-term labor, 13% in temporary labor, and 65% in subsidized contracts. Since then, the shift has accelerated. In 2005, precarious forms of employment represented nearly one quarter of the total. At the moment, 87% of first hires involve contracts of less than three months. Turnover is also exploding: we have gone from 38 acts of hiring and firing for every 100 positions in a company in 1982 to 177 in 2011. At the same time the share of fixed-term employment has nearly tripled, going from 5% to 13%, while average duration has been cut by two-thirds. At the beginning of the 1980s, half of those with fixed-term contracts or interim labor or internships went on to permanent employment the next year. Today, barely over one fifth follow the same path. So unstable jobs are less often playing the role of trampolines for jumping into stable employment. The main victims of this precariousness are the young and those with low qualifications.[7]

This rise in precariousness led in England to the increase in the laboring poor (more than 1.4 million today), and in Germany since the Hartz reforms to "minijobs" (450 Euros without contributions or social benefits) which in 2013 involved some seven million laborers, about 20% of the active German population.

The consequences of precariousness are not simply economic and financial but also psychological and social. First, there is the desocialization factor. As uncertainty about the future increases, the old points of reference become unclear. As competition becomes harsher, all other members of society are seen as adversaries or rivals. There are also consequences for health: in a precarious situation, one does not have the means to get medical treatment. But it is above all labor's loss of meaning that is a source of misery. Many studies demonstrate the moral suffering of salaried laborers when their labor appears useless or absurd to them, i.e., "without qualities" (Richard Sennett). Dostoevsky said: "If you want to reduce a man to nothingness, it is enough to give his labor a character of complete uselessness, even absurdity." In Great Britain, more than a third of the population considers its own labor meaningless. In France, one third of inhabitants would like to switch jobs, and 32% say they

---

[7] Cf. Serge Paugam, *Le salaire de la précarité* [*The Wages of Precariousness*] (Paris: PUF, 2000).

are tempted by a manual trade or handicraft.[8]

A precarious laborer, especially if he is in debt, will not take the risk of engaging in social protest or any action of solidarity. He will be less inclined to activity in a labor union, more vulnerable to the demands of productivity, but also to employment blackmail (which might force him, e.g., to accept a cut in salary to avoid having his company move). He can be more easily subjected to constraints of every sort, beginning with time constraints that place him in a permanent state of urgency. When he has less assurance as to his future, forced to live from day to day, he will find himself called upon to engage more intensely with his labor.

This is why offering precarious employment has become an economic strategy for employers, who figure on increased competitiveness and an ability to adjust more rapidly to changes in economic circumstances. MEDEF's[9] constantly-repeated refrain is well-known: the more easily one can fire, the less hesitantly one can hire. So how do we explain that precariousness has constantly progressed in tandem with unemployment?

Bertrand Russell wrote in 1932: "Modern production methods have made comfort and security possible for everyone: instead, we have chosen abundance for some and famine for others." One of the paradoxes of modern labor is in fact that we are producing ever more goods and services with ever fewer men, but that those who labor must do so all the more. As Juliet Schor saw at the beginning of the 1990s,[10] labor is continually becoming more intense within businesses now able to capture "performance measures" for the evaluation of all employees in real time. Jobs are eliminated, but those who still have one

---

[8] *Cf.* Jean-Laurent Cassely, *La révolte des premiers de la classe. Métiers à la con, quête de sens et reconversion urbaines* [*The Revolt of the Top of the Class: Dumb Jobs, the Quest for Meaning, and Urban Reconversion*] (Paris: Arkhè, 2017).

[9] The MEDEF (Mouvement des entreprises de France [Movement of the Enterprises of France]) is the largest employer federation in France. — Trans.

[10] Juliet Schor, *The Overworked American: The Unexpected Decline of Leisure* (New York: Basic Books, 1992).

must work harder and more productively. We never worked so hard before work became unnecessary. This does not prevent employers from repeating that the French "do not work hard enough" while, contrary to what many imagine, they work longer hours than the Germans, Dutch, Scandinavians, and Americans. Work-related suicides are getting more common, and France shares with Japan the world record for cases of burn out.

David Graeber has shown that the ideology of debt and the ideology of labor mutually support one another, since monetary creation through debt involves harder work to pay off the debt, while because of unemployment, individuals and households are forced to go into debt to maintain their standard of living.[11] This debt is the cause of their growing docility (one is afraid to lose one's job, afraid of not being able to pay one's debts), a reflection of their vulnerability. Hence the ambivalence of feeling: people want a job at any price, but they also want to see the place work occupies in their lives reduced.

The promise of "independent labor" (the "Uberization" of society) is deceptive as well, for precariousness is the rule there even more than among salaried laborers. In the post-industrial world, which privileges knowledge more than machines, everyone is invited to "become his own company" (to be "an entrepreneur of himself") in order to make the best use of his intangible assets, with salaried laborers free to become "slashers,"[12] multitasking workers running from one activity to another, seeking out new clients while improvising as amateur lawyers or accountants on the side. "Uberization" is merely a new name for the parceling out and atomization of labor. Precariousness becomes the rule, for the results aimed at are within an ever-shorter time horizon. More than ever, we are losing our lives trying to earn a living.

---

[11] David Graeber, *Debt: The First 5000 Years* (Brooklyn: Melville House, 2011). *Cf.* by the same author *The Utopia of Rules: On Technology, Stupidity, and the Secret Joys of Bureaucracy* (Brooklyn: Melville House, 2015).

[12] An athlete who is quick and agile. — Trans.

On the pretext of "flexibility," we seek men who can be drafted to work and taxed at will, who must constantly adapt to the demands of an economy whose servants, if not slaves, they are expected to be. The generalization of precariousness represents the emergence of the replaceable, interchangeable, flexible, mobile, disposable man. It is the complete reduction of the person to his labor power, i.e., to a certain part of himself that can be treated as a commodity. It is submission to the imperative of profitability, the sale of oneself extending to all aspects of existence. Philippe Simonnot has wittily written: "Slavery has found in paid employment a legal covering that renders it compatible with the rights of man." It will get even better tomorrow thanks to robotics: robots never get sick, they can work unceasingly, and they have no labor unions. A dream come true!

CRITIQUE OF VALUE

In his 1947 *Letter on Humanism,* Heidegger stated that he saw in the philosophy of Karl Marx "the most profound" thought of our time. Profound means complex, and the complexity of Marxian thought hardly needs to be demonstrated, as witnessed by the diversity of intellectual currents that have claimed the label. The results have been so unconvincing that Michel Henry was able to define Marxism as "the totality of misinterpretations that have been made of the thought of Marx."

It was precisely as a reaction against its original anticapitalism and against the positions of a now archaic "traditional" or "orthodox Marxism" that critical value theory (*Wertkritik*) was formulated beginning around 2000, a movement that offers an original and instructive angle of approach to Marx's thought. The school formed in Germany around the journals *Krisis* and *Exit!* Its principal representatives have been Robert Kurz (1943–2012), Norbert Trenkle, Roswitha Scholz, and Claus Peter Ortlieb in Germany, Jean-Marie Vincent (1934–2004) and Anselm Jappe in France, and Moishe Postone (1942–2018) in the US. Knowledgeable of the Frankfurt School (Adorno and Horkheimer, as well as Marcuse), all of them have done plenty of reading in Karl Polanyi and Georg Lukács, but they appeal especially to Isaac I. Roubine (*Essays on Marx's Theory of Value,* 1924) and Alfred Sohn-Reithel (*La pensée-marchandise* [*Thought as a Commodity*]), also making references to André Gorz, Guy Debord, and Jean Baudrillard.

Robert Kurz distinguishes between the "exoteric Marx" and the "esoteric Marx." What are we to understand by this? The answer is simple. The exoteric Marx, the best known, is the Marx who theorized the class struggle, that of the *Communist Manifesto* and the *1844 Manuscripts*; the esoteric Marx is that of *Capital* and the *Grundrisse,* the mature Marx. The former limits himself to criticizing capital from labor's point of view, making the class struggle the engine of history. The second emphasizes the forms of social life historically specific to capitalism: commodity, labor, value, money.

"Traditional Marxism" has generally kept to exoteric Marxism, i.e., to class relations reduced to the exploitation of surplus value, socialism being defined by collective property in the means of production. This is a sterile conception for a number of reasons. First, because the Soviet system has collapsed after achieving the results everyone knows. Second, because today we have entered into a post-proletarian period, that of a deterritorialized speculative capitalism in which the working class has lost its importance, where producers have been transformed into consumers (which has allowed them to be integrated into the system), while forms of social identity not based on class membership assert themselves ever more vigorously.

The esoteric Marx does not limit himself to analyzing the opposition between capital and labor but deals with commodities and the fetishistic character of commodity production, abstract labor, the distinction between value and wealth, and the nature of capital as an "automatic subject." His critique does not stop at the level of class antagonism but goes much further.

The theoreticians of critical value theory concentrate on the first chapter of Marx's *Capital*, the one Althusser strongly recommended not reading because it was both too "Hegelian" and too "complicated" ("One gets bogged down there and gives up, " *L'Humanité*, March 21, 1969).

In the *1844 Manuscripts* Marx had already blamed liberalism for seeking to replace old forms of power and dependence with a new form of abstract domination imposed on supposedly "free and equal" individuals (i.e., unbound from any traditional relations of interdependence preventing their alienation) by means of the law of value, this law taking the form of an objective constraint. In *Capital*, Marx developed this idea systematically, taking an interest in the content of production and no longer merely its distribution. He gradually abandons his universal theory of labor and the ahistorical centrality of the class struggle, and instead devotes himself to uncovering the specificity of the capitalist system, which is no longer regarded simply as one "stage" among others in the history of modes of production. He understands that the essence of capital finds its origin in a historically specific practice proper to the modern

West, which is the practice of labor, and that capitalism is based on fetishized social relations going well beyond the mere class struggle.

This is exactly what critical value theory also affirms. It claims that Marx's theses, far from having universal transhistoric validity, are historically relative to modern capitalist society, and that the heart of Marxian thought is what allows us to understand — beyond classic problems of domination — the "social construction of capitalism." There follows a general redefinition of capitalism, which is henceforth no longer defined by mere exploitation (in which case it would not differ fundamentally from the systems that preceded it). What is proper to capitalism is not the appearance of a new politico-economic class, but the emergence of a society entirely mediated by new categories.

Marx writes: "My departure point is the simplest social form that the product of labor takes in contemporary society: the commodity" (*Critical notes on Adolph Wagner's Treatise of Political Economy*). Elsewhere he says the commodity is an object full of "metaphysical subtleties and theological hair-splitting." What characterizes form-commodity as analyzed by Marx is that it is constituted by labor, that it exists in an objectivized form (it represents a social-historical imagination constitutive of certain social practices), and that it has a dual nature.

Every commodity has both a use value and an exchange value: on the one hand, it is a concrete object with its own qualities, on the other a purely quantitative and abstract value-object. This distinction is not new, since it goes back at least to Aristotle. But it takes on a new meaning in the modern world: value, formerly more important, is effaced in favor of exchange value. The novelty of capitalism is the way it privileges exchange over mere production, the generalization of exchange having been made possible by man's gradual separation from his own means of existence, subsistence, and production.

Exchange value, i.e., the value a thing acquires when it is exchanged, is defined by a pure universal and abstract quantity, something that allows it to be expressed by a price. It is a value without any relation to its particular objective qualities, which are incommensurable, a value as such that only relates to the quantity of money corresponding to its price. "To produce directly for the market is to produce for a domain of equivalence where everything is as good as everything else" (Jean Vioulac). Capitalism's goal is to pass through the domain of commerce everything that previously escaped it. In the capitalist world where almost no one works to satisfy his own needs, everything without use value for its possessor, but only exchange value, is a commodity. Now the very concept of exchange presupposes the equivalence of all things. More exactly, the exchange of different things implies they can all be reduced to a "neutral" universal equivalent: money. It is in this sense that Marx could write: "Money itself has become the community and cannot tolerate any other community superior to it."

The essence of what a commodity is worth is its capacity to be exchanged even before the exchange occurs. So it presupposes the existence of capital, i.e., that capitalist social relations have become dominant. Whereas use value does not express the social value of production (being a commodity is a matter of indifference to it), exchange value is a mode of socialization that imposes its own structure on a whole society. A commodity *has* value by its material form and its use value, but it *is* a value by its exchange value, which makes it into a social form of mediation. Form-commodity can thus be defined as a structuring social relation specific to capitalist social formation, a specific form of social practice and social relations.

Commodity "fetishism," described by Marx as a "new secular religion" (he is comparing the relation of individuals to commodities with the attitude of "primitive" societies to fetishes), is in no way defined as an immoderate appetite for commodities, nor is it a mere mystification, but results from the automatic, anonymous, and impersonal character of a system in which social relations are only possible by means of commodities and where everyone must submit to the law of the market. Commodity fetishism resides mainly in attributing a natural character to capitalist categories (labor, commodity), endowing objects which are only ever human products with an autonomous, impersonal life, and in an inversion of the subject-object relation, the reification of persons dominated by the objects they produce: under the effect of norms internalized by the reign of value, relations between men are increasingly calqued upon relations of things or objects. Commodity fetishism is expressed by a reversal of the relation between man and his own products: henceforth, things direct men.

This form of abstract domination analyzed by Marx absolutely cannot be understood in simple terms of class domination. "Commodity" and "capital" constitute in fact a dynamic system of a peculiar kind that increasingly determines the aims and means of human activity, even when it has no determinate proprietor.

But what then is to be understood by "value?" Value is entirely different from material wealth (it is precisely liberalism's error to confuse them). Nor can it be reduced to "labor-value" as we frequently find in "Marxism," which makes labor the only source of wealth. Marx in fact distinguishes clearly between wealth, corresponding to the quantity of goods produced, and value, constituted by the human labor time socially necessary to its production. The growth of material wealth can very well coexist with a lessening of value. Value, which constitutes the dominant form of wealth in the capitalist system, is in reality a "self-mediating" form of wealth. At the same time, it constitutes the social form commodities take in exchange and allows all commodities to be made equivalent with one another; in other words, it is an alienated social relation. Marx's great merit, as Costanzo Preve remarked, is to have grafted the qualitative category of alienation (*Entfremdung*) onto the quantitative category of value (*Wert*).

Marx defines capitalism as the system based on the "self-valorization of value," which distinguishes it from all preceding systems. Capital in fact can only accumulate by a movement toward autonomization and the self-valorization of value. This movement corresponds to a process without any subject, and this is why it is vain to try to identify those responsible for it (its hidden masters). Similarly, "surplus value" cannot be reduced to a mere surplus produced by workers for the benefit of their boss, but represents an accelerated form of artificial growth that forms part of the limitlessness of capital.

The scheme A-M-A', where A refers to money, M to the commodity, and A' to the surplus money obtained by the exchange—the profit being greater insofar as the difference between A and A' grows—is a summary of how capital valorizes itself. A certain quantity of value (capital) buys commodities in order to produce itself, thus increasing its own quantity by means of surplus value. The commodity becomes the mediator of money, whereas formerly it was the other way around: value is both the point of departure and the point of arrival. The production of commodities is no more than a means for getting ever more money. Commodities transform the world to make money return to itself in ever-increasing proportions.

From this we understand that the goal of capitalism is not to satisfy needs but, by satisfying them, to develop exchange so that any sum of money ends up being transformed into a larger sum. The essence of capitalism is the way it seeks to transform human energy into money so that this money produces ever more money. This involves making money an end in itself (Marx's "money *qua* money"), at the risk of arriving at a contradiction, since the unlimited supply of commodities always meets with a limited effective demand. In this case we see a crisis of valorization, with capital no longer valorizable finding a natural refuge in speculation.

Let us now see how things stand with labor. Critical value theory (to which we owe a famous *Manifesto Against Labor*) refuses to consider labor as an eternal and universal category, as the young Marx still believed it to be. Like commodities, modern labor, radically different from mere traditional activity, has characteristics proper to it. Capitalist society is in fact the only society to have made wage work the only mode of interaction between its members. In it, social relations are constituted by labor, which is not the case in other societies. The key idea is that with capitalism, labor ceases to be a mediation of the interactions between man and nature to become a historically specific form of objectivizing social activity. It stops being a means and becomes, as a productive activity, an end in itself that allows capital to form and accumulate.

As Denis Collin notes, "the commodity-form must not be

conceived as a transhistoric form. One must start from its full development in the capitalist mode of production to grasp its essence." The same goes for labor or time. It is only in capitalism that the function of labor is to obtain products taking the form of commodities. It is in this respect that "capitalism marks a qualitative break with all other historical forms of social life" (Moishe Postone).

Labor itself has a double character: concrete and abstract. Concrete labor creates use-value; abstract labor creates exchange value. These are not two different kinds of labor (and abstract labor is not "immaterial" labor either), but two different aspects of all labor. In the capitalist system, labor doubles: all labor is both concrete and abstract. To these two forms of labor correspond two forms of social wealth: material wealth and value. The former depends on the goods concretely produced and possessed, but only the latter, representing the objectification of abstract labor, constitutes a self-mediating form of social relations.

Abstract labor can only be quantitatively evaluated because it involves uniform homogeneous time indifferent to particularities and individuals. (It is for this reason that the bourgeoisie has never ceased domesticating time). Labor is called "abstract" when the concrete or specific qualities of a given activity are no longer considered, but it is approached only from the perspective of valorizing labor as measured by abstract quantity and reified by the time socially necessary for its realization.

So abstract labor has a historically specific social function: it mediates a new form of interdependence or social mediation of which capital and commodities are the product. In a society where the commodity is the fundamental structuring category of the whole, explains Moishe Postone, labor and its products are not socially distributed by means of traditional power relations:

On the contrary, it is labor itself which replaces this relation by serving as a quasi-objective means by which one acquires the products of others. A new form of interdependence emerges where no one consumes what he produces, but where everyone produces and exchanges commodities to acquire new ones which are the product of others. By thus serving as a means, labor and its products fulfill the function formerly carried out by obviously social relations.

But the role played by labor in capitalist society runs into a decisive contradiction resulting from capitalism's need to expend ever more labor power on the production of commodities in order to guarantee the valorization of capital—whereas, conversely, it finds itself obliged (in order to stand up to competition) constantly to improve productivity, which involves producing ever more commodities per unit of time, and therefore constantly reducing the labor time necessary for this production, going so far as to render the labor superfluous: structural unemployment develops and the number of "superfluous men" increases. As Claus Peter Ortlieb writes: "Capital relies on the exploitation of labor, but at the same time it gradually expels labor from the process of production, thus destroying its own basis." In other words, productivity augments wealth but not value (especially since the machines that replace labor do not themselves produce value). Hence the tendency for profit rates to sink, as recognized recently by the liberal economist Patrick Artus of the bank Natixis.

It is this contradiction (considering the expenditure of human energy as an end in itself while trying to make labor increasingly superfluous; trying to produce ever more with ever less labor time while continuing to make labor time the basis of value) that explains why our enormous gains in productivity have never resulted in any significant reduction in working hours, nor in an increasing level of overall affluence. The capitalist dynamic thus saps the foundation on which capitalism rests. Today's financial crises are less the result of speculation or debt than of a fundamental structural crisis of the valorization of capital.

So critical value theory does not hesitate to forecast the exhaustion of capitalism, which is currently attaining its objective limits even as it takes over all social reproduction. Capitalism is destroying itself because it has itself created the basis for the devalorization of value and because the quantity of superfluous labor has now passed the quantity of labor created by the extension of the markets.

For the classic critique of capitalist society from labor's point of view, critical value theory has proposed substituting a critique of labor (and of the centrality of labor) as a specific invention of capitalism. As Robert Kurz writes: "To criticize capitalism from labor's point of view is a logical impossibility, because one cannot criticize capitalism from the point of view of its own substance." Labor under capitalism is not an activity exterior to the system and opposed to capital and that must be "liberated," but a foundation of capitalism, a form of social activity that must be abolished. Capital is not opposed to labor, for it is nothing but accumulated labor. The struggle between capital and labor occurs within the capitalist system but does not allow us to leave it. All labor, in other words, is today alienated simply because it is labor. All objectification of human activity in modern labor constitutes a form of alienation.

By reducing capitalism to a system in which the wicked owners of the means of production limit themselves to exploiting workers by extorting surplus value from them in order to increase their profits, "traditional Marxism" misses the essential point. In reality, capitalism is a system where commodities reign and men merely carry out their logic under the abstract influence of value in motion. "All social groups are preformed by value and thus constituted in a capitalist fashion," emphasizes Robert Kurz. Workers and capitalists are merely the "accomplices of a process larger than either of them," and the class struggle, which is certainly real, is itself merely a contradiction within the mode of life common to both. The working class is a central element of capitalism, but it does not incarnate its antithesis, its negation. The subject of history is neither the proletariat nor humanity but labor, of which capital represents the objectivized form. Removed from the capitalists in order to be directed by the workers, industrial production would not change its nature because it represents the materialization not merely of productive forces but also of productive relations.

While it was Marx's ambition to make a universal critique of political economy, traditional Marxism limited itself to formulating an alternative political economy. The principal error of many "Marxists" is to have remained prisoners of a philosophy of progress that owes much more to capitalism than to socialism, and consequently of a sort of religion of production. Most "orthodox" Marxists never stopped believing in the liberating character of the growth of productive forces (this is why Soviet communism was never anything but a form of state capitalism). Their intention was not to escape productivism but to change the owners of the means of production while establishing a more "just" form of distribution. The same thing happened as regards labor: "traditional" Marxism wanted to break wage-slavery but never questioned the very principle of modern labor. In other words, it wanted to liberate labor but not liberate us from it.

Far from being in the least "conservative," capitalism is eminently revolutionary in the sense that it involves a permanent upheaval in social relations even as it constantly reconstitutes the identity underlying it: it ceaselessly encourages the new while always re-engendering the same. This tendency always to maximize exchanges does not result merely from the "greed" of property-owners, as maintained by a superficial critique ever on the lookout for scapegoats (bankers, speculators, etc.), but constitutes a tendency inherent in the capitalist system. What is alienating is not so much the ruling classes as a process with no subject: the self-movement of things created by themselves (the "automatic subject"). Capitalism involves limitlessness as a condition of its own survival. The result is a society where the totality of social life, based on an imagination of abstract and "fluid" equality, is subjected to a new form of heteronomy in which only capital is autonomous and where it is no exaggeration to say value replaces the social bond. As Moishe Postone concludes: "The dream contained in the form capital is that of absolute limitlessness, an idea of freedom as complete liberation as regards matter and nature. . . . Humanity can only awaken completely from that state of somnambulism by abolishing value."

To criticize the unequal division of wealth remains sterile as long as one does not question its substance, which is the abstract form of value. Any real critique of capitalism ought to center not merely on the exploitation of workers but on categories such as commodity, value, and labor. As Moishe Postone writes: "The struggle against capitalism is a struggle against men and value, and not between the proletariat and the bourgeoisie, labor and capital." The logic of capital extends to the totality of social groups. At that point, as Maxime Ouellet writes, "To emancipate society from capitalism means escaping the ontology of labor and value which drives individuals into a war of all against all and subjects them to the depersonalized domination of self-interested calculation."

Is this too radical or too abstract an analysis? A new utopia? As Hegel said: "One can measure the extent of a spirit's loss by that in which it finds satisfaction."

BIBLIOGRAPHY

The Krisis Group, *Manifesto Against Labour* (Paris: Lignes, 2002).

Robert Kurz, *Read Marx: The Most Important Texts of Karl Marx for the 21st Century* (2000).

_____. *Lire Marx* [*Read Marx*] (Paris: La Balustrade, 2002).

_____. *Avis aux naufragés. Chroniques du capitalisme mondialisé en crise* [*Notice to the Shipwrecked: Chronicles of Globalized Capitalism in Crisis*] (Paris: Lignes, 2005), a collection of articles in translation.

_____. *Vies et mort du capitalisme* [*Lives and Deaths of Capitalism*] (Paris: Lignes, 2011).

Anselm Jappe, *Les aventures de la marchandise. Pour une nouvelle critique de la valeur* [*The Adventures of Merchandise: For a New Critique of Value*] (Paris: Denoël, 2003).

_____. *Crédit à mort. La décomposition du capitalisme et ses critiques* [*Credit to Death: The Decomposition of Capitalism and its Critiques*] (Paris: Lignes, 2011).

_____. *La société autophage. Capitalisme, démesure et auto-destruction* [*The Autophagic Society: Capitalism, Excess, and Self-Destruction*] (Paris: La Découverte, 2017).

Serge Latouche and Anselm Jappe, *Pour en finir avec l'économie. Décroissance et critique de la valeur* [*To End the Economy: Degrowth and Critique of Value*] (Paris: Libre et solidaire, 2015).

Moishe Postone, *Marx est-il devenu muet?* [*Has Marx Become Mute?*] (La Tour-d'Aigues: L'Aube, 2003).

_____. *Temps, travail et domination sociale* [*Time, Work, and Social Domination*] (Paris: Mille et une nuits, 2009).

_____. *Critique du fétiche-capital* [*Critique of Fetish Capital*] (Paris: PUF, 2013).

Éric Martin and Maxime Ouellet, *La tyrannie de la valeur* [*The Tyranny of Value*] (Montreal: Écosociété, 2014).

Alfred Sohn-Rethel, *La pensée-marchandise* [*Thought as a Commodity*] (Bellecombe-en-Bauges: Éditions du Croquant, 2010).

Isaac I. Roubine, *Essays on Marx's Theory of Value*, 1924.

MONEY, OR THE UNIVERSAL EQUIVALENT

In *Capital*, Marx writes that "Money is the commodity whose character is absolute alienation, for it is the product of the universal alienation of all other commodities." Yes, but how did it get to this point?

Cupidity, the desire for money, the taste for the power conferred solely by material possession—these have always existed. It is the place they occupy in public discourse that has changed. The novelty lies in the good conscience with which reverence for money as a value *per se* is now regarded. What is new is not the desire to possess, nor even the social consideration attached *de facto* to the one who possesses, but the idea now found everywhere that this desire is both moral and natural, "normal" in a word, since it answers to the most legitimate form of human behavior: the permanent search by every individual for his private best interest, so that he who possesses can really think, with regard to this common idea, that *he is worth what he has*.

We know the three great sources of crime: money, power, sex. Each allows us to acquire the others (in variable proportion), but money remains the surest means. Not long ago, men were rich because they were powerful; today they are powerful because they are rich. In the past, even if people were happy to enrich themselves, they were not necessarily proud of it. Today, not having money is a source of shame: from being a misfortune, poverty has become a disgrace. Alain Caillé rightly speaks of the "social and symbolic exclusion resulting from the radical delegitimation of all that does not relate exclusively to functionality and performance." In a world where material success symbolizes effectiveness set up as a dominant value, the poor or the unemployed can only be incompetents, i.e., ultimately parasites. And above all, in a world where ever more is produced with ever fewer men: useless, superfluous men.

Georg Simmel demonstrated that the intrinsic nature of an economy based on money was to dismiss the question of ends in favor of means. As soon as wealth is put on a pedestal, the means used to acquire it all inevitably become legitimate in some sense. Wouldn't one be stupid to be honest when the world around you provides the spectacle, and thus implicitly the example, of so much insolent wealth dishonestly acquired? If the whole world is corrupt, why not me?

Strictly speaking, we can only talk of a market when land, labor, and money are exchanged as commodities "like others," and the totality of prices are formed by the effects of anonymous and impersonal transactions. So there cannot be a market where the economic sector has not achieved a certain autonomy. Now, what especially characterizes "archaic" or traditional societies is precisely that economic activity is never perceived as autonomous, but is integrated, "embedded," within a network of social relations and obligations that prevent it from going beyond its role and provoking an irresistible growth in commercial relations.

If money today is at once a standard of value (commodity), an accounting unit, a means of exchange, and a reserve of value (sign of capital), its birth is explained by the development of exchange, whose specific means it constitutes. What is proper to capitalism is that exchange value occupies a preponderant place in the process of production, to the point where production becomes independent of human needs and subordinate to the accumulation of exchange value, which becomes an end in itself. Hence the Marxian definition of money:

> The exchange of commodities is the process wherein the social exchange of substances, i.e., the exchange of the particular products of private individuals, is at the same time the creation of determinate social relations of production into which individuals enter as they exchange substances. Emerging mutual relations of commodities crystalize in the form of distinct determinations that the general equivalent possesses, and the exchange process is thus also that of money formation.

"General equivalent": that is indeed the correct term. As a

universal equivalent, money is what allows everything to be evaluated, to be quantified with a number. Reducing all goods to a common denominator, money thereby makes exchanges homogeneous thanks to the adoption of a common measure destined from the beginning to limit evaluative divergences. Aristotle already observed: "All things exchanged must be somehow comparable. It was to this end that money was invented, and it becomes in a sense an intermediary, for it measures all things." By creating a perspective from which the most different things can be numerically evaluated, money makes them somehow equal: it reduces all the qualities that distinguish them to a simple logic of more and less.

In fact, money is pure quantity, or more exactly, quantity is its only quality—which amounts to saying that with money, quality is systematically reduced to quantity. Now, any quantity can always be increased by one unit. To any number it is always possible to add another, so the best automatically gets confounded with the most. One *never has enough* of that of which one can *always have more*.

Shakespeare said that gold is the "common whore of mankind." The same can obviously be said of money: it turns all social relations into relations of prostitution. Péguy said so as well: "All the abasement of the modern world comes from that world considering as negotiable values what the ancient and Christian worlds considered non-negotiable." In fact, the rise of modernity is characterized by the ever more extensive inclusion within the logic of commercial relations of things or sectors that previously did not come under that logic. Not only does it go without saying that any modern town must have more banks than libraries or museums, but money has gradually taken power in all those sectors from which it long remained more or less excluded. Applied to every domain of human existence, the model of the market is now taken as the universal and paradigmatic key. School is becoming the antechamber to the hiring office: you go there to "learn a trade," not to acquire knowledge, still less to have your character formed. Sports and culture, art, science, religion, even private life have in turn submitted to the logic of profit. Now that the practice of copyrighting living organisms is in the process of creating bio-things, we are driven to manage ourselves like a stock portfolio.

Everything is becoming convertible into cash, available on the market. Even non-economic ends are pursued through economic activity. Money measures all human activities simply because of its overaccumulation. Such is the principle of limitlessness that corresponds to the essence of capital. Based on the postulates of self-interest, the dynamics of commercialization are devouring everything. The world of money does not know completeness, limits. It implies *hybris*, lack of measure: "ever more, never enough."

Jean-Joseph Goux writes:

> The reign of money is the reign of the *only* measure by which all things and all human activities can be evaluated. . . . A certain monotheistic configuration of the form-value *universal equivalent* clearly appears here. Monetary rationality, based on the only measure of values, is part of the same system as a certain theological monovalence.

At the end of this development, society is no longer the locus of the common (or common things), of shared values, but a *market society* where economic reason subordinates all social relations to itself, i.e., the locus of generalized competition, the war of all against all, where everyone wants to maximize his own interest at the expense of others. On the one hand, money liberates the individual from communitarian attachments, from the social bond; on the other, by isolating him from his fellows, it makes him more vulnerable than ever and makes his newfound liberty an empty and meaningless shell.

Money thus institutes a new relation to reality. It generates a formidable movement of homogenization and quantification. Any way of life is a system of subjectivation. Marx saw this: commodity fetishism involves the reification of social relations, the increasing commercialization of human relations. The reign of commercial value consecrates the destitution of all other values. By getting used to evaluating all things in terms of money, man also gets used to considering everything from a quantitative point of view and, at the same time, to considering as "irrational" and hence meaningless, or even non-existent, all qualities that cannot be counted, i.e., reduced to a quantitative evaluation. *Value*, which formerly referred to things that were by definition non-negotiable, has been reduced to an always conditional, hypothetical *price*, since it can always be the object of a transaction. The generalization of universal equivalence induced by the money relation drives us to consider men equivalent as well. We say they have become equal, whereas in reality they have only become interchangeable. Beings transformed into objects really do become interchangeable: one man is as good as another, just as every penny is worth the same.

Can we deny that we need money? Obviously not. We also need toilet paper. But that is no reason to worship it. The value of money is mainly what we attribute to it: anyone who attaches too much value to it already has too much of it; anyone who attaches no value to it, whatever the quantity he possesses, remains its master. The problem is that today the rich and poor live according to the same values and aspire to the same things, even if they cannot have the same quantity of those things.

What is left that cannot be evaluated in money? What cannot be bought or sold? It is not easy to say. Feelings? Perhaps. But what share does the desire for security occupy in love that seems to itself disinterested? Shedding one's blood? Yes, but do we not do so with the hope that someone will, if necessary, shed his for us? Doesn't this apparently disinterested gesture disguise the conscious or unconscious desire to benefit from reciprocity? If I help others, it is in the hope they will help me as well. Biologists are very clever at making altruism appear to be disguised selfishness. Fresh air? Trees? Mountains, the sea, and the sky? Yes, undoubtedly. But a day may come when we shall have to pay to breathe oxygen or bathe in unpolluted water. If everything in life can be bought or sold, gratuitousness can only reside in the giving of one's own life. Then the question becomes whether one believes there are things worse than death. If our answer is no, we are already lost.

What is born of money will die by money.

INDEX

Numbers in bold refer to a whole chapter or section devoted to a particular topic.

131; of progress, 2, 70, 72–73, 253; of reason, 74; of the dominant class, 1; of the Rights of Man, 1, 4, 37, 52, 221, 234, 253, 274; of Sameness, 11, 106, 110; of work, 142, 273; scientistic, 187; see also Constructivism; liberalism

idleness, 129n23, 158, 263

illiberal democracy, 215–16, 218

illiberalism, 215–16

immigration, 16–18, 20, 25, 51, 72, 227

independence, as freedom, 106; individual, 10–11, 41, 46–47, 57, 106, 256; of the state, 31, 218

independent labor, 273

individualism, 4, 6, 14, 32, 37, 40, 44, 46n6, 57, 66–68, 71, 79n17, 92, 111, 125, 142, 185, 197, 213, 216, 226, 247, 257; anarchistic, 5; aristocratic, 6; biopsychic, 6; bourgeois, 134; impure, 175, 201; liberal, 50, 81; Marxian, 53n12, 184; methodological, 206; modern, 42, 53n12, 67, 71; possessive, 7, 81; religious, 41; social, 6; vs. individuation, 6

inner man, 4, 256

instincts, in Hayek, 165, 166, 178, 180, 186

instituted order, 194–95

institutional investors, 230, 233

institutions, 37, 61, 79n17, 97, 155, 210, 238, 255, 260; collective, 212; Hayek's view of, 166, 177, 190, 194, 196, 198–200; human, 177, 198; liberal, 165; public, 248; social, 84;

see also: Constructivism

internet commerce, 157

Internet, 157, 236; stocks, 236–37

internships, 270

intrinsic good, 18, 89, 101

invisible hand, 35, 51, **53–57**; Hayek's view, 169, 174, 193, 202

Israelewicz, Erik, 229, 230n3

Ivan Illich, 260

J

Jappe, Anselm, 275, 284–85

Jefferson, Thomas, 105

job (social role), 6, 264, 266, 270, 273

jobs, 24, 29, 239–40, 266, 268–71

Joffrin, Laurent, 232, 243–44

Johannet, René, 142

Joseph, Carens, 16–17

Jospin, Lionel, 239

Julliard, Jacques, 241, 248

July Monarchy (French), 135

justice, 13, 14, 19–20, 28, 30, 58, 82, 84–85, 87, 90, 100, 134, 241; Hayek's view of, 179–204; see also: social justice

Juvin, Hervé, 61

K

Kahn, Sylvain, 216

Kant, Immanuel, 84, 93, 154n70; Kantianism, 62, 75, 82, 84, 86, 94, 100, 107, 216

Kelsen, Hans, 182

Keynes, John Maynard, 3n4, 163n5, 266; Keynesianism, 228, 246

kin groups, 43

King, Charles, 82

Kirk, Russell, 253, 259

Klein, Melanie, 117–18

ABOUT THE AUTHOR

Alain de Benoist (b. 1943) is a political philosopher and historian of ideas. The author of a hundred books and thousands of articles, his recent books in English include *Ernst Jünger: Between the Gods & the Titans* (Middle Europe Books, 2022) and *The Populist Moment: The End of Left vs. Right* (Middle Europe Books, 2025).

www.ingramcontent.com/pod-product-compliance
Lightning Source LLC
Chambersburg PA
CBHW020458270326
41926CB00008B/658